100 THINGS
ASTROS FANS
SHOULD KNOW & DO
BEFORE THEY DIE

Brian McTaggart

TRIUMPH
BOOKS

Library of Congress Cataloging-in-Publication Data

Names: McTaggart, Brian, 1970–
Title: 100 things Astros fans should know & do before they die / Brian McTaggart.
Other titles: One hundred things Astros fans should know and do before they die
Description: Chicago, Illinois : Triumph Books LLC, [2016]
Identifiers: LCCN 2015041350 | ISBN 9781629371962
Subjects: LCSH: Houston Astros (Baseball team)—History. | Houston Astros (Baseball team)—Miscellanea.
Classification: LCC GV875.H64 M37 2016 |
DDC 796.357/64097641411—dc23
LC record available at http://lccn.loc.gov/2015041350

This book is available in quantity at special discounts for your group or organization. For further information, contact:

Triumph Books LLC
814 North Franklin Street
Chicago, Illinois 60610
(312) 337-0747
www.triumphbooks.com

Printed in U.S.A.
ISBN: 978-1-62937-196-2
Design by Patricia Frey
Photos courtesy of AP Images

100 THINGS
ASTROS FANS
SHOULD KNOW & DO
BEFORE THEY DIE

To my late father, Patrick, the pride of Donegal
Thank you for always pushing me and believing in me.

To my late sister, Bridget
The world hasn't been as bright since you left.

To Lisa, Erin, Emily, and Amy
You are my driving force and my source of inspiration.

Contents

Foreword *by Craig Biggio* xi

Introduction xv

1 The Judge 1

2 Craig Biggio. 3

3 The Astrodome: The Eighth Wonder of the World 7

4 Nolan Ryan. 10

5 The Colt .45s 12

6 Biggio Reaches Hall of Fame. 15

7 Jeff Bagwell 19

8 Killer B's 21

9 Tombstone 23

10 Houston Becomes AL Town 25

11 Mike Scott. 28

12 Biggio's 3,000th Hit 31

13 Larry Dierker. 34

14 Altuve Wins Batting Title 36

15 1980 NLCS. 42

16 First-Round Playoff Blues 44

17 Lance Berkman 46

18 The Big Unit Hits Houston. 49

19 Ken Caminiti. 51

20 Crawford Boxes Spook Pitchers. 54

21 Nolan Ryan Spins Fifth No-No. 57

22 Hurricane Ike 59

23 Jeff Bagwell's MVP Season 61

24 2015 Astros Breakthrough. 63

25 Phil Garner 66

26 Six Pitcher No-Hitter 68

27 Drayton McLane. 71

28 Biggio Moves to Second Base 73

29 Bagwell Trade Alters History 76

30 Cesar Cedeno 80

31 Sunshine Kids 82

32 Joe Niekro. 84

33 The 2004 Season. 85

34 Roy Oswalt 88

35 Hatcher's Game 6 Home Run. 91

36 Visit the Hall of Fame. 94

37 Pettitte, Clemens Come Home 96

38 Astrodome Scoreboard Dazzles 99

39 Jeff Kent's Walk-Off Home Run. 101

40 John McMullen. 104

41 26-Game Road Trip 106

42 22-Inning Game 108

43 Jose Cruz. 110

44 The Toy Cannon 113

45 Tal Smith 116

46 Jim Deshaies Strikes Out the First Eight Batters. 118

47 Art Howe 121

48 Lima Time 123

49 Three Consecutive No. 1 Picks. 125

50 Rainbow Jerseys. 127

51 Enos Cabell 130

52 Trading for Carlos Beltran 132

53 J.R. Richard. 134

54 Notable Announcers 137

55 Chris Burke's Walk-Off Home Run 140

56 Astros Reach Fall Classic 142

57 Darryl Kile 145

58 Alan Ashby 147

59 Brad Ausmus. 149

60 Kerry Wood K's 20 Astros 152

61 Astros Overcome Pujols' Home Run off Brad Lidge 154

62 Watson Breaks a Barrier 156

63 1980 NL West Tiebreaker. 160

64 Tal's Hill. 162

65 Watch a Game from the Crawford Boxes 164

66 1986 NLCS. 166

67 Rusty Staub. 168

68 Glenn Davis 170

69 The Talent and Tragedy of Dickie Thon 173

70 Hello, Analytics. 175

71 Rainout in Astrodome. 178

72 Other Astros Hall of Famers 180

73 Aspromonte Homers for a Blind Child 185

74 Terry Puhl. 188

75 Shane Reynolds. 190

76 Joe Morgan 192

77 Watson Scores Millionth Run 194

78 Billy Wagner 196

79 Crazy Injuries 199

80 Hunter Pence 201

81 Go to Spring Training 203

82 Bill Doran 205

83 Yogi Berra 207

84 Norm Miller and the 24-Inning Game 209

85 Bill Virdon 211

86 Bob Watson and *The Bad News Bears* 213

87 Carlos Correa 215

88 Buy Astrodome Memorabilia 218

89 Cardinals Hack the Astros 220

90 Back-to-Back No-Nos 222

91 Tour Minute Maid Park 224

92 Hal Lanier 226

93 Go to FanFest 228

94 Dave Smith 230

95 Big Game Brandon Backe 232

96 Go to a Double A Game 234

97 The Don Wilson and Jim Umbricht Tragedies 236

98 Famous Brawls 238

99 Walk Around the Astrodome 241

100 Eat Chicken and Waffles in a Cone 245

Acknowledgments 249

Sources 253

Foreword

When I went to big league spring training camp for the first time, I arrived in the clubhouse and asked the first guy I saw, "Hey, where's Yogi Berra?" Yogi, who scouted me while I was at Seton Hall, was a coach for the Astros and the only person I knew. It turns out the man I was talking to was longtime equipment manager Dennis Liborio. He quickly put me in my place. He goes, "Who the [bleep] are you?" *Welcome to the big leagues, right?* Dennis became a close friend and confidant through the years after teaching me an early lesson about knowing my place.

When I reached the big leagues at 22 years old in 1988, I joined a team full of veterans like Nolan Ryan, Buddy Bell, Billy Doran, and Terry Puhl. They had a wealth of service time and knowledge, and I soaked up as much as I could. After games some of the players would sit around a cooler and drink a couple of beers while talking baseball, and I'd sit nearby and listen without saying a word. They were good people and great baseball players. To have the opportunity to watch these guys play the game every day, respect their job, prepare like they did every day—day in and day out—and then come to work every day with the intentions of winning baseball games and getting to the playoffs, that was huge for me. I didn't say much my first couple of years in the big leagues obviously, but by being quiet, my eyes and ears were open, and I learned a lot from those guys. The early years were the most beneficial for me because I had the opportunity to be around such classy people.

I didn't know anything about the Houston Astros until I got drafted by them in the first round in 1987. I didn't know a lot about the city or the town or the fans. I was born and raised on Long Island but soon found out what the Astros are all about. It's about playing the game the right way, playing the game every day.

It's something I take a lot of pride in because it's the only team I ever played for. It's the only team I ever wanted to play for—once I got here and got drafted by them. For me to be able to spend 22 years—20 in the big leagues and two in the minor leagues—in one organization and one city, that's a pretty cool thing.

When the veteran players moved on, I was joined by guys like Jeff Bagwell, Ken Caminiti, and Luis Gonzalez, and we grew up together in the big leagues. The Astros Way was already here before me—it was the Joe Morgans and Billy Dorans—and all we did was continue the way that you're supposed to play the game. To break in and have as many guys like that around me, it was great. To come up together in the '90s, to hang out together, and start winning and getting to the playoffs in '97, '98, and '99 with that group of guys, it was really special. We were the same team that lost a lot of games and the same team that won a lot of games together. In baseball you're together for eight months a year and you don't necessarily have to be friends. But we actually were friends on the field and off the field, and our families got together, which made it all the more gratifying. We did a lot of things together, and that's why it was so rewarding to do it with that bunch of guys. We were pretty much all a bunch of homegrown guys from the organization.

Before we knew it, Houston was becoming a baseball town. We were changing the culture. The Astros had a lot of success, but they didn't have a lot of sustained success and they had a lot of second-place finishes. When you're about to take a culture of fans from hoping to get to the playoffs to expecting to get to the playoffs every year, that's hard to do. That takes a lot of success and a lot of playing the game the right way. You've got to have a good front office making the right moves and the right players on the field and the right coaching staff. To be able to change that culture, that's a pretty cool thing, and I take a lot of pride in that.

I never really wanted to play for any other organization. Sometimes the way the business goes, players have to move on, and sometimes it's because of the player, and sometimes it's because of the front office, but for us we were able to make it work here. To be able to get 3,000 hits with one team—well, it's a pretty small list of guys who have done it with one organization, and I was able to enjoy it with the fans along the way. The fans take ownership of it. From the beginning when I was a catcher and then transitioned to second base and then went to the outfield and came back to second base, we enjoyed the ride together. They were part of the journey along with me. When you talk about reaching the Hall of Fame, it was for my family, No. 1. And it was also for the fans to finally say, "We have a guy in there." Nobody can take that away from us.

That's why it was really special for me to be able to enjoy the Hall of Fame weekend with so many Astros fans. Standing at that podium and looking out at a bunch of Astros out there was amazing. There were 45,000 or 50,000 people out there, and 30,000 of them were Astros fans. I can't put into words the feeling I had looking out there. They said they were coming and they did. That's kind of the relationship I had with the fans over 20 years. They respected and appreciated the way that I played the game, and I respected and appreciated them. I took great pride in playing the game the right way for the fans for 20 years.

Those same Astros fans—along with new and old fans—will enjoy *100 Things Astros Fans Should Know & Do Before They Die* as Brian McTaggart is uniquely qualified to bring you the stories of many of the franchise's greatest moments, events, and characters that are brought to life in this book.

—Craig Biggio
National Baseball Hall of Fame, 2015

Introduction

The history of the Astros is about as rich as you can get for a team that has never won the World Series. The list of characters and great players who have come through Houston is impressive, and the city changed the way sports would be watched forever when the Astrodome opened for the Astros in 1965. There have been playoff triumphs and much heartbreak. There have been Most Valuable Players, Rookies of the Year, and Cy Young winners. Many of the team's stories have been told throughout the years, but I thought it was time that the franchise's greatest stories, characters, players, events, and games come together in one book. Thus, *100 Things Astros Fans Should Know & Do Before They Die* was born.

The idea behind the book is taking 100 chapters and ranking them in order of importance. Chapter One was easy. Judge Roy Hofheinz built the Astrodome and spearheaded baseball coming to Houston. He got it all started, so he gets the book started as well. Players like Craig Biggio, Jeff Bagwell, and Nolan Ryan were easy choices of high importance, but so were some key events as well. Biggio reaching the Hall of Fame in 2015 and the Astros overcoming a terrible start to win the National League pennant in 2005 ranked high as impactful moments in team history. Ranking the chapters became more difficult and less clear as the process went along, but you can easily flip to the ones that are most important to you and read them first.

I can't remember exactly when I went to my first Astros game, but it was sometime in the mid-to-late 1970s when my father took me to the Astrodome for the first time. I was in awe of the place. I still am. I feel like I grew up there. As the years went on, I attended more games and when I got my driver's license in 1986 I went all the time. Of course, the 1986 season was a memorable one, but I'm sad to say I missed Mike Scott's no-hitter because it was a day game and I did have to go to school. Priorities.

In 1989 I started working the scoreboard at the Astrodome and was paid to watch Astros games. *Good deal, huh?* I did that for several years before branching out into journalism, but through the years, I saw more Astros games in person than many people. I witnessed a lot of the great moments and games in team history and I saw many of the team's great players in person as a fan, scoreboard operator, and later as a beat reporter for the *Houston Chronicle* and for MLB.com.

I remember Ken Caminiti's debut and Scott's dominance. Through the years I saw a lot of the team's most memorable moments, too: the 22-inning game in 1989, Darryl Kile's no-hitter in 1993, playoff games in the late 1990s, the final game at the Astrodome in 1999, the first game at Enron Field in 2000, Chris Burke's 2005 National League Division Series-clinching walk-off homer, Albert Pujols' shocking homer off Brad Lidge in the 2005 National League Championship Series and Roy Oswalt's gem in St. Louis two days later, Craig Biggio's 3,000th hit, Mike Fiers' no-hitter, and the 2004 and 2005 playoff clinchers on the final day of the season. It's been quite a ride.

All those memories and more are detailed in this book, which I hope serves as a fun trip down memory lane for every Astros fan. And those who haven't been fans for a while can hopefully learn a lot about the Astros while trying some of the suggestions of things you—and other baseball fans—should do before you die.

1 The Judge

He's one of the most important historical figures in the history of Houston and one of the men responsible for bringing Major League Baseball to Houston. Roy Hofheinz, known as "the Judge," left an unforgettable imprint on the city's political and sports landscape. He graduated from the University of Houston law school at 19, was a member of the Texas Legislature at 22, and served as a Harris County judge at 24. Hofheinz later became a popular and, at times, controversial young mayor to a city on the rise during a colorful tenure, in which he helped Houston thrive and become a progressive community, while also having a profound, positive impact on civil rights.

Perhaps his biggest contribution to the city of Houston was the acquisition of the first National League franchise in the southern United States. Hofheinz, his partner R.E. "Bob" Smith, and several other influential figures brought big league baseball to Houston and laid out plans for what would soon become the Astrodome. Known as the "Eighth Wonder of the World," the first air-conditioned domed stadium changed the way sports was played and viewed across the country.

He was a master salesman, an impeccable leader, and terrific orator and wasn't afraid to take risks. He went against the grain. Without the gumption of Hofheinz, the Astros and the Astrodome may have never existed. Baseball in Houston would have looked dramatically different without Hofheinz's can-do spirit and remarkable vision. "He was just a dynamic, exciting individual that could really captivate an audience," said longtime Astros executive Tal Smith, who was hired by Hofheinz as a staffer in helping to build the Astrodome. "He's the best orator I've ever heard. His presentations were just outstanding."

Hofheinz was born on April 10, 1912, in modest means in Beaumont, Texas. In *You Be the Judge* by Hofheinz's daughter, Dene Hofheinz Anton, she detailed her father's first money-making project, which entailed setting up a soda pop stand. After serving two terms as Houston's mayor in the 1950s, Judge Hofheinz was lured to join the Houston Sports Association (HSA) by R.E. Smith, who made millions in Texas' booming oil business. The HSA was formed in 1957 by prominent businessmen and lifelong baseball fans George Kirksey, William Kirkland, and Craig Cullinan to help bring a baseball team to Houston, and Hofheinz became a key player because of his political clout and ability to get things done. Kirksey and Cullinan helped organize the Continental League, which eventually led to Houston being awarded a National League expansion franchise in 1960.

With the Astrodome being built for $35 million, the Colt .45s of the National League played their first game on April 10, 1962, the date of the Judge's 50th birthday. There was no better way to blow out the candles than by watching Houston beat the Chicago Cubs 11–2 on that day at Colt Stadium, the makeshift facility in the parking lot of what would become the Astrodome. The Astrodome opened to much fanfare in 1965, and the Astros were born. Hofheinz continued to be the Astrodome's biggest promoter and was one of the key members in the introduction of an artificial playing surface in the Astrodome now referred to as Astroturf. During his time as owner of the Astros, his vision created an excitement for baseball in Houston that laid the foundation for the great success of the franchise.

Former Astros pitcher Larry Dierker said Hofheinz was so convincingly persuasive that around 1968, when the team couldn't get a sponsor for its pregame radio show, he talked players into doing the interviews for free, even though players on other teams were getting paid for similar interviews. "They told us we were going to do the interviews, and there weren't going to be any gifts," Dierker said. "Obviously, it created quite a stir. The next day Judge Hofheinz went into the clubhouse and held a meeting with the players and delivered a speech and laid out the opportunities we had as young men to be stars in the community and to build upon that for our baseball careers and future careers and how much it would mean to us having all this good publicity. By the time he got done talking, guys were lined up to go on the show. That was the Judge."

Ever the showman Judge Hofheinz developed Astroworld, an amusement park that was built across the freeway; purchased the Ringling Brothers and Barnum and Bailey Circus; and developed four hotels in the area as part of his Astrodomain project. Hofheinz suffered a stroke in 1970 that confined him to a wheelchair. Five years later with the Astrodomain in debt, control of the team was passed to two credit companies, and Hofheinz sold his remaining stock. He died of a heart attack on November 22, 1982, but left a magnificent, inimitable legacy.

2 Craig Biggio

He ran out every ground ball, whether it was the first day of spring training or the first game of the World Series. It didn't matter to Craig Biggio. If he had a chance to put on an Astros uniform and play baseball, he was going to give it his all. For 20 years Biggio, with his boyish good looks, filthy batting helmet, and dirty

The greatest Astro of them all, Craig Biggio, circles the bases after hitting a two-run home run against the St. Louis Cardinals on May 30, 2006.

uniform, weaved his way into the hearts of Astros fans, as well as the record books. He retired in 2007, as perhaps the greatest Astro of them all, with 3,060 hits—including more doubles than any other right-handed hitter in history—and eventually a plaque on the wall in the Baseball Hall of Fame. "What a gamer," former Astros manager Art Howe said. "He made my job easy for five years, that's for sure."

Biggio grew up in blue-collar Long Island, New York, as an undersized two-sport star—football and baseball—in a family of air traffic controllers. Biggio had other plans. He quickly separated himself from his peers with his athletic prowess, earning a scholarship to Seton Hall University in New Jersey. He soon put himself on the radar of major league scouts, and Hall of Fame catcher Yogi Berra, who was serving as an Astros coach at the time, went to scout the promising young catcher in person.

The Astros drafted Biggio in the first round in 1987, and he was in the majors a year later, taking over as starting catcher for Alan Ashby. He quickly blossomed into an All-Star before being moved to second base in 1992. There he became a superstar. He was among the best players in the game in the mid-to-late 1990s and helped the Astros win four division titles in a five-year span (1997–99, 2001). He and longtime teammate Jeff Bagwell became franchise cornerstones and eventually reached the World Series together in 2005, Bagwell's final year. "I was an East Coast kid and all I ever wanted to do was get to the World Series," Biggio said. "Hopefully the team that drafted me was the team that we were going to get there with."

Biggio moved to the outfield for two years when the Astros signed Jeff Kent. He returned to second base in 2005 and played the final three seasons of his career at the position. Biggio wound up hitting 291 home runs with 1,175 RBIs, 414 stolen bases, and a .281 average. "Craig's never going to talk that much about it, and you can talk about his athleticism and talk about his skills and all that stuff, but you don't become what Craig became if you're just not driven and you just don't have a lot more qualities about yourself that don't show up in the box score," said Bill Doran, who helped Biggio learn second base and was ultimately unseated at the position by Biggio. "He had all those intangibles."

Biggio became the 27th player in major league history to reach the 3,000-hit plateau after he hit a seventh-inning single against Colorado Rockies pitcher Aaron Cook on June 28, 2007, at Minute Maid Park. A hustling Biggio was thrown out at second base trying to stretch the historic hit into a double. Biggio's No. 7 was retired by the Astros in 2008. He received the ultimate honor on July 26, 2015, when he was inducted into the Hall of Fame, becoming the first player to be enshrined with an Astros cap on his plaque. His impact on baseball was secure, but his impact on those who played with him was bigger. "More than anything it was an attitude," said former Astros shortstop Adam Everett. "It was an attitude of how to come to work every day and how to play the game. You can tell kids all the time, 'Hey, play the game hard,' but until you see a guy literally run until his last game he played, and he hits a pop up and runs it out under 4.5 [seconds] and he tries to stretch a single into a double for his 3,000th, that was Biggio. That was the way he played."

Former Astros general manager Gerry Hunsicker, who was the assistant general manager of the New York Mets before coming to Houston, said Biggio never got the national recognition he deserved. He said if Biggio was playing in New York, Boston, or Chicago, he would have been on billboards. But he didn't need the spotlight. Biggio embraced Houston, raised a family there, and was a pillar in the community. He helped raise millions for the Sunshine Kids organization that supports kids with cancer. Biggio wore a yellow sun pin on his batting practice cap throughout his career and was as proud of the work he did for kids as he was any of his on-field achievements. "Craig was a once-in-a-lifetime player. He was a manager's dream in the sense you just pencil his name in the lineup every day," Hunsicker said. "He brought his A game every day. He gave everything he had to win day in and day out. It's no coincidence that the greatest stretch in franchise history was with Biggio."

The Astrodome: The Eighth Wonder of the World

When the Astrodome opened on April 9, 1965, its historical significance wasn't lost on anybody who was in the building that night. The vision of Judge Roy Hofheinz, the magnificent Astrodome—the "Eighth Wonder of the World"—ushered in a new era in the way sports would be watched forever. It had air-conditioning, a roof, and cushioned seats. And when the New York Yankees came to Houston for an exhibition game against the newly named Astros, 47,876 fans—including President Lyndon B. Johnson—were on hand to witness history. Even the players couldn't help being nervous.

Astros catcher Ron Brand was behind the plate when Yankees great Mickey Mantle led off the game in the top of the first inning. The Hall of Fame had asked Brand to ask Mantle to take the first pitch so the ball could be sent to Cooperstown. "So he came up and I politely said, 'Mickey, they want you to take the first pitch,'" Brand said. "Mantle said, 'Okay,' and he smoothed the dirt. He said, 'Shoot, I'm too nervous to swing anyway.'" Mantle led off with a single and homered in the sixth. He's credited with the first home run in the $35 million Astrodome, though Bob Aspromonte of the Astros hit the first regular-season home run by an Astros player in the

Dome. "When you circle the bases and have 50,000 people in the stadium, it was a long-lasting feeling," Aspromonte said.

Hofheinz, his partner R.E. "Bob" Smith, and several other influential figures brought big league baseball to Houston and laid out plans for the Astrodome. Hofheinz presented the idea of the stadium to the National League owners in 1960, around the same time Houston was awarded a National League franchise. During the January 3, 1962, groundbreaking, members of the Harris County Commissioners and Houston Sports Association simultaneously fired Colt .45 pistols into the dirt.

Hofheinz, a political leader in Houston, was inspired to design the Astrodome after a trip to see the Colosseum in Rome. It was Dene Hofheinz, the Judge's daughter, who one day asked her daddy if it would be possible to play baseball indoors while they were driving home from a minor league Houston Buffs game that had been rained out. "He didn't say anything right at first," she said. "When he got really quiet, I thought, *Oh no, I'm in trouble.* Then a little bit down the road, he said, 'What have you been doing, little doll? Have you been taking my smart pills?' I didn't understand fully that was a compliment."

The franchise began as the Colt .45s for its first three years (1962–64) and played in Colt Stadium, a makeshift ballpark in the parking lot of what would become the Astrodome. The oppressive heat and humidity and pesky mosquitoes that made watching games at Colt Stadium sometimes unbearable were a thing of the past with the Astrodome. Judge Hofheinz was very involved in the design of every inch of the Astrodome—from the color of the seats to the length of the dugouts, which were extended longer than any others so more seats could be marketed as premium. On the seventh floor was Hofheinz's apartment, which included a billiard parlor, six-hole miniature golf course, barbershop, beauty parlor, shooting gallery, lap pool, and bowling alley.

The Astrodome wasn't without its issues. The 4,596 skylights in the roof that provided natural light also made it difficult for fielders to catch pop-ups because of glare. When the skylights were painted with translucent acrylic coating, the grass died. That forced Hofheinz to go in search of a solution. "We had to overcome those things," said longtime Astros executive Tal Smith. "Initially, if you had said we're going to play indoors, there's going to be a roof over your head, it's going to be air-conditioned, and we're not going to be able to grow grass, I don't think that would have flown."

Instructed by the Judge, Smith worked with Chemstrand, a division of the Monsanto Chemical Company, which was testing a new nylon material dubbed Chemgrass. The product passed several tests for the Astros, and Hofheinz convinced Monsanto to call it Astroturf in the deal. It soon became standard in nearly every stadium and ballpark.

The Astros wound up playing in the Astrodome for 35 years, leaving for a downtown ballpark after the 1999 season. Along the way the Astrodome played host to the NFL's Houston Oilers, the University of Houston football team, and several marquee events, including the NBA All-Star Game, NCAA Final Four, the "Battle of the Sexes II" tennis match between Billie Jean King and Bobby Riggs, and the "Game of the Century" in 1968 when Elvin Hayes led Houston past UCLA and Lew Alcindor before 52,000 fans. The 474-foot scoreboard, which featured snorting bulls and shooting guns when a home run was hit, was removed in 1989 to accommodate 10,000 more seats for the Oilers, who wound up leaving town a few years later anyway. Despite being vacant the Astrodome stood tall 50 years after it opened and will always remain a special part of Houston's history. "It has history as a structure," former Astros pitcher Larry Dierker said. "There's never been anything built on the planet like that before."

4 Nolan Ryan

The only thing that made more news than the signing of Nolan Ryan prior to the 1980 season to join his hometown Astros was his departure from Houston following the 1988 season. Ryan pitched nine of his incredible 27 seasons in Houston and cemented himself as a Texas legend by going to the Rangers for five years to finish his career, throwing his sixth and seventh no-hitters while in his 40s. He was inducted into the Hall of Fame in 1999 with a Rangers cap on his plaque, but there's no denying his impact on the Astros—or the impact the Astros had upon Ryan. "Ever since the Colt .45s came in, I had hoped that someday I would be able to play with the Astros and be at home," Ryan said. "It was a dream come true for me."

Lynn Nolan Ryan was born on January 31, 1947, in Refugio, Texas, and grew up in Alvin, just south of Houston. He listened to Colt .45s games on the radio as a teenager. New York Mets scout Red Murff discovered him as a hard-throwing sophomore pitcher at Alvin High School, and the Mets drafted him in the 12th round in 1965. He made his major league debut at age 19 late in the 1966 season and appeared in 103 games for the Mets in 1968–71, winning a World Series title in 1969. Ryan was traded to the California Angels prior to the 1972 season and became a star in Southern California. In eight years with the Angels, he won 138 games and struck out 2,416 batters in 2,181⅓ innings, made the All-Star team five times, and threw four no-hitters to tie Sandy Koufax's record.

Ryan and his 100-mph fastball were free agents following the 1979 season. The Astros, who had tried to trade for him a couple of years earlier, signed Ryan for $4.5 million over four years on November 19, 1979, making him the first player in history to make $1 million in one season. "There was always interest in bringing

Nolan Ryan home," former Astros general manager Tal Smith said. "Dick Moss was Ryan's agent and was very in-depth and very good at what he does. He reached out to [Astros owner John] McMullen. As it turned out, we created the first $1 million player in free agency."

The signings of Ryan and former National League Most Valuable Player Joe Morgan that offseason gave the Astros a formidable club. The team was in contention for most of 1979, and the "Ryan Express" was added to a pitching rotation that included J.R. Richard and Joe Niekro. "Playing with the Astros for nine years was very beneficial to our family and stability of our home life, so I was very appreciative of that," Ryan said. "I had some very good friends from those teams."

Ryan made his Astros debut on April 12, 1980, against the Los Angeles Dodgers and homered off Don Sutton, one of only two homers he hit in his career. Ryan went 106–94 with a 3.13 ERA

Morganna the Kissing Bandit

Not many people could bring Nolan Ryan to his knees. Morganna Roberts certainly wasn't just anybody. Roberts, the busty dancer with a penchant for athletes, became known in the 1970s and 1980s for running onto fields at athletic events and kissing players, earning the nickname, "Morganna, the Kissing Bandit." It began in 1969 when she jumped onto the field at Riverfront Stadium in Cincinnati and kissed Pete Rose, beginning a "career" in which she kissed more than 50 athletes.

On April 9, 1985, at the Astrodome, Morganna rushed onto the field and headed to the pitcher's mound, where Ryan was doing his work in the first inning. Ryan dropped to one knee, put out both arms, and let Morganna plant a kiss on his cheek as the fans cheered wildly. Morganna was arrested, but Harris County prosecutors dropped the case at the request of attorneys for the Houston Sports Association. "We won the case on the gravity defense," she said. "I just leaned over the fence, and gravity took its toll and took me into the arms of Nolan Ryan and Dickie Thon. Who is gonna argue with Isaac Newton?"

in 282 career starts in Houston, but he never received much run support. He threw his record-breaking fifth no-hitter with the Astros on September 26, 1981, and broke Walter Johnson's all-time strikeout record by whiffing future Astros manager Brad Mills on April 27, 1983, in Montreal for strikeout No. 3,509. Ryan made two All-Star teams with the Astros and won league ERA titles in 1981 (1.69) and 1987 (2.76). In 1987 he led the league in strikeouts and ERA despite going 8–16 because of poor run support. "We just weren't a team that scored a lot of runs," Ryan said, "but we were very competitive, so we had a couple of chances to get to the World Series and didn't quite get there."

Ryan was a free agent following the 1988 season, and McMullen offered him a reduced salary. He wound up signing with the Rangers, which made Astros fans furious—especially when Ryan won his 300th game, recorded his 5,000th strikeout, and threw two more no-hitters in Rangers gear. "My thought and hopes and intent when I signed with Houston were that I would retire as a Houston Astro," he said. "John McMullen wanted me to take a 20 percent pay cut because he felt like the salaries were getting out of hand and thought I wouldn't leave as a free agent because it was my home and I was at the end of my career. I went to Arlington…and enjoyed it so much up there that I just stayed and ended up playing five years up there."

5 The Colt .45s

They were cast-offs from other organizations and they played in a temporary stadium that was built in five months in a parking lot where the mosquitoes made more noise than the fans. But on the day they got together for their first game, they were invulnerable. The Houston Colt .45s, one of two expansion teams in the National League, played their first game on April 10, 1962, and beat the Chicago Cubs 11–2. Third baseman Bob Aspromonte led off the game with a single for the first hit in franchise history and wound up scoring the first run. Bobby Shantz pitched a complete-game five-hitter (and was traded away a month later). All nine players who started the game for the Colt .45s played the entire nine innings on a hot day in Houston. "We were just excited about playing, starting with a new team. We were just trying to win a game," said starting center fielder Al Spangler.

Spangler, who had the first RBI in team history when he tripled home Aspromonte in the first inning, was taken by the Astros from the Milwaukee Braves in the expansion draft and couldn't help but wonder what he had gotten himself into. "I was with Milwaukee and I supposedly had a shot at playing center field for the Braves in '62, but they called me and told me I was sold to Houston, Texas," he said. "I said, 'Where the hell is Houston, Texas?' We ended up buying a house in Houston in August of '62 and we've lived here ever since."

The Colt .45s won their first three games, sweeping the Cubs, before the losses began to mount. They finished with a 64–96 record for manager Harry Craft, but it was the first step for a franchise that would later become known as the Astros beginning in 1965 with a move into the Astrodome. "When you come in for the first Major League Baseball game in the city of Houston and to get those people fired up like we did, it was really inspirational for a lot of the players, and we felt really good about it," said Aspromonte, who hailed from Brooklyn.

The Colt .45s averaged more than 11,000 fans for the 1962 season, but by the end of 1963, attendance had dropped below 9,000 per game. In an effort to create a few headlines, manager Harry Craft fielded an all-rookie starting lineup on September 27, 1963, that had an average age of 19 years old. It wasn't until Carl Warwick entered the game as a pinch-hitter in the eighth inning of a 10–3 loss to the New York Mets in the final series of the season at Colt Stadium that a veteran player took the field for Houston. Jay Dahl, a 17-year-old lefty, became the youngest pitcher to start a game since Joe Nuxhall in 1945 at 16 years old. That was the only career major league game for Dahl, who died in a car accident less than two years later. Among the other rookies to start for Houston were Joe Morgan, Rusty Staub, and Jimmy Wynn, who joined Aaron Pointer as the only two Colt .45s players in the lineup who were old enough to vote at the time. Pointer, interestingly, later became an NFL referee and is the brother of the member of the Pointer Sisters singing group.

Two days later, in the only game he ever appeared in, rookie John Paciorek went 3-for-3 with four runs scored and three RBIs in the season finale, a 13–4 win against the Mets. He ended up battling injuries and never stepped foot on a big league field again, finishing with a 1.000 career batting average.

Houston's origins in professional baseball can be traced to the minor league Houston Buffaloes, who began play in the late 1880s as the Houston Babies. The Buffs were affiliated with the St. Louis Cardinals from 1920 to 1942 and 1946 to 1958 and were the Triple A affiliate of the Cubs from 1960 to 1961. They played at Buff Stadium, which sat on the Gulf Freeway across from the University of Houston. Hall of Famers Dizzy Dean, Joe Medwick, and Tris Speaker spent time playing for the Buffs. But Houston had major league dreams.

On June 19, 1958, the Houston Sports Association formally applied for admission into the National League. About a month later, Harris County voters approved an $18 million bond issue for a new sports complex, clearing the way for businessmen George Kirksey and Craig Cullinan to begin traveling the country to gain support for a major league team in Houston. The city flirted with the newly formed Continental League—which had appointed Branch Rickey as president—when Major League Baseball wouldn't support expansion, though league owners eventually changed their mind. On October 17, 1960, the National League awarded expansion franchises to Houston and New York after a masterful presentation by Judge Roy Hofheinz, who brought with him a scale model of what would become the Astrodome. The team earned its nickname through a contest. Houston salesman William T. Neder came up with Colt .45s, writing in his entry, "The Colt .45 won the West and will win the National League."

Winning the National League? That would have to wait until the Astros finally won the pennant in 2005. The Colt .45s played their final home game on September 27, 1964, and Colt Stadium was shipped to Mexico to be used in the minor leagues. "This was not really a baseball city like you expect St. Louis and Boston and even Cincinnati and other places to be," longtime Astros executive Tal Smith said, "but still the anticipation of the Dome stadium deal, Major League Baseball, and the quick development of Colt Stadium made it fascinating."

Biggio Reaches Hall of Fame

The streets of Cooperstown, New York, were awash with Astros fans in all shapes, sizes, and ages. There were hundreds of fans in orange shirts with No. 7 on the back, rainbow jerseys from a previous era, and signs and banners at every turn. Astros fans had waited more than 50 years for this moment—with the final three years being the longest.

If there was ever to be a player to reach the Hall of Fame to represent the Astros, Craig Biggio was the perfect trailblazer. "It's very significant," said longtime Astros executive Tal Smith. "He's the first player signed by the Astros to make the Hall of Fame, first one to spend his entire playing career with the club. Hopefully, it's the first of many."

Biggio spent all 20 years of his career with the Astros and embodied everything the blue-collar Houston fans loved: he played the game hard, always hustled, and rarely walked off the field when he wasn't covered from head to toe in dirt. The pine tar on his helmet may as well have been an oil-stained hardhat. He was Houston.

That's why thousands of Astros fans made the difficult trip from Houston and points all around Texas to Cooperstown's National Baseball Hall of Fame to see Biggio's induction into the Hall of Fame. "It's really special," Biggio said. "When you think about the amount of people that were here from Houston and made the journey to get here…Obviously it's not easy to get here. For them to come and enjoy this and enjoy this together, it was a great day. It was a blast."

Biggio took his spot among baseball's legends on July 26, 2015, getting enshrined alongside Randy Johnson, John Smoltz, and Pedro Martinez. They were elected on their first time on the ballot, while Biggio narrowly missed in 2013 (39 votes) and 2014 (two votes) before finally getting enough support from the Baseball Writers' Association of America. The fact Biggio wasn't elected his first time on the ballot was a letdown considering his impressive credentials. A first-round draft pick out of Seton Hall in 1987, Biggio quickly blossomed into an All-Star catcher before being moved to second base in 1992, where he became a superstar. He was among the best players in the game in the mid-to-late 1990s and helped the Astros win four division titles in a five-year span (1997–99, 2001). He was there when the Astros reached the World Series in 2005. Biggio retired with 3,060 hits, including more doubles (668) than any right-handed hitter in history. When he hung up the cleats, he was 15th all time in runs scored (1,844), 10th in plate appearances (12,504), and first in times hit by pitch (285) in the modern era.

On a warm Sunday afternoon before 45,000 fans—many of whom were wearing orange Astros jerseys—Biggio delivered a heartfelt and poignant speech. More than 50 living Hall of Famers, including his former teammate Nolan Ryan, shared the stage behind him as he gave his speech. "What an incredible honor it is to be standing in front of these great men," Biggio said as he began his speech. "I've played against a lot of them, I admired a lot of them, I respected all of them."

The inscription on his Hall of Fame plaque reads:

GRITTY SPARK PLUG WHO IGNITED ASTROS OFFENSE FOR 20 MAJOR LEAGUE SEASONS, BECOMING FIRST PLAYER IN HISTORY WITH AT LEAST 3,000 HITS, 600 DOUBLES, 400 STOLEN BASES AND 250 HOME RUNS. TRANSITIONED FROM ALL-STAR CATCHER TO GOLD GLOVE SECOND BASEMAN TO EVERYDAY OUTFIELDER, AMASSING 3,060 HITS, INCLUDING 668 DOUBLES— MOST BY A RIGHT-HANDED BATTER—AND A MODERN-DAY RECORD 285 TIMES HIT BY A PITCH. A SEVEN TIME ALL-STAR WON FIVE SILVER SLUGGER AWARDS AND FOUR GOLD GLOVE AWARDS.

"When you look at it and the first word is gritty, that's kind of the player that I was," Biggio said.

In his speech, Biggio spoke about his late parents, Lee and Johnna Biggio. He called his mother, who died in 2009, the "rock."

"I know she's happy today," he said. "I miss you so much." He spoke glowingly about his sons, Conor and Cavan, and daughter, Quinn. He and his wife, Patty, celebrated their 25th wedding anniversary earlier that year.

He gave credit to his youth baseball coaches and praised former Astros owner John McMullen, a New Jersey man who scouted Biggio personally while he was at Seton Hall. "He was like a father figure to me," he said. "We did a lot of things together off the field. Dr. McMullen kept baseball in Houston when the franchise was struggling. How many owners come watch a prospect work out in the gym in the middle of winter? McMullen and Yogi Berra did that." Berra, a catcher like Biggio, also scouted Biggio at Seton Hall and was an Astros coach when he made his major league debut. Berra wasn't able to attend the ceremony and died later that year.

Biggio spoke admirably about former Astros owner Drayton McLane, who owned the team for much of Biggio's tenure, and former Astros coach Matt Galante, who was instrumental in helping Biggio make the move to second base from catcher. "If it wasn't for him, I wouldn't be here today," Biggio said.

Biggio reached the major leagues about the same time as Ken Caminiti and three years before Jeff Bagwell and he was close friends with both. Caminiti, of course, died tragically in 2004, but Bagwell was able to attend the Hall of Fame ceremony. "We played 15 years together and changed the culture in Houston by making it a baseball town," Biggio told the audience. "We both got to live our dreams together by playing in the big leagues side by side. Thanks for being here today. It really means a lot." Bagwell, who has Hall of Fame aspirations himself, summed the achievement up quite succinctly. "I'm so freakin' proud of him," he said.

7 Jeff Bagwell

Jeff Bagwell was one of the most feared sluggers of his generation. A look at his gaudy offensive numbers will tell you that. He's the franchise's career leader in homers, RBIs, batting average, and walks. Those who watched Bagwell play on a day-to-day basis for the Astros will bring up other things he did on the baseball field that were as impressive as his clout. He was one of the more heady players in the game. He was a terrific and smart base runner, even though he wasn't fast. He was a Gold Glove-winning first baseman. And for 15 years, he and longtime teammate Craig Biggio were the heart and soul of the Astros. "It's all about my teammates," Bagwell said. "If they think I was a good teammate and enjoyed playing with me, then that's all that matters to me."

Bagwell is emblazoned in our minds as a barrel-chested slugger, who uncorked powerful swings from his patented crouch stance and hit tape-measure homers. That's not the guy the Astros got when general manager Bill Wood pulled off an infamous trade in 1990 that plucked Bagwell away from the Boston Red Sox in exchange for veteran relief pitcher Larry Andersen. He was a skinny third baseman who was blocked in Boston's system, and with Ken Caminiti established at third base in Houston, the Astros shifted Bagwell across the diamond to first base. He was in the Opening Day lineup in 1991 and would be for 15 consecutive seasons. He hit .294 with 15 homers and 82 RBIs in 156 games in his rookie season. "The fact he was Rookie of the Year for me, that was a pretty good sign of things to come," said Art Howe, who managed the Astros from 1989 to 1993. "I think it was his first game in the big leagues against the Cincinnati Reds, and the 'Nasty Boys' were pitching against us and I think they had the lead and he's leading off the top of the ninth. [Rob] Dibble's on the mound and he's blowing them away and he knocks Bagwell down. I don't know how he got out of the way of it. The next pitch, [Bagwell] hit a rocket up the middle. That told me we had our hands on a great player."

Bagwell blossomed into one of the most feared sluggers in the league by 1994, hitting .368 with 39 homers and 116 RBIs in only 110 games and winning his only Gold Glove Award en route to unanimously being named National League Most Valuable Player in a strike-shortened season. Not that the work stoppage mattered to Bagwell because his season ended when he was hit by a pitch and broke his hand two days before the players went on strike. Bagwell, who also missed the final 20 games of the 1993 season after being hit by a pitch on the hand and was on the disabled list for a month in 1995 with his third such hand break, averaged 34 homers and 115 RBIs in his career and hit .297. He stole 202 career bases. "Baggy was just a great teammate, first and foremost," former Astros slugger Lance Berkman said. "Everybody that played with him loved playing with him. He wasn't really a rah-rah guy but a quiet presence and was very professional."

Bagwell's career was cut short when an arthritic right shoulder forced him to retire following the 2005 season. He underwent capsular release surgery on his shoulder that May and missed 115 games. He returned for the final few weeks of the regular season and served in a pinch-hit role because he could no longer throw a ball. He was the designated hitter for the Astros in the World Series, going 1-for-8 in the Fall Classic in his final appearance in an Astros uniform as a player. "For me it was bittersweet," Bagwell said. "I really couldn't play."

In his first five appearances on the Hall of Fame ballot, Bagwell topped out at 59.6 percent of the vote, leaving him shy of the 75 percent needed to get to Cooperstown. He received 71.6 percent of the vote in 2016, leaving him just 15 votes shy of the Hall of Fame. Those who know him think he should be a lock. "The shoulder hampered what he could do, but he would have played at the same level without that shoulder injury," former manager Phil Garner said. "A Hall of Fame player has to have overall greatness. Some players had excellent defensive skills and might have gotten into the Hall of Fame, some have excellent offensive skills and might have gotten into the Hall of Fame, and here's a player that's a complete package."

8 Killer B's

When the Astros were rolling through the playoffs in 2004 and 2005, a loud buzzing sound filled every corner of Minute Maid Park when someone shot a home run into the Crawford Boxes or came up with a big hit. It was terrific if you loved the Astros, and if you were a visiting player, nothing short of annoying. There was no doubt the Killer B's were at the heart and soul of the Astros' lineup and highlighted the team's long playoff runs in those two seasons.

Beginning in the mid-1990s with Jeff Bagwell, Craig Biggio, Derek Bell, and, yes, Sean Berry, the Killer B's were the driving force behind the Astros' offense. For the next 10 years, any player whose last named started with a B became a member of the fraternity. That ranged from everybody from Carlos Beltran to Chris Burke, but it started and ended with the two franchise icons—Bagwell and Biggio. When Bagwell retired after the team's World Series run in 2005—and was followed by Biggio two years later—the Killer B's essentially died. It went down in history as one of Houston's most memorable sports eras.

Just like Phi Slama Jama, Luv Ya Blue, and Clutch City in the years before, Houston fans got swept up in Killer B mania, dressing as bees in the stands and holding up signs of the players' heads on black and yellow bee bodies during the playoff runs in 2004 and 2005. Former Astros general manager Gerry Hunsicker gets credit for coming up with the term after he traded for outfielder Bell in 1994.

"It was one of those deals—distraction is not the right word—but something we didn't pay too much attention to it as a player," Lance Berkman said. "The original Killer B's were Sean Berry and Bagwell and Biggio and Derek Bell. You kind of felt like an imposter, or at least I did, getting thrown in that mix because we weren't on the original Killer B's."

Bagwell and Biggio were among the best players in the game by the mid-1990s when the club made a blockbuster deal with the San Diego Padres on December 28, 1994. The Astros sent Ken Caminiti—a future MVP—Andujar Cedeno, Steve Finley, Roberto Petagine, and Brian Williams to the Padres for Bell, Doug Brocail, Ricky Gutierrez, Pedro Martinez (not the Hall of Famer), Phil Plantier, and Craig Shipley. Bell was terrific his first year in Houston, hitting .334 with eight homers and 86 RBIs. Berry was traded to the Astros following the 1995 season and paid immediate dividends in 1996, hitting .281 with 17 homers and 95 RBIs. The Killer B's were in full force.

Neither Bell nor Berry spent a long time in Houston, but a new decade dawned and Bagwell and Biggio were still carrying the Killer B flag. Beltran joined the fun when the Astros traded for him in June 2004 and he carried them through the playoffs with eight homers in 12 games. And former first-round pick Chris Burke crashed the party in 2005 by playing in 108 games in the regular season and famously hit a walk-off homer to cap an 18-inning win against the Atlanta Braves in Game 4 of the National League Division Series.

Burke had no idea he qualified as a Killer B until late in the 2005 season when he heard the deafening buzz sound when he came to the plate. "I was like, 'What's happening right now?'" Burke said. "I just went from kind of a rookie that played a role on the team—to all of a sudden they're doing the buzzing noise, and I'm up to bat. The year before I wasn't even on the roster, and that was the buzz they would play when Beltran would come up and Bagwell and Biggio. It was a really cool moment for me."

9 Tombstone

If you have been a sports fan in Houston for any length of time, you've probably dealt with heartbreak. There was the Oilers' loss to the Pittsburgh Steelers in consecutive AFC Championship Games following the 1978 and 1979 seasons, the Astros' crushing losses in the 1980 National League Championship Series to the Philadelphia Phillies and in the 1986 NLCS to the New York Mets, and the Oilers blowing a 32-point lead to the Buffalo Bills in the playoffs following the 1992 NFL season. ESPN Classic may as well have been a horror network for Houston fans.

So when the star-studded Astros, who were coming off a season in which they were a game away from reaching the World Series, got off to a terrible start in 2005, the *Houston Chronicle* piled on. The paper ran a large graphic on the front page of the June 1 sports section featuring a tombstone with an Astros logo on it, signifying the Astros' season was over. It certainly was a terrible beginning for a team with high expectations, but it was a little early to bury the Astros, even though they got off to a 15–30 start that season and were 19–32 at the end of May and in last place in the National League Central. They trailed the first-place St. Louis Cardinals by 14 games.

The *Chronicle*'s premature tombstone became the Houston sports version of "Dewey Defeats Truman." The Astros posted the best record in baseball from June 1 until the end of the season and won the NL wild-card on the final day of the season and wound up winning the NL pennant. The *Chronicle* was forced to eat crow as the Astros celebrated their first NL pennant four and a half months later. "Just from what I remember, it was more of a joke than anything else," Astros slugger Lance Berkman said. "Nobody got upset about it. It was kind of like, people write stuff and say stuff all the time that you just kind of have to not pay much attention to it and try to keep going about your business. It was a veteran club, so nobody really gave it too much thought. It was kind of a joke, really."

In addition to Berkman, the Astros were loaded with veterans who had been through the playoffs wars—Craig Biggio, Jeff Bagwell, Roy Oswalt, Brad Ausmus, Roger Clemens, and Andy Pettitte had extensive postseason resumes. And the Astros didn't have to reach too far back in their memory bank for a reminder that it's a long season. The 2004 club sputtered all year and was four games under .500 in mid-August before rallying for a 36–10 finish to win the wild-card, so there wasn't going to be any panic. "Sometimes when you have an event like that with the tombstone in the paper, it solidifies everybody," former manager Phil Garner said. "It kind of puts it on the table. The 800-pound gorilla in the room is out in front of everyone, and you deal with it."

When pitcher Brandon Backe beat Greg Maddux and the Chicago Cubs at Wrigley Field on May 25, that was the start of a 44–18 run that was the best in the majors, including a 22–7 record in July. Thanks to the wild-card, the Astros were back in the pennant race. They won 13 of their final 18 games to reach the playoffs before beating the Atlanta Braves in four games in the NL Division Series and beating the Cardinals in six games in the NLCS. The Astros were swept in the World Series by the Chicago White Sox, but a team that was left for dead wound up with one of its finest seasons. "That season was so crazy," closer Brad Lidge said. "The one thing I recall that season that's amazing to me is at 15–30, we literally—even though everybody in the world around us and probably rightfully so felt we had no chance to get back in— had such a lack of panic in the clubhouse. We could look around and see the talent and know we're going to be okay. Secondly, we had a bunch of guys that just didn't care we weren't doing well in a good way. We didn't feel the pressure. We needed a winning streak and we knew we could do it…The rest is history."

10 Houston Becomes AL Town

Some of the greatest teams in Astros history—the 1980 club that fell just shy of the World Series and the 1986 team that lost a heart-breaking National League Championship Series to the hated New York Mets—were built on pitching, speed, and defense. They were built for artificial turf. They were built for the spacious Astrodome. They were built for the National League.

The American League was a foreign concept for Houston baseball fans. Even before the Astros, the minor league Houston Buffs were an affiliate of the St. Louis Cardinals (1920–42, 1946–58) and the Chicago Cubs (1960–61), two storied NL teams. It wasn't until interleague play started in 1997 that baseball fans in Houston began to get acquainted with the American League. The idea of teams like the Cleveland Indians, New York Yankees, and Texas Rangers coming to Houston on occasion was a novelty that some fans liked and some didn't. The purists thought it was blasphemous that teams from each league could meet each other prior to the World Series. Others came to embrace interleague play, relishing in the chance to see the Yankees and Boston Red Sox for the first time. They played the Rangers each year in what became known as the Lone Star Series. Little did they know they would be seeing quite a bit of the AL in the years to come.

Former baseball commissioner Bud Selig had a desire to even the competitive balance in the AL, which for years had 16 teams, and the NL, which had 14. Why should AL teams have to go through more teams to reach the World Series? Selig wanted to put 15 teams in each league and establish a wild-card game, but baseball couldn't force an owner of a team to switch leagues.

When longtime Astros owner Drayton McLane sold the team to Houston businessman Jim Crane in 2011 for $610 million, a condition of the sale was the Astros would move to the AL after 51 years in the NL. The move was met with anger by Astros fans, who wanted no part of the designated hitter and didn't care to see the team switch to the AL West, where road games would routinely begin much later at night than they did in the NL Central.

Selig said that it was McLane—and not Crane—who accepted the stipulation of the move. Crane and his group had originally agreed to buy the team for $680 million, but he got a $70 million discount—split between Major League Baseball and McLane—because he was now buying an AL club. Thus, the Astros moved into the AL West with the Rangers, Seattle Mariners, Oakland A's, and Los Angeles Angels of Anaheim. McLane previously had said he was against a move to the AL West because it would result in an increase in the number of late West Coast start times. (The Astros played in the NL West from 1969 to 1993, a division that included the Cincinnati Reds and Atlanta Braves, but they had called the NL Central home since 1994.)

With the Astros in the AL, all six divisions now had five teams as MLB realigned for the first time since the Milwaukee Brewers moved to the NL from the AL in 1998. The new format made it necessary for year-round interleague play because there were an odd number of teams in each league. A move to the AL would also require the Astros to start using a designated hitter, something they were required to do only in games in AL ballparks during interleague play.

Sean Berry was the first DH in Astros history when he grounded back to the pitcher in an interleague game against the Kansas City Royals on June 16, 1997. Berry went 1-for-4 that day. Through the year several players took turns at DH for the Astros, including stars Craig Biggio, Jeff Kent, Lance Berkman, and Jeff Bagwell and lesser known players like Jack Howell, Eric Munson, and Todd Self.

The Astros made their AL debut on March 31, 2013, in a Sunday night game at Minute Maid Park that was aired nationally on ESPN. Texans defensive lineman J.J. Watt threw out the first pitch, and Grammy Award-winning singer Lyle Lovett, who is from the Houston area, performed the national anthem before a sold-out crowd. The Astros even had new uniforms for the occasion, getting rid of the brick red pinstriped uniforms in favor of a more traditional orange and blue look from the team's past. If the move to the AL was met with distaste from fans, the new uniforms wound up being a huge hit.

Veteran Rick Ankiel, who was signed in the offseason but didn't make it through the year in Houston, belted a three-run homer in the sixth inning in the season-opener against the Rangers to break the game open and send the Astros to an 8–2 win. Bud Norris threw five and two-thirds innings to get the win, and veteran lefty Erik Bedard worked the final three and one-third innings for a rare save. Norris' jersey and a ball used in the game were sent to the Hall of Fame. What's more it was the Astros' 4,000th win in franchise history. (3,999 came in the NL.)

The win was gratifying, but they quickly became harder to come by. The Astros, with a payroll of only $20 million, suffered a franchise-record 111 losses in 2013 before improving by 19 games in 2014, going 70–92. It was only a year later they were in the thick of the AL playoff race, and most of the fanbase had gotten over the AL blues. They didn't care which league the Astros were in. They were just glad their team was once again contending for the playoffs.

11 Mike Scott

Perhaps the worst thing Roger Craig ever did was teach Mike Scott the split-fingered fastball. Craig made the pitch famous when he was the pitching coach of the Detroit Tigers, who won the World Series in 1984. Scott was a fledging pitcher who went 5–11 with a 4.68 ERA for the Astros in 1984 when general manager Al Rosen suggested to him that he seek out Craig that winter to learn to throw the split-fingered fastball. Scott, acquired from the New York Mets in exchange for Danny Heep on December 10, 1982, was 30 years old and threw a flat fastball without much movement, but the split-fingered fastball broke sharply as it crossed the plate.

The results were immediate. Scott went 18–8 with a 3.29 ERA in 1985 and quickly became a star. He went 18–10 and led the

Jim Deshaies (left) and Kevin Bass (right) carry Mike Scott off the field after his no-hitter clinches the 1986 National League West title for the Astros.

league in ERA (2.22), shutouts (five), innings pitched (275⅓), and strikeouts (306) in 1986 en route to the Cy Young Award. He sewed up the award when he pitched a no-hitter to clinch the National League West division title. Allegations that Scott was scuffing the baseball to give him an advantage followed Scott throughout that season with Craig—now the manager of the San Francisco Giants—leading the charge.

Scott and the Astros steadfastly denied the balls were being doctored. Nothing was proven. "It was tough, annoying," former Astros manager Hal Lanier said, "especially when we played the

Giants. Roger Craig made a big, big thing about it. There were other clubs also. The Cubs made a big deal about it. They had cameras on him throughout the games every time he started. The Mets during the playoffs were keeping baseballs. Mike and I talked and I said, 'Mike, just go out there and do what you're doing, what you've done all year.'"

Scott took the mound against the Giants on September 25, 1986, with a chance to clinch the NL West. He plunked Dan Gladden with the first pitch but proceeded to become the first pitcher in baseball history to throw a no-hitter in a clinching situation, beating the Giants 2–0. "We knew [clinching] was going to happen, but it's more fun if you win, and everybody can run on the field," Scott said. The triumphant pitcher leapt into the air when he got rookie Will Clark to ground out to first baseman Glenn Davis to end the game and spark a huge celebration. "The pitch wasn't that good," said Scott, who gripped the ball by spreading his pointer finger and middle finger wide across the baseball. "He happened to ground it out and when I look back I still kind of hold

Coneheads

After the Astros clinched the National League West title in 1986 on a no-hitter by Mike Scott, relief pitchers Charley Kerfeld, Larry Andersen, and Aurelio Lopez donned conehead masks during the postgame celebration. The masks fit neatly onto their heads and prevented champagne from getting into their eyes. Andersen was with the Cleveland Indians in 1979 when he saw Texas Rangers pitcher Sparky Lyle don a conehead mask during the national anthem. He decided to pick one up for himself.

The coneheads were as much of a celebration of the Astros' division title as champagne and beer. When Kerfeld, Andersen, and Lopez were posing for a picture while wearing the masks in the clubhouse following the victory, Astros bench coach Yogi Berra walked by and quipped, "You guys make quite a pair."

"There was three of us," Andersen said. "That's Yogi."

my breath, hoping he doesn't get a base hit because it wasn't a very good pitch. He happened to ground out to first, and that was it."

Scott was just as dominant in the postseason, beating the Mets twice in the National League Championship Series before being denied a chance to finish them off in Game 7, when the Mets rallied to win Game 6 in 16 innings. Scott was so dominant he was named the Most Valuable Player of the NLCS despite the Astros losing the series.

Astros catcher Alan Ashby got accused of scuffing baseballs, along with some of the infielders. "Who's to say what was going on?" he said. Ashby played with Gaylord Perry with the Cleveland Indians when he won 15 in a row in 1974. Perry had thrown a spitball at one time in his career but was still able to get into opponents' heads when he wasn't throwing it. Ashby said the suspicion worked in Scott's favor, too. "There was nothing wrong with having Roger Craig and others accuse us of chicanery," he said.

Scott won 110 games in nine seasons with the Astros, winning 20 games in 1989 and making the All-Star Game for the third time. The Astros retired his No. 33 in 1992. "Sometimes I felt like I could drop my glove by my side and watch him pitch," Davis said. "I didn't have to get ready because he was going to dominate. For the most part, it was art in motion. He was just brilliant."

12 Biggio's 3,000th Hit

Astros second baseman Craig Biggio always ran out of the box with a double in mind. He retired with more doubles than any other right-handed batter in history and he always took pride in being able to get to second base with one swing of the bat. That meant Biggio was in scoring position and—with his speed—had a good chance to score on any hit.

Biggio entered the 2007 season—his 20th with the Astros—with 2,930 hits, putting him in line to become the 27th player to reach 3,000. That's hallowed ground. He hadn't yet announced his retirement, but most believed Biggio was going to hang up the spikes at the end of the season. The Astros weren't contenders in 2007, so Biggio reaching 3,000 was going to be the crowning achievement of the season. The team installed a digital counter to keep track of Biggio's hits inside Minute Maid Park. The Astros wanted to make sure they cashed in, and as Biggio got closer to the 3,000 mark, he mapped out a schedule with manager Cecil Cooper in which he would get periodic days off so he could reach the milestone at Minute Maid Park. After going 3-for-5 in a game against the Texas Rangers in Arlington on June 24, Biggio was four hits shy of reaching 3,000 with a three-game series in Milwaukee still looming.

Biggio sat out the first game of the series and went 1-for-4 in the second game, putting him three hits shy. Cooper left him out of the starting lineup in the final game of the series against the Milwaukee Brewers. That all but assured Biggio would get 3,000 before the home crowd. A sellout crowd of 42,537 packed Minute Maid Park on June 28 eager for a shot to witness history. Biggio started at second base and hit leadoff. He grounded out in his first at-bat before stealing the show.

Facing Colorado Rockies pitcher Aaron Cook, Biggio singled to center in the third inning for hit 2,998. He beat out an infield single in the fifth for hit No. 2,999, filling the ballpark with anticipation for his next at-bat. The crowd roared when Biggio came to the plate in the seventh inning, and Biggio lined a single into right-center field for his 3,000th hit. Biggio tried to stretch the single into a double and was thrown out at second base by Rockies center fielder Willy Taveras, a former teammate of Biggio. That didn't dampen the celebration one bit. "Everybody thinks I wanted to get a double," Biggio said. "I wasn't trying for the double. There were two outs, and we were losing 1–0 in the seventh inning, and I was trying to make sure that Brad [Ausmus] scored and also make sure I got myself in scoring position. Then, hopefully, I could score on another single. Obviously, Willy wanted nothing of that and threw me out by 10 feet."

Biggio's wife, Patty, and daughter, Quinn, came onto the field to hug Craig, along with his sons, Conor and Cavan, who were serving as batboys and didn't have to go far to join in the celebration. More than 40 family members and friends of the Biggios, from both Houston and his native New York, celebrated along with the fans. Biggio lifted Quinn high in the air as Patty let her emotions get the best of her. Biggio then spotted Jeff Bagwell in street clothes in the dugout and dragged his teammate of 15 years onto the field to celebrate with him.

"I wanted it to happen at home," Biggio said. "For the integrity of the game, you let the chips fall where they may. But the right thing happened, and we were able to get it done, and anybody who had a ticket that night got to enjoy it, and the people at home got to enjoy it. Like I said, 20 years playing here and to be able to give that back to the fans is a pretty cool thing."

Biggio didn't stop at 3,000. He singled to right field in the ninth inning for his fourth hit of the game and he singled again in the 11th to cap off a 5-for-6 night. Carlos Lee finished the night with a walk-off grand slam, scoring Biggio to win the game. The grand slam proved to be only a sidebar to a night that belonged to No. 7.

13 Larry Dierker

Larry Dierker made his major league debut for the Astros on his 18th birthday and has remained a part of the organization since. He won 137 games in 13 seasons with the Astros, made two All-Star teams, and threw a no-hitter. When he retired he owned the franchise records for innings pitched, starts, complete games, and shutouts. And his Astros career was just getting started.

Dierker, known for his Hawaiian shirts and cerebral nature, went from the mound to the broadcast booth. He spent 18 seasons an Astros broadcaster, calling some of the greatest moments in team history. The Astros stunned the baseball world when they plucked him from the booth after firing Terry Collins in 1996 and named him manager. "It certainly was an out-of-the-box decision and left a lot of people scratching their heads," former Astros general manager Gerry Hunsicker said. "Those of us that knew Larry knew he had a great baseball mind. He was a student of the game. He also had a relationship with some of our core players, namely Craig Biggio and Jeff Bagwell, and we thought that might work in his favor. We also thought he might have a major impact on the pitching. Looking back, he obviously was the most successful manager in franchise history."

Dierker guided a talented Astros club to four playoff appearances in five years. The Astros won a club-record 102 games in 1998, and Dierker was named National League Manager of the Year. That cemented his place as an Astros legend. His No. 49 was retired in 2002, one year after he was let go following a fourth first-round playoff loss. "The first thing that comes to my mind is how lucky I was in my career in a couple of ways to retrieve something near the end that everyone wants to experience that some people don't ever get to experience," Dierker said. "The first one didn't have to do with managing but pitching. I ended up pitching the no-hitter right at the very end of my career. My arm was so sore I could hardly go out there. I wasn't even throwing between starts. Somehow I lucked into throwing a no-hitter right at the very end of my career, and it was such a thrill."

Once Dierker became manager, the pitchers loved him. He challenged them to work deeper into games and pitch out of their own messes. Jose Lima, Darryl Like, Mike Hampton, Chris Holt, and Shane Reynolds flourished under Dierker. "He came in and helped us tremendously because he told us at spring training, 'Look, guys, when we get to the fifth inning, sixth inning, and get in a little trouble, don't look over your shoulder to the bullpen and dugout like we're going to come get you,'" Reynolds said.

Dierker was signed as an amateur free agent by the Colt .45s in 1964 and made his major league debut on September 22, 1964. He struck out Willie Mays looking to end the first inning of that game. Dierker became the franchise's first 20-game winner when he went 20–13 with a 2.33 ERA in 1969 and made the All-Star team en route to being named the team's Most Valuable Player. It was during that season that Dierker had one of the best games of his career, when he threw 12 innings against the Atlanta Braves on September 13 and allowed four hits, four walks and struck out five. He got a no-decision in a 3–2 loss, and the Astros faded in the final three weeks. "That was a momentous game for me because it was the first year in Astros history," Dierker said. "We were actually a contending team in September, and that one game blew us right out of contention and seemed to launch [the Braves] on a streak that took them to the NL West title."

In his 14-year career, which ended with an 11-game stint with the St. Louis Cardinals in 1977, Dierker went 139–123 with a

3.31 ERA, 106 complete games, and 25 shutouts. Nearly 40 years after his last game, he still holds the club record for games started, complete games, innings pitched, and shutouts. On July 9, 1976, against the Montreal Expos, he threw a no-hitter in the Astrodome. After finishing his career with St. Louis in 1977, he returned to Houston and directed the group and season ticket sales office for the Astros. He began broadcasting games a year later and became a fixture on the radio game broadcasts with Milo Hamilton, though he did TV as well.

During a game against the San Diego Padres on June 13, 1999, Dierker collapsed in the dugout while suffering a grand mal seizure. The seizure was caused by a tangle of ruptured blood vessels that was called an arteriovenous malformation (AVM). Two things saved Dierker's life: the AVM occurred in the frontal area of the brain, which was easy to access and didn't affect any of his motor skills, and the Astrodome was only 10 minutes from the Texas Medical Center. "What would have happened if I had the seizure in the middle of the night in a hotel on the road?" Dierker said. "I would have died. You just thank God. The surgeon fixed it so quickly and completely that within a week I was playing golf. I wanted back in the dugout within a week." It took a month, but with peach fuzz-length hair and a scar atop his head, Dierker returned to the dugout on July 15, 1999, and led the Astros to the division title.

14 Altuve Wins Batting Title

The incredible numbers Jose Altuve posted throughout his minor league career still weren't enough to make most people believe he could perform at that level in the major leagues. After all, he was a 5'6" second baseman who wasn't highly touted coming up or even listed on any prospect lists coming through the system. Altuve, signed by the Astros as a 16-year-old out of Venezuela, was a career .327 hitter in the minor leagues and was hitting a combined .389 between Class A Lancaster and Double A Corpus Christi in 2011 when the Astros called him up midseason after trading Jeff Keppinger. *Who was this little guy?* No one knew what to expect, except for Altuve. He hit safely in his first seven games in the big leagues and didn't stop, batting .290 and reaching the All-Star Game in 2012.

Anyone who still doubted his talents could only watch in awe at what Altuve did during his record-breaking 2014 season. Altuve, blessed with great hand-eye coordination and bat control, became the first Astros player to win a batting crown when he led the major leagues with a .341 batting average, as well as smashing Craig Biggio's club record by rapping out 225 hits. He also stole 56 bases, which led the American League.

Altuve didn't clinch the batting title until the final day of the season, going 2-for-4 in an 8–3 loss to the Mets at New York's Citi Field. The Astros had originally decided to keep Altuve out of the lineup for the season finale to help protect his three-point lead over Detroit Tigers designated hitter Victor Martinez, but interim manager Tom Lawless called Altuve back into the office just prior to the start of the game. There had been a change of heart, and the team released a statement via Twitter about 30 minutes prior to the first pitch saying Altuve was playing. "We decided to make the change and play him, and whatever happened, happened," Lawless said. "And it happened that with his two hits he became the batting champion. It was a moot point what happened before."

After the game Astros teammates, coaches, and staff gave Altuve a champagne toast in the clubhouse. "I'm pretty excited, but what made me happier is all the support and the things my team has done for me," Altuve said. "After the game they were happy for me, and all came to me and said 'Congratulations,' and that made my season way better."

Altuve had the most hits by a second baseman in a single season since 1936, and he joined Joe Mauer (2006) and Alex Rodriguez (1996) as the only AL players 24 years old or younger to win a batting title in the previous 20 seasons.

On the day Altuve was born, his father was watching a baseball game at a field next door to the hospital where his wife was giving birth in Venezuela. Carlos Altuve wound spend much of his free time the next few years throwing baseballs to his oldest son with hopes he would inherit his father's love of the game. "He always told me," Jose said, "you've got to hit to make the major leagues."

Altuve first caught Houston's attention while playing second base for the Venezuelan 16-and-under national team. The Astros sent Omar Lopez to see another player, a shortstop named Angel Nieves, in Venezuela. Lopez drove four hours to watch Nieves, but he couldn't take his eyes off "the little guy." Al Pedrique, then a special assistant under general manager Tim Purpura, went to see Altuve, and his ability to put the bat on the ball couldn't be ignored. Pedrique met with Altuve's family and offered him $15,000 to sign. His father was an assistant engineer at a chemical company (his mother was a housewife), so money wasn't an issue. Still, $15,000 was too much to pass up. "I was putting that money in my pocket before I answered that," Altuve said. "I always believed the hardest thing for me was an organization giving me the opportunity."

Altuve's rise was a quick one. He spent only one year playing for the team's Venezuelan Summer League in 2007 before the Astros made a decision to bring him to the U.S., which was unprecedented for a player so young. He hit a combined .302 between

Jose Altuve takes a swing during 2014, a year in which he hit .341, recorded 225 hits, and stole 56 bases.

Greeneville and Tri-City in '09 and .301 in '10 between Class A Lexington and Class A Lancaster.

Altuve credited the work he did with hitting coach John Mallee for helping put him in position to win the batting title in '14. After all, Mallee established three goals for Altuve in the spring of that year: become more disciplined in the strike zone, make the All-Star team, and win a batting title. He did all three. "That caps off him as a person, the hard work he put in," Mallee said. "He went out and finished the job. He did it on the field."

It was earlier that season, when Mallee was forced to take an alternate route to Minute Maid Park, that he saw how much

Willy Goes Streakin'

For all the great players the Astros have had in their history, it's Willy Taveras who owns the club's longest hitting streak. Taveras was a solid player. He had streak-of-lightning speed and was a popular member of the 2005 World Series team, but he certainly wasn't close to the kind of offensive force of players like Cesar Cedeno, Craig Biggio, Jeff Bagwell, Lance Berkman, or Jose Altuve.

Still, Taveras set the franchise record for consecutive games with a hit when he hit in 30 in a row from July 27, 2006, through August 27, 2006, breaking Jeff Kent's previous record of 25 games set in 2004. Taveras hit .349 during the streak, which included 38 singles, five doubles, one triple, and one homer. Somehow, Taveras managed to maintain his streak despite going 0-for-11 in the middle of it.

How did he do that?

Taveras singled in his first at-bat in an 8–6, 18-inning loss to the Chicago Cubs and went 0-for-8 the rest of the game. The next game he was hitless in his first three at-bats before beating out a bunt single in the seventh inning to extend his hitting streak.

His hit streak, though, wasn't as unusual as Tony Eusebio's during the 2000 season. Eusebio, a burly backup catcher for the Astros, set a club record with a 24-game hitting streak accomplished over 45 games (but over 51 days) because he didn't play every day.

Altuve meant to the organization. Mallee's detour carried him past a side of the ballpark he had rarely seen, a side with a massive Jose Altuve banner hanging of the diminutive second baseman. "I told him when I came in, I said, 'Do you realize how important you are to this organization, to this city?'" Mallee said. "'To drive by and see your picture up there every day from where you came from and how hard it's been for you to get where you are, that should make you have pride and want to work and be the best you can be because you are the Houston Astros.'"

Altuve was coming off a pretty good 2013 season in which he hit .283 with 52 RBIs and 85 strikeouts and 32 walks in 152 games. He worked hard in the offseason to get in shape—in order to beat out more ground balls he said—and reported to camp quicker and 10 pounds lighter. Still, he was skeptical about tinkering with his approach because he had a couple of solid big league seasons under his belt. Mallee wanted him to change his mechanics to better identify off-speed pitches because he used to stride early to the ball. Mallee added a knee tuck to help load the hips, allowing him to wait to put his front foot down until he was ready to swing. "He was able to time up pitches a lot better because he wasn't committed early," Mallee said.

The improvement in his batting average was only the beginning. He struck out much less in 2014 than he did the year before and had a much higher average on balls in play. He also became a terrific two-strike hitter. Altuve put in the work and got the results, even though he admitted he thought Mallee's aspirations were crazy at first. "But he's not as crazy as I thought," he said.

15 1980 NLCS

The Astros boarded a flight for Philadelphia emotionally drained and exhausted after a grueling four games to end the 1980 regular season. They had gone into Dodger Stadium for a three-game series against the Los Angeles Dodgers to end the season with a three-game lead in the National League West and found themselves tied after 162 games after losing three consecutive one-run games. Behind the pitching of Joe Niekro and a big home run by Art Howe, the Astros won a one-game playoff on October 6, 1980, to win the division title in one of the most clutch wins in franchise history. When the celebration ended, they had to fly across the country to meet the Phillies in Game 1 of the best-of-five National League Championship Series the following day.

It turns out the drama was only beginning for the Astros.

The Phillies, who featured Hall of Famers Mike Schmidt and Steve Carlton as well as eventual all-time hits leader Pete Rose, won Game 1. The 3–1 victory before 65,277 at Veterans Stadium in Philadelphia was the only game of the series not decided in extra innings. Astros starter Ken Forsch and Carlton battled for five innings before Greg Luzinski hit a two-run homer in the sixth that put Philadelphia ahead 2–1. The Astros had Nolan Ryan on the mound for Game 2 and wound up winning 7–4 in 10 innings, scoring four times in the 10th inning on RBIs by Jose Cruz, Cesar Cedeno, and Dave Bergman. The win was a boost to the Astros' psyche because they were going home for three games—the first home playoff games in franchise history—and needed only two wins.

The Astrodome was rocking on October 10, 1980, for Game 3. Niekro threw 10 scoreless innings and set the stage for the Astros to win in the 11th when Joe Morgan tripled off Tug McGraw and limped into third on a bad knee, and pinch-runner Rafael Landestoy scored the winning run on a Denny Walling sac fly. The Astros—who lost Cedeno to an injury in the game—were one win from the World Series. "The three games back here at the Astrodome, we had a lot of occasions where the crowd noise is really deafening," former general manager Tal Smith said. "It was quite a scene."

Game 4 was played under protest by both teams following a controversial call in the fourth inning. The Astros led 2–0 going to the eighth inning, but they had blown great scoring chances in the sixth and seventh when they had the bases loaded. A run was taken off the board in the sixth when Gary Woods left third base too early on a fly ball off the bat of Luis Pujols, resulting in an inning-ending double play after the Phillies successfully appealed. The Phillies scored three runs in the eighth to take the lead, and—after Terry Puhl tied it with an RBI single in the ninth—Philadelphia scored twice in the 10th to win and tie the series. "Even though, yeah, in Game 5 we had Nolan Ryan on the mound, it never should have went to a fifth game," said Puhl, who set an LCS record by hitting .526 (10-for-19) in the series. "Lots of sore spots in that one."

The decisive fifth game, which was played before a college football game between Houston and Texas A&M in the Astrodome didn't end until 2:41 AM, led to more open wounds for the Astros. They had a 5–2 lead entering the eighth inning with Ryan on the mound and coughed it up. The Phillies scored five times to take a 7–5 lead, only to watch the Astros tie it in the bottom of the ninth inning on RBIs by Landestoy and Cruz. In the 10th inning, the Phillies got doubles from Del Unser and Garry Maddox to win 8–7. Maddox was carried off the field after catching the final out off the bat of Enos Cabell while Cruz shed a tear in the dugout. "I drove home that winter back to California, and everywhere I stopped for gas everybody saw the games because they were so thrilling," Cabell said. "It was really exciting because we had come so far, and in '80 we had lost J.R. Richard, too. We were thinking we had a team that was going to win for five, six, seven years…We thought we were going to be that good. It was really disheartening for the fans and really tough for us."

16 First-Round Playoff Blues

It was just the Astros' luck. They snapped an 11-year playoff drought by winning the National League Central division in 1997 and had to face the juggernaut Atlanta Braves and their pitching rotation that included future Hall of Famers Greg Maddux, Tom Glavine, and John Smoltz. The Braves, who won 14 division titles from 1991 to 2005, were a thorn in the Astros' side and eliminated them from the playoffs in 1997, 1999, and 2001. The Astros finally broke their Braves curse by beating them in the National League Division Series in 2004 and 2005, but some of the most talented teams ever assembled by the Astros couldn't get past the Braves in the first round of the playoffs, as well as the San Diego Padres in 1998. "I'd rather go through that than never get the chance of competing," former Astros closer Billy Wagner said. "I mean, people don't realize, when you're playing the Braves and you have to go through Maddux, Smoltz, and Glavine…holy cow."

The 1997 Astros took the division despite winning only 84 games. Still, Houston's first baseball championship since the 1986 NL West title had baseball fans excited. In Game 1 in Atlanta, Maddux threw a complete game to beat the Astros 2–1, and Glavine got the win as the Braves took a 2–0 lead in the series with a 13–3 win in Game 2. The Braves polished off the sweep behind a complete game by Smoltz in a 4–1 win in Game 3 in Houston. The Braves beat the Astros in four games in 1999 and swept them in 2001, leaving the Astros without a playoff series victory in their history. "I don't think I really ever felt guilty that I should have been able to do something about it as a manager—either inspire somebody or come up with a sneak small ball attack or manipulate something," former manager Larry Dierker said, "to stop us from being so feeble offensively in the playoffs through the series that I managed."

The 1999 NLDS, though, was particularly hard to swallow for the Astros. After the Astros and Braves split two games in Atlanta, they came to the Astrodome for Game 3. The game was tied 3–3 in the 10th inning when the Astros had the bases loaded and no outs. They were poised to win. With one out Tony Eusebio hit a hard grounder that Braves shortstop Walt Weiss made an unbelievable play on to get a force out at the plate. The Braves wound up winning in 12 innings and took the series with a 7–5 win the next day. "The Braves were an extraordinary powerhouse back then," former general manager Gerry Hunsicker said. "It was unfortunate we had just come along at the same time. They had tremendous success. I think part of it was we had a lot of right-handed hitters that didn't match up real well with the Braves back in that era. Part of it might have got into our heads after the second go-around and having a hard time beating them during the season. I think it definitely was a contributing factor."

The Astros won 102 games in 1998 and were positioned to make a long playoff run, especially with the Braves not standing in their way in the first round. And the Astros had acquired future Hall of Fame pitcher Randy Johnson at the trade deadline, and he made 11 starts and went an amazing 10–1. In the playoffs the Big Unit had a 1.93 ERA in two starts, but the Astros were shut down offensively. Kevin Brown allowed one run in two starts, and

Sterling Hitchcock handcuffed them in Game 4 as the Padres won the series in four games. "The '98 one was the tough one to me," Wagner said.

The Padres wound up winning the NL pennant and losing to the New York Yankees in the World Series. "We should have been playing the Yankees," Wagner said. "I don't think anybody would disagree with that part. Gosh, we were solid. We had an awesome team. There was so many things that went on in that series with San Diego. Everything that could happen, happened. It was a great series, but it was very frustrating because we all felt like we had the better team."

17 Lance Berkman

He was one of the Astros' most feared sluggers in history, as well as one of their most colorful characters. At the height of his career, Lance Berkman was once being heckled by fans at Wrigley Field because of his perceived extra weight, which he chalked up to big jowls. The fans threw a pair of Twinkies onto the field, and Berkman opened the wrapper and ate one of them during a pitching change and stuffed the other one in his back pocket. "They went absolutely crazy," he said. "They gave me a standing ovation. I ended up hitting a homer in my next at-bat."

That was the wild, wonderful world of Berkman's tenure with the Astros, where he joined fellow Killer B's Jeff Bagwell and Craig Biggio to help take the franchise to new heights in the 2000s. A proud native Texan, Berkman was drafted in the first round after leading Rice to the College World Series and quickly became a star. The wise-cracking switch-hitter blasted 326 home runs and drove in 1,090 in his 12 seasons (1999–2010) with the Astros and was a fan favorite. He's generally regarded, along with Bagwell and Biggio, as one of the top three offensive players in club history.

When he was drafted by the Astros with the 16th overall pick in 1997, Berkman—a first baseman at Rice—figured he was headed to the outfield because Bagwell held that position, but he otherwise didn't know much about the Astros. They hadn't scouted him or talked to him, even though he had played college ball in the same city. "It was totally out of left field—pardon the pun—to be drafted by the Astros," he said. "My first reaction was kind of like, 'Oh, I didn't expect that at all.' And then as I started to realize I was getting to stay close to home and having the opportunity to be a part of an organization that's in the same town where I went to college—and knowing after having talked to them I was expected to play left field—you get your head around that, and it was very exciting."

Lance-A-Lot of Homers

Lance Berkman dazzled the home fans at Minute Maid Park during the 2004 Home Run Derby, blasting a total of 21 homers, including one that measured 497 feet. It was the longest of the competition. Impressive as Berkman's feat was, it wasn't good enough to win.

That's because Baltimore Orioles shortstop Miguel Tejada bashed a record 27 home runs to edge Berkman for the title. The previous record was 26 set by Sammy Sosa in 2000 and matched by Albert Pujols in 2003. Berkman, a switch-hitter, was a better left-handed hitter in his career, but he batted exclusively right-handed during the derby to take advantage of the Crawford Boxes in left field, which sit just 315 feet from home plate. Most of Berkman's homers sailed well over the Crawford Boxes.

Berkman admitted he really had no clue what he was doing during his first derby in Milwaukee in 2002 despite teammate Jeff Bagwell telling him not to swing at every pitch, which he promptly did. Berkman was better prepared two years later to rise to the moment.

Berkman quickly became an All-Star, hitting .331 with 55 doubles, 34 homers, and 126 RBIs in 2001. He finished third in the National League Most Valuable Player voting in 2002 by hitting .292 with 42 homers and 128 RBIs. He hit 45 homers and a set club records for RBIs (136) in 2006 and earned his fifth All-Star honor with the Astros in 2008 by hitting .312 with 29 homers and 106 RBIs. By this time the "Big Puma"—the self-depreciating name he gave himself for his lack of quickness—had moved back to first base to replace Bagwell, who had retired.

In the playoffs Berkman was even more clutch. He was a career .317 hitter in 52 career playoff games, mostly with the Astros in the 2000s. His dramatic grand slam into the Crawford Boxes at Minute Maid Park in Game 4 of the 2005 National League Division Series against the Atlanta Braves got the Astros within a run in the eighth inning, and they eventually won in 18 innings on a Chris Burke walk-off homer. "It's a great memory," he said. "A lot of times a home run is a rally killer because now the bases are empty, and they still have a lead and sort of the worst thing that can happen has happened, and you survived it, and it gives the other team a mental edge. Sure enough, we get out of that inning and then we come to the ninth down a run, and that's when [catcher Brad Ausmus] hit the homer [to tie the game]."

Berkman's only regret about his time in Houston was that the Astros never won a World Series. He was traded to the New York Yankees in 2010 when the club started rebuilding. Berkman joined the St. Louis Cardinals in 2011 and enjoyed another great year, hitting .301 with 31 homers and 94 RBIs while helping them win the World Series. In Game 6 of the 2011 World Series against the Texas Rangers, a graying Berkman tied the game with a clutch single off Scott Feldman in the 10th inning when the Rangers were one strike away from winning.

18 The Big Unit Hits Houston

Astros general manager Gerry Hunsicker saw opportunity. The 1998 Astros had been in first place most of the season with a powerful lineup that included Craig Biggio, Jeff Bagwell, and Moises Alou, and a strong pitching staff. They were bound for the postseason and poised to make a long run into October. Hunsicker was sold on his team. He was thinking about October. He was thinking of the New York Yankees. Joe Torre's club was on its way to a 114-win regular season and was undoubtedly World Series-bound. Hunsicker thought his team could get there, too, and wanted to make sure they matched up. "When you have a good team," Hunsicker said, "pile on to give yourself as much reinforcement as you can to get through the playoffs, and, of course, that year the Yankees were arguably the best team in the American League and they had a lot of talented left-handed hitters, and adding a dominant left-handed starter like Randy Johnson really would give us a great chance against them if we got to that point,"

Johnson was the intimidating 6'10" left-hander who blossomed in Seattle. He won the 1995 Cy Young Award and made his fifth All-Star team in 1997 while finishing second in the Cy Young for the second time. Johnson was just 9–10 with a 4.33 ERA through 23 starts in 1998 and was set to become a free agent at the end of the season, so the Mariners wanted to get something for him. The Cleveland Indians and Yankees were the two teams heavily involved in Johnson trade talks. The Astros stayed out of the headlines before stunning the baseball world as the July 31 deadline hit. Hunsicker pulled off the deal, sending prospects Freddy Garcia, Carlos Guillen, and a player to be named later (pitcher John Halama) to Seattle for the Big Unit. News of the deal came down late at night. "It was definitely the most exciting trade I ever made because it was made at literally the deadline," Hunsicker said. "It was in the middle of an exciting season already, and we obviously got a future Hall of Famer in the trade, which was something that Houston fans weren't accustomed to. Those kinds of players just didn't come to Houston. It was very close to not happening."

In the hours leading up to the deadline, Hunsicker called owner Drayton McLane and team president Tal Smith and told them the trade wasn't going to happen. The next couple of hours were somewhat gut-wrenching for Hunsicker because of the lack of negotiations. "It was a Friday night, and I was at a church meeting, and he kept calling me," McLane said. "We talked and made counteroffers. I kept encouraging him to call back to Seattle's general manager." Hunsicker had reengaged with the Mariners and upped the ante. "I knew we had to overpay to get him [because] we had a tremendous team that in my mind was going to get to the playoffs," Hunsicker said. "As we painfully found out in hindsight, getting to the playoffs is hard. Getting to the World Series and winning it is even harder."

Johnson was nothing short of magnificent for the Astros. He made 11 starts and went 10–1 with a 1.28 ERA. The Astrodome was filled to capacity every time he started. He was a rock star with a mullet. "I was going from the Kingdome, which was a band box, and now I was pitching in the Houston Astrodome," Johnson said. "I was also going and playing for a first-place team. Billy Wagner was my closer. So everything just kind of fell into place, and it was my best two months of my career."

Johnson's brilliance was wasted. The Astros' mighty offense was shut down in the playoffs. The San Diego Padres beat them in four games in the National League Division Series. Johnson made two starts and lost them both, but he was terrific. He struck out 17 and walked only two and allowed 12 hits and three earned runs in 14 innings. He signed a four-year, $52.4-million deal with the Arizona Diamondbacks in the offseason and wound up winning four Cy Young Awards. But the two-month stretch in Houston remains legendary. "It was the most exhilarating stretch of my career," Hunsicker said. "To see the city that excited was really a special feeling."

19 Ken Caminiti

Craig Biggio and Jeff Bagwell were set to play the biggest game of their careers—Game 5 of the 2004 National League Division Series against the Braves in Atlanta—when they were forced to deal with heartbreaking news. Ken Caminiti, their former teammate with the Astros, had been found dead of a heart attack at the age of 41.

The news stunned the baseball world and the Astros, who proceeded to beat the Braves 12–3 to win their first playoff series in history. Biggio and Bagwell celebrated with heavy hearts, taking solace in the fact Caminiti would have wanted them to play. "He was a gentle giant," Biggio said. "He looked like a big bad ass with his Fu Manchu and his beard and all that stuff and he looked like the intimidator, but he was the furthest thing from it. Cammy would give you the shirt off his back. To have to play the Braves… losing one of your best friends was hard. The thing that got me through it was he would want me to play."

Caminiti won the National League MVP with the San Diego Padres in 1996 but cut his teeth in the major leagues with the Astros. He was drafted in the third round out of San Jose State by the Astros in 1984. He broke into the major leagues with the Astros with a bang, hitting a homer and a triple in his first game

Prior to Game 5 of the 2004 NLDS, Craig Biggio and strength and conditioning coach Gene Coleman watch a video tribute, honoring former Astros third baseman Ken Caminiti, who died at the age of 41.

on July 16, 1987, one year before Biggio made his debut. With his hard-nosed style of play and cannon for an arm, Caminiti quickly became a fan favorite, and by 1991 he, Biggio, Bagwell, and Luis Gonzalez were the cornerstones of a young team on the rise. Biggio, who broke into the big leagues as a catcher, had the best seat in the house to watch Caminiti's wizardry at third base. "You're seeing every play and watching him make some plays, and you're like, 'Wow, a normal human being doesn't make those plays,'" Biggio said. "He would knock the ball down on the third-base line, and the ball falls out, and he picks it up and throws from his butt and throws a seed across the diamond."

Caminiti was one of the top defensive third basemen in the NL, but he never won a Gold Glove until he put up gaudy offensive numbers after being traded to the Padres. He was traded to the Padres after the 1994 season in an 11-player trade that brought Derek Bell and Doug Brocail, among others, to Houston. The Astros also sent future All-Star and Gold Glove outfielder Steve Finley to the Padres in the deal. Caminiti bashed 26 homers in 1995 for San Diego and won the MVP in 1996 after hitting .326 with 40 homers and 130 RBIs. He returned to the Astros in 1999 for two injury-plagued seasons—he hit three homers in the 1999 NLDS—before finishing with the Braves in 2001.

Caminiti struggled with substance abuse throughout his career and admitted in 1994 to having alcoholism. A year after he retired, he told *Sports Illustrated* he used steroids during his 1996 MVP season. Caminiti's remains are buried on Cambo Ranch in Sabinal, Texas, which was co-owned by Caminiti and Biggio. When Biggio was inducted into the Hall of Fame in 2015, he made sure Caminiti's wife and three daughters were there to share the moment with him.

"People ask me what kind of person he was," Biggio said. "Everyone knows what kind of player he was. He was a warrior. He played in any kind of pain. He had an obligation to the people who depended on him. He was the guy you'd want in your foxhole. He was a great guy, too. He was one of those people that would give you the last dollar he had. If you needed something, he'd be there for you, no questions asked. I always said that if I was in trouble and had one telephone call, he'd be the one I'd want to call."

20 Crawford Boxes Spook Pitchers

Workers were putting the finishing touches on Enron Field in the spring of 2000 when the Astros left spring camp in Florida and flew home for an exhibition game against the New York Yankees at the new Houston ballpark. When the team buses arrived at the ballpark, the players made their way to the field to check things out. They had heard about the short porch in left field, atop which sat the Crawford Boxes seats. Getting a chance to see it for the first time, though, put it into better focus and brought a stark reality: this wasn't the Astrodome. "From the first day they saw this park, it got in their head," general manager Gerry Hunsicker said. "And there's absolutely no question in their mind it was a huge factor that year."

The Astrodome, which housed the Astros for the previous 35 seasons, was always known as a spacious pitcher's park despite efforts to move in the walls in the 1990s. Enron Field returned Houston to natural-grass and—sometimes—open-air baseball, but it also brought the offense. The left-field line was only 315 feet from home plate where it was met by a 19-foot wall, which made it look much closer. If you were a pitcher, you couldn't help but be taken aback. "There's no question the difference between pitching in the Astrodome and pitching in Minute Maid Park, which was then Enron Field, was dramatically different because long fly balls that were outs in the Dome were home runs in Enron," Astros manager Larry Dierker said. "And for a pitcher, the difference between an out and a home run is gigantic. It's way more than between a single and a double, an out or a single, or something like that. They're throwing balls they're used to getting outs on, and it's at least a run, and if there's anybody on, it's more than a run."

The Astros were coming off their third consecutive division title in 1999 and had many of the same pitchers on their 2000 roster. They ranked third in the National League in 1999 in ERA at 3.83 and gave up the fewest home runs at 128. The first year at Enron Field, they were last in ERA in 5.42 and gave up 234 home runs, which was the second-highest total in the major leagues. Right-hander Jose Lima, coming off a pair of terrific seasons, allowed a whopping 48 homers in 196⅓ innings, and four other pitches gave up at least 20—Scott Elarton (29), Octavio Dotel (26), Chris Holt (22), and Shane Reynolds (20). "You're so worried about leaving one over the plate too much and them not hitting it good but just

300 Club

In 2009 the Astros became the first team in major league history to have three players hit their 300th home run in the same season for the same team.

Catcher Ivan Rodriguez, who spent less than a full season in Houston, hit his 300th career homer on May 17 at Wrigley Field. Lance Berkman, who's second on the team's all-time home runs list, hit his 300th career home run June 13 in Arizona. And outfielder Carlos Lee slugged No. 300 on August 8 against the Milwaukee Brewers at Minute Maid Park.

In recognition of their achievement, the Astros presented each player with a specially made, framed shadow box containing the lineup card, milestone home run ball, and bat from their historic nights.

getting enough of it to get it into the Crawford Boxes and the next thing you know you start nitpicking," Reynolds said. "You fall behind, you start walking people, and then you give up a home run, and it hurts you a lot worse than maybe the solo one. I think it did affect some guys individually early, but I think everybody kind of got used to it and learned how to deal with it."

Even Dierker had to change his strategy. He was the type of manager who wanted to save his relief pitchers and pinch-hitters until later in the game, but with his starters throwing more pitches and fewer innings, he started going to his bench and bullpen earlier than he wanted. He tried to convince the pitchers that pitching at Enron Field would benefit them because the offense would score more runs behind them, but the Astros struggled on offense the first three months, which only compounded things. "[The pitchers] had good reason to be afraid because it was so much different than what they were used to," Dierker said. "What I was unsuccessful in selling to them is that it wasn't that much different than pitching a game at Wrigley Field with the wind blowing out or pitching a game at Coors Field."

The Astros starting swinging the bats in the second half of the 2000 season—despite losing Craig Biggio to a devastating knee injury—and went 44–34 in the second half after starting 28–56. It wasn't until guys like Roy Oswalt and Wade Miller, pitchers who had never thrown in the Astrodome, came up in the early 2000s that the angst of pitching at Enron Field began to ease. "You can pitch well there, and a lot of guys have had great seasons there," Dierker said. "A lot of it was psychological."

21 Ryan Spins Fifth No-No

Nolan Ryan had a great admiration while growing up for Sandy Koufax, the Dodgers' Hall of Fame lefty who capped his career with a brilliant six-year stretch that matched the dominance of any pitcher in major league history. Ryan, who was reared about 30 miles south of Houston in the rural town of Alvin, Texas, was a budding young power pitcher himself when Koufax retired at the age of 30 in 1966. That's the same year Ryan broke into the major leagues with the New York Mets at age 19.

When Koufax retired his record of throwing four no-hitters was believed to be unreachable. Ryan matched it by throwing four no-nos with the California Angels in a 25-month span from 1973 to 1975. By the time the 1981 season rolled around, Ryan—in his second year with the Astros—thought his no-hit days were behind him at age 34. He was wrong. On September 26, 1981, on a Saturday afternoon in the Astrodome against Koufax's former team, the Dodgers, Ryan threw his fifth no-hitter to break Koufax's record. "The fifth on a personal basis was very meaningful to me," he said, "because I grew up as a Sandy Koufax fan and held Sandy in high esteem in the fact he and I were tied with four no-hitters. I surpassed that, and it was very rewarding for me." He walked three batters and struck out 11 in the Astros' 5–0 win, getting Dusty Baker to ground out to third base for the final out in NBC's *Game of the Week*. His teammates picked him up on their shoulders and carried him off the field.

Ryan, of course, went on to throw seven no-hitters after tossing a couple with the Texas Rangers in 1990 and 1991, but the fifth no-no stands out. That record no-hitter came against a Dodgers team that went on to win the World Series that year, the only one of Ryan's seven no-hitters that came against the club that went on to win it all.

Ryan had the kind of stuff—a 100-mph-plus fastball—that made him a threat to throw a no-hitter each time out, but his curveball was terrific on that September day against the Dodgers. "You never know about those kinds of days," Ryan said. "Things have to go right, and normally you have good stuff and you're making your pitches. That's the way I looked at that game. I had a good breaking ball. If I look back at what I call high-strikeout games, it's not only because I had a good fastball but because I had a good breaking ball and was throwing it for a high percentage of strikes. That runs pretty true in that game."

Astros outfielder Terry Puhl got an assist in the no-hitter. He made a long running catch of a Mike Scioscia fly ball in right-center field for the final out in the seventh inning. The rest was easy for Ryan. He retired the final six batters he faced. And when third baseman Art Howe threw across the diamond to first baseman Denny Walling for the final out, Walling lifted the ball into the air before the Astros mobbed Ryan. "When I threw the fifth," Ryan said, "there was so much time between the fourth and fifth, I thought that part of my career was behind me."

Ryan had a long career, including two more no-hitters ahead of him, but behind the plate that record-breaking day in Houston was Alan Ashby, who caught three no-hitters in his career. Ashby grew up in Southern California and also admired Koufax. In fact Ashby was in the stands at Dodger Stadium for two of Koufax's four no-hitters, so being able to catch Ryan's record-setting no-no was extra meaningful for him as well. "Made no sense at all," he said. "To be there that day and be interviewed after that game by Bryant Gumbel…It was all kind of just like, *What the heck is this? Who threw me into their dream?* Pretty wild."

22 Hurricane Ike

The Astros were surging in September of 2008, winning 14 of 15 games to pull even with the Philadelphia Phillies and get within three games of the Milwaukee Brewers for the National League wild-card spot. The Astros had somehow put themselves in the playoff hunt with 15 games remaining. But something else was brewing. Hurricane Ike was bearing down on the Houston area from the Gulf of Mexico and was expected to make landfall within 48 hours of the Astros' 6–0 win against the Pittsburgh Pirates on Thursday, September 11. Roy Oswalt threw a shutout that day in a game that lasted two hours, nine minutes. "Somebody said there was a hurricane on the way, so I was trying to be as quick as possible," Oswalt said.

There was no way the Astros would be able to play their weekend series against the Chicago Cubs when much of the area was evacuating the impending storm. Astros owner Drayton McLane and baseball commissioner Bud Selig spent much of Friday trying to hammer out an alternative. Meanwhile, Astros players and staff were trying to make sure their families were okay. Some players, including Brad Ausmus and Geoff Blum, flew their families home to California and out of harm's way, and few minds were on baseball. Minnesota, Atlanta, and Cincinnati were among the sites considered to move the game before it was finally announced on Saturday the Astros and Cubs would play two games at Milwaukee's Miller Park on Sunday and Monday.

The decision didn't sit well with the Astros. They weren't wild about the idea of having to play the first-place Cubs in Milwaukee, which is 90 miles from Wrigley Field. "It definitely didn't help us that we had to go play the Cubs 45 minutes from their home stadium when we were supposed to play a home game," Lance Berkman said. "It's one of those things where at the time as a player you kind of feel like, 'Man, this really isn't fair.' What they could have done is cancel those games and play them at the end of the season."

Intercontinental Airport in Houston was shut down, but the Astros got clearance to fly to Milwaukee on Sunday morning. Ike was battering Houston at the time. The roof caved in at Hunter Pence's apartment, and it was raining in his bedroom. "It was a disaster," he said. Blum was with David Newhan and Mark Loretta at Ausmus' house and was trying to follow what was happening with the storm and the rescheduling while a kayak floated down the street. Like it or not, they had to head to the ballpark to get ready for a flight no one wanted to make. "One of the more eerie things I've experienced is being in downtown Houston with all the windows blown out and no electricity and going to the airport and there's one plane," Blum said. "You're like, 'What in God's name is going on?'"

Things only got worse for the Astros. Carlos Zambrano threw a no-hitter in the first game at Miller Park before 23,441 Cubs fans, and Ted Lilly followed with a one-hitter the next day. That was the start of a five-game losing streak that all but ended the Astros' playoff hopes.

"People point to that and say, 'Oh it ruined our season,' but it's been my experience that teams that are good enough generally end up getting there, and teams that don't quite have enough sort of fade back," Berkman said. "I felt like we were in that latter category. We just didn't have quite enough that year to get it done."

Selig took out a full-page ad in the *Houston Chronicle* explaining the decision to play in Milwaukee: "I recognized the advantage the Cubs would have in playing in such close proximity to Chicago, and had there been a better option, I would have taken it. All of us involved in the decision regret the frustration the Astros and their fans felt about playing two games in Milwaukee. As commissioner my job is to balance many competing needs, while also finishing the season on time, so the postseason can begin as scheduled. Hurricane Ike disrupted many things, including the baseball schedule, and I regret its impact on Astros fans. I have heard your complaints and I understand the impact this storm has had on the lives of Texans and Houston-area residents in particular."

23 Jeff Bagwell's MVP Season

The numbers were mind-boggling. Jeff Bagwell, then the Astros' 26-year-old slugger, turned in the greatest offensive season in Astros history in 1994. He bashed 39 home runs, drove in 116 runs, scored 104 runs, posted a .368 batting average, and had a .451 on-base percentage with a 1.201 OPS (on-base plus slugging percentage). He led the league in runs, RBIs, slugging percentage, and total bases. And he did it in only 110 games.

Bagwell's season was cut short when he was struck by a pitch thrown by Andy Benes of the San Diego Padres and broke his hand on August 10. As it turns out, Bagwell only missed one game because the players went on strike August 12. The rest of the regular season, including the World Series, was lost. Bagwell joined Orlando Cepeda in 1967 and Mike Schmidt in 1980 as the only National League players to earn unanimous votes for Most Valuable Player and was the only Astros player to win an MVP award in the NL. He became the first player since Carl Yastrzemski in 1967 to finish first or second in his league in average, runs, RBIs, and homers. His 39 home runs almost doubled the 20 he hit in 1993.

Less than a week before he broke his hand, Bagwell smashed his 38th home run of the season in the Astrodome, breaking Jimmy Wynn's long-standing club record for home runs in a season. Bagwell went on to hit 225 more home runs with the Astros. "It's something to be proud of, don't get me wrong," Bagwell told the *Houston Chronicle* in 1994. "I was aware of the home run and RBI records and I started thinking about it too much the last couple days. Now I can relax and get back to business as usual."

There, though, was nothing usual about his 1994 season. Bagwell hit .336 against right-handers and .457 against left-handers. He batted .373 with 23 homers and 58 RBIs at home and .362 with 15 homers and 58 RBIs on the road. Bagwell's worst month when it comes to batting average was .301 in May. He smashed 13 homers in June and hit .409 with 11 homers and 29 RBIs in 24 games in July. "People don't realize how great a slugger Bagwell was," former Astros general manager Gerry Hunsicker said. "He was a great hitter, but he was among the top sluggers of his era. To do what he did playing a big part of his career in the Astrodome was even more incredible, which arguably was historically still the toughest hitters' park ever constructed. He got pitched around a lot. He certainly had great discipline with all the walks he acquired, but the frustration of having to hit—maybe pitches he didn't want to hit—was just very difficult for him. He was just a very special hitter. The other thing that people don't realize is that he was a Gold Glove first baseman. Until you don't have a defensive first baseman like Bagwell, you don't realize how important the defensive part of that position is. Again, very special player. He was a quiet leader. He led by example, as did Biggio. He commanded tremendous respect from all of his teammates, and you can't put a value on veteran leadership like we had with Bagwell and Biggio. It makes a huge difference in trying to be successful over a 162-game season."

24 2015 Astros Breakthrough

The expectations surrounding the Astros in 2015 were as high as they had been in several years, but they were still generally predicted to be also-rans in the American League West. Coming of a 70–92 season that was a 19-game improvement from the 111-loss club of 2013, the team made some significant offseason improvements by adding Luke Gregerson, Pat Neshek, and Will Harris to the bullpen and acquiring Colby Rasmus, Luis Valbuena, Hank Conger, and Jed Lowrie to bolster the lineup. Under first-year manager A.J. Hinch, the Astros would have been considered a success had they finished with a .500 record.

It didn't take long for the Astros to quiet the naysayers. They won 14 of 15 games in late April and early May and jumped out into first place in the American League West at 18–7. With an improved bullpen and power coming from up and down the lineup—led by Evan Gattis, Chris Carter, George Springer, Valbuena, and Rasmus—the Astros spent 139 days in first place before an 11–16 September allowed the Texas Rangers to surpass them and win the division with the Astros finishing second at 86–76. For the first time in 10 years, the Astros made the postseason.

"Coming off of a 19-game improvement, we really felt we had another large improvement inside of us and we accomplished it during the season, and it got us into the postseason," general manager Jeff Luhnow said. "We're pleased with the progress of the team, we're pleased with the progress of the organization. A.J. and his staff did a tremendous job of allowing the players to be themselves and be the best players they could be this year, and the result is what we saw on the field."

The Astros traveled to the Bronx to face the Yankees in the American League wild-card game and rode six scoreless innings from 20-game winner Dallas Keuchel and got solo homers from Rasmus and midseason addition Carlos Gomez to win 3–0 and advance to the AL Division Series against the defending AL champion Kansas City Royals. The Astros were underdogs in the best-of-five series, but when they won Game 1 in Kansas City 5–2, the series became a dogfight. The teams split two games in Kauffman Stadium before Keuchel, fueled by a raucous crowd in Houston, pitched them to a 4–2 win in Game 3.

Game 4, though, was heartbreaking. The Astros led 6–2 in the eighth inning after hotshot rookie shortstop Carlos Correa homered for the second time, and Rasmus followed with a solo shot. Six outs from advancing to the American League Championship Series, the Royals rallied against the Astros bullpen by scoring five runs in the eighth and two in the ninth to steal a 9–6 win to even the series. Game 5 in Kansas City was a mismatch. The Royals won 7–2, ending the Astros' season and went on to win the World Series.

Keuchel (20–8, 2.48) was the second Astros lefty to win 20 games in a season and won the AL Cy Young, and Collin McHugh went 19–7. Correa, the No. 1 overall pick in 2012, made his debut in June and was spectacular, hitting .279 with 22 homers and 68 RBIs in 99 games while coming up big in the playoffs en route to being named Rookie of the Year. In addition to Correa, rookie pitcher Lance McCullers Jr. and outfielder Preston Tucker had promising debuts.

Meanwhile, steady All-Star second baseman Jose Altuve became the only player in franchise history to have at least 200 hits in two seasons and won his first Gold Glove. The Astros finished with 230 homers, which was second in the AL and the second most in franchise history. The team also turned a triple play in May in Detroit, and Mike Fiers threw a no-hitter in August. A major league record-tying 11 different players hit at least 10 homers. Houston became Crush City as baseball took center stage in the city's sports landscape for the first time in a decade. "It was great," Hinch said. "The biggest thing that I think you could ask out of your team is belief. In spring training and into the season, into a very successful April, May, June, and in July, that belief grew. And for a team that was

Dallas Keuchel, who went 20–8 with a 2.48 ERA, anchored the pitching staff and helped lead the Astros' resurgence in 2015.

experiencing a lot of firsts—with a lot of new players, a new staff, a new manager, new additions to the team—that belief grew and that confidence grew. It's very satisfying for me to have that culture develop to where the expectation every night is to win."

25 Phil Garner

Phil Garner is one of the most beloved sports figures in the history of Houston. In addition to having one of the most famous mustaches and nicknames—Scrap Iron—the hard-nosed Garner, a World Series hero as an infielder for the Pittsburgh Pirates in 1979, played seven of his 16 big league seasons in Houston, where he was a leader in the clubhouse and a steady player on the field. He later managed the Astros to their first World Series berth in 2005 and was adored by his players and the media alike.

Garner, a product of the University of Tennessee, began his career with the Oakland Athletics in 1973 and hit .500 in the World Series for the Pirates in 1979. He was traded to the Astros on August 31, 1981, and became a fixture in Houston before being dealt to the Los Angeles Dodgers in 1987. "Great teammates, great fun, good players, and a good team, and good guys to be around," Garner said of his time with the Astros. "As a player it was great fun, and as a coach for three years, I had the wonderful experience of being with [manager] Art Howe, and [general manager] Bill Wood was terrific to work with…We had a great core of players that you just loved being around, that you know you've got a chance to win when the season starts. I'm very grateful and very blessed to have been a part of it."

Garner was so respected as a player he went immediately into coaching upon his retirement following the 1988 season. He served as a coach for the Astros from 1989 to 1991 and replaced Tom Treblehorn as manager of the Milwaukee Brewers in 1992. He won 563 games in eight seasons as Milwaukee's manager but never made the playoffs. Garner took over as manager of the Detroit Tigers in 2000 and won 145 games in two years before being fired six games—all losses—into the 2002 season.

Garner continued to make his home in Houston, so when the Astros were preparing to fire manager Jimy Williams at the All-Star break in 2004, general manager Gerry Hunsicker called Garner to gauge his interest. The Astros, having signed Andy Pettitte and Roger Clemens in the offseason, were stumbling to an unacceptable 44–44 record at the All-Star break and needed a spark.

"I knew he was local and I knew he would be warmly received in the Houston market and I knew that some of our players, like Bagwell and Biggio, knew him and that he would be a very comfortable fit," Hunsicker said. "It's not easy to make a change in midseason, but those characteristics and his easygoing demeanor, his ability to communicate with players, his knowledge of some of the players we had, all made him a very comfortable fit."

Garner was at a ranch in South Texas with his son, Eric, for his granddaughter's birthday when Hunsicker called him. He scurried back to Houston to meet with the Astros but didn't want news of his interest in the job to leak because of his respect for Williams, who was a National League coach at the All-Star Game in Houston that year and was loudly booed by the fans at Minute Maid Park during pregame introductions. Williams was replaced by Garner the next day. "I was excited about the opportunity because of the club," Garner said. "I never had the number of quality players I thought the Astros had."

The Astros eventually rallied behind Garner, going 36–10 down the stretch in 2004 to win the National League wild-card on the final day of the regular season. They beat the Atlanta Braves for their first playoff series win in franchise history before losing to the St. Louis Cardinals in the National League Championship Series. "Phil was hot," former Astros second baseman Chris Burke said. "He was really hot." In 2005 Garner guided the Astros to the playoffs after a 15–30 start and into the World Series, where they were swept in four games by the Chicago White Sox.

Garner, who won 82 games in 2006, was fired along with general manager Tim Purpura late in the 2007 season. The decision to fire Garner didn't sit well with the players, who loved playing for him. "I really felt like he did a great job when he came in midseason and just basically asked us, 'Hey, what do you think is the problem here? What can we do to fix it?'" former Astros slugger Lance Berkman said. "I felt like the way he came in and went about winning the club over was well done. The guys all loved Gar. Gar's a guy that is fun to play for. He provided that spark that was missing."

26 Six Pitcher No-Hitter

How are you supposed to celebrate a no-hitter, in which six pitchers took the mound? The Astros weren't quite sure what to do when they accomplished that unused feat against the New York Yankees on June 11, 2003, at Yankee Stadium. Hideki Matsui ended the game by hitting a grounder to Jeff Bagwell at first base, and Bagwell flipped to closer Billy Wagner for the final out of the first no-hitter thrown against the Yankees in 45 years. Wagner pumped his fist, slapped his glove, and that's about as far as the celebration went.

Chasing Perfection

The Astros wound up on the wrong side of history on June 13, 2012, at AT&T Park in San Francisco when Giants pitcher Matt Cain threw the 22nd perfect game in history. It was the first perfect game and only the fifth no-hitter ever thrown against the Astros, who were smack dab in the middle of a rebuilding mold.

Less than 10 months later, the Astros were staring another perfect game in the face. Japanese-born right-hander Yu Darvish of the Texas Rangers sent down the first 26 batters he faced at Minute Maid Park. The only thing that stood between him and perfection was Astros infielder Marwin Gonzalez, who was in the lineup for Cain's perfect game the previous season.

Gonzalez came through, stroking the first pitch he saw—a fastball on the outside corner—up the middle and into the outfield with two outs in hte ninth to end Darvish's bid for a perfect game. Gonzalez, a career .234 hitter in only 205 big league at-bats entering the season, struck out swinging and grounded out to first base in his first two at-bats against Darvish and wasn't about to suffer through another perfect game. "We didn't want to lose like that," Gonzalez said. "And I'm grateful I got the hit and he didn't get a perfect game."

They sported wide smiles and high fives, but nothing really to indicate the remarkability of the feat. "I get the flip from Bagwell and step on first and I'm raising my hands and I'm all excited, and Bagwell and Jeff Kent are looking at me like I'm an idiot," Wagner said. "It probably would have been a little more exciting if the team knew what was going on, but it was still pretty awesome to be a part of those guys and to go up there and do something at Yankee Stadium that hadn't been done in 45 years. That was unique."

The game was only the Astros' second in history against the Yankees. Astros starter Roy Oswalt was forced to the trainer's room in the second inning with a strained groin. Pete Munro followed Oswalt and threw two and two-third innings, Kirk Saarloos tossed one and one-third innings, Brad Lidge threw two innings, and Octavio Dotel and Wagner each worked an inning. The pitchers combined for 13 strikeouts, including four by Dotel in the eighth inning. "It was the first time I ever set foot in Yankee Stadium," Lidge said. "It was a special moment. I was up to four or five in the morning answering phone calls and I wasn't tired. I was wired all night from what we accomplished, and it was funny because some of the guys—Jeff Kent is one of them—didn't even know we threw a no-hitter. Billy Wagner was going into that game to finish it no matter what."

Wagner was definitely aware the Yankees had been held without a hit. When manager Jimy Williams called down to the bullpen, Wagner jumped up and began warming up. He wanted a chance to finish it off. "I would die to be there," Wagner said. Dotel and Wagner combined to strike out six batters in a row before Matsui grounded out. Astros left fielder Lance Berkman made a tumbling catch in the fifth inning to rob Alfonso Soriano of a hit and save the no-hitter.

After the game Yankees manager Joe Torre, who led the Yankees to four World Series titles in five years, spoke of the embarrassment of the situation, telling reporters, "This is one of the worst games I've ever been involved in." He called it the low point for the Yankees since he started managing the team.

The gravity of the accomplishment wasn't lost on Wagner. "It's Yankee Stadium! Babe Ruth, all the greats have been there," he said. "It was unbelievable how that went down. From that seventh on, there was no chance they were going to do anything. None."

The Yankees, showing the class of their organization, left bottles of champagne at the lockers of all six pitchers after the game.

27 Drayton McLane

Drayton McLane admits he had a lot to learn about baseball when he purchased the Astros late in 1992. He had only been to a handful of Major League Baseball games in his life but grew up listening to St. Louis Cardinals games on the radio in the 1940s and 1950s. He changed his allegiances when the Houston franchise was born in 1962. McLane, who grew up in central Texas, was running the grocery distribution business started by his grandfather when he was approached in 1992 about being part of a group to buy the Astros.

McLane joined friends Robert Onstead, the founder of the Randall's grocery store chain, and Ben Love, the president of Texas Commerce Bank, and put in a bid to buy the Astros from John McMullen. The group was involved in intense negotiations for six months before the deal fell through and the group broke up. McLane wasn't about to give up. "I thought, *I've never done anything worthwhile that I didn't stick with until it got done*," he said. "I called the others and asked them if they objected if I tried to do this on my own. They said, 'You're crazy.'"

Crazy, maybe. Determined, definitely. McLane purchased the Astros from McMullen in November 1992 for $117 million, taking over a franchise that hadn't been to the playoffs since 1986. Unlike McMullen, who lived in New Jersey, McLane brought a down-home presence to the Astros and attended most of the games, sitting right behind home plate. He always made it a point to mingle with fans and the players, asking everyone if they were "charging" or "are you ready to be a champion?"

One of the first big splashes McLane made was signing free agent pitchers Greg Swindell and Doug Drabek, a pair of local products who had solid careers. Neither was able to enjoy much success in Houston. Swindell went 12–13 with a 4.16 ERA in 1993, and Drabek lost 18 games that year. He made the All-Star team a year later, but he wasn't the same guy who had won a Cy Young with the Pittsburgh Pirates. "I'll give Drayton credit for this," former general manager Bill Wood said, "he wanted to do what we can do to make the club better. I thought we needed to improve our pitching at that point, and the two guys we zeroed in on just didn't come through the way we hoped they would."

Still, the 1993 Astros posted their first winning record in four years, going 85–77. That began a run where the Astros finished with a winning record in 13 out of 14 seasons. The Astros won the National League Central division four times in a five-year span (1997–99, 2001). They advanced to the National League Championship Series in 2004 and went to the World Series the next year. "I remember when Jason Lane caught the ball in right field, and we clinched (the 2005 NL pennant), but we've had other memories," McLane said. "There's been a lot of glorious memories."

Perhaps McLane's biggest legacy in Houston was leading the charge to build a new ballpark. He made more than 150 speeches in a three-month span in 1996 as he stumped for a county referendum that helped fund the ballpark. It barely passed, garnering 51 percent of the vote. The $250 million ballpark opened in 2000 as Enron Field to much fanfare. The retractable roof gave Houston fans outdoor baseball for the first time since 1964 at Colt Stadium. "I just thought if we were going to be a really, really good franchise, we needed a new stadium," he said. "I felt it needed to be downtown. I knew in Houston we would never be successful if we didn't have a retractable roof because of how hot it gets here."

McLane announced in 2010 it was time to sell the club. He said his sons, Denton and Drayton III, had no interest in walking in their father's footsteps, and with his health still in tiptop shape and five grandsons constantly grabbing at his pants legs, he and his wife, Elizabeth, decided it was time to move on. "I'm a firm believer you can manage something too long," he said. He sold the Astros to Jim Crane in 2011 for $610 million.

28 Biggio Moves to Second Base

It was a makeshift glove that was nothing more than a hard piece of foam that was barely big enough to cover Craig Biggio's hand. No one could have known at the time it would turn out to be the tool that would be instrumental in getting Biggio into the National Baseball Hall of Fame more than 20 years later.

Biggio was a first-round draft pick of the Astros as a catcher out of Seton Hall in 1987, and it didn't take him long to make his mark in the major leagues. He won the Silver Slugger award at catcher in his first full season in the big leagues in 1989 and made the National League All-Star team at catcher in 1991 during a season in which he hit .295. Astros management recognized they had a talented hitter and they also understood the wear and tear Biggio would endure if he stayed at catcher. Especially at the level of intensity at which Biggio played the game, which was go-go all the time. There was no second gear.

Astros general manager Bill Wood and manager Art Howe decided to try to prolong Biggio's career by getting him out from behind the plate and moving him to second base. Biggio was certainly athletic enough to make the transition, but the move was unprecedented. And they didn't even know if Biggio would be on board with it. But Biggio, too, was acutely aware how moving from catcher could benefit him and was willing to give it a shot. "At first, he wasn't real keen on it because he was a catcher," Howe said. "It's pretty tough to ask a guy who was an All-Star, 'We want you to change positions.' But…he had great speed. And his durability—he wasn't a big guy. He was catching with all that equipment on back there, and there was a guy named Dave Parker that seemed like every week he was running over a catcher, and in the back of my mind, I said, 'I don't want to see that collision at the plate.'"

Enter Matt Galante. The Astros coach was considered one of the best infielder instructors in the game and was saddled with the task of turning Biggio, the All-Star catcher, into Biggio, the second baseman. If anyone was up for this kind of challenge, it was Biggio. He was eager and determined to make himself into not just a second baseman, but also one of the best to play the game. And there was no turning back. "It was the hardest thing I've done in my life," he said. "Put it this way. It was never done ever in the history of the game: a catcher to go to second base, and I had to learn it in the big leagues. Think about it: if it didn't go as well as it did, I'm home already. I play a couple of years and I'm done."

To further help with the transition, Bill Doran, a popular second baseman for the Astros in the 1980s who was traded to the Cincinnati Reds in 1990, flew to Houston prior to the start of spring training in 1992. Biggio and Doran went to the Astrodome, where the floor was covered in dirt for rodeos, tractor pulls, and motocross. There was no baseball field. So the pair drew a field on the dirt and discussed angles and the nuances of the position. "He said, 'Look man, if you're going to play this position, you've got to let me show you the shortcuts here and there and do this thing right,'" Biggio said. "I mean, who does that? I'll never forget that."

When Biggio arrived at Osceola County Stadium in Kissimmee, Florida, a few weeks later, Galante took away Biggio's infield glove and handed him his makeshift paddle. The transformation from catcher to second baseman was to begin in earnest. Galante, the longtime Astros coach and fellow New Yorker whom Biggio considers a father figure, worked tirelessly one-on-one with Biggio that spring. The pair disappeared each morning prior to workouts and worked on the position on a turf half-field at the team's spring training complex. "I have a paddle in my hand and I'm saying, 'What am I doing here? This is crazy,'" Biggio said. "I just made the All-Star team the year before and now I have a paddle in my hand?" The goal of the paddle was to help Biggio field the ball gently and with two hands and help his hands and feet work together.

Biggio went on to play second base for the Astros for the next 11 seasons before he moved to the outfield in 2003–04 when the Astros signed Jeff Kent. Biggio returned to second base for the final three seasons of his 20-year career and retired following the 2007 season with four Gold Gloves. Biggio was so indebted to Galante for helping him make the transition that he gave him the first of the four consecutive Gold Gloves he won from 1994 to '97. "There were no bad habits to break," Galante said. "It was almost like taking a little baby and teaching him how to walk because he had never walked before. It was pretty easy. He was very attentive and did what I asked him to do."

When Biggio was inducted into the Hall of Fame in 2015, he made sure Galante was there and he singled him out in his acceptance speech. "We had six weeks to learn it in spring training," Biggio said. "No pressure, huh, Matt? A typical day with Matty was we started at 7:00 AM, go to a half-field when the sun was coming up, work for an hour and a half until 8:45 or so, then go practice with the team from nine til around noon, grab a sandwich, go to the half-field again, get some more work done. Then we go back, play the game. When the game was over, we went back to the half field again. We did that every day in spring training for six weeks. I thank God for Matt Galante and I'm so grateful. When I won my first Gold Glove, I gave it to him. Matt, thank you for everything, for being a great coach, a great teacher, but a better person and a better friend."

29 Bagwell Trade Alters History

Twenty-five years after it was made, the trade that sent a skinny infielder named Jeff Bagwell to the Astros from the Boston Red Sox in exchange for veteran relief pitcher Larry Andersen is considered one of the most lopsided trades in baseball history, and it had nothing to do with Andersen. He was a solid veteran relief pitcher who had a nice career and was a fan favorite because of his fun-loving personality, but the guy he was traded for put together a Hall of Fame resume.

Bagwell was the National League Rookie of the Year in 1991 at 23 years old, won the NL Most Valuable Player in 1994, and was one of the greatest sluggers of his generation. He played 15 years in Houston and was a career .297 hitter with 449 homers, 1,529 RBIs, and 202 stolen bases, in addition to his terrific defense and skillful base running. Andersen spent 17 seasons in the big leagues and appeared in 15 games down the stretch for Boston in 1990, helping them reach the playoffs. Still, it's a deal the Red Sox would like to have back.

Bagwell came up as a third baseman with Boston, but he was blocked in the organization by Scott Cooper and Tim Naehring.

With Ken Caminiti established at third, the Astros moved Bagwell to first base, where he would play for the next 15 seasons. Former Astros general manager Bill Wood, who pulled off the trade, said the Astros had a valuable piece in Andersen, a veteran with an unhittable slider. "He was pitching well that particular year," Wood said. "He was a valuable piece to anyone in the hunt, and Boston, of course, was interested in him, and we had our scouts look at the Boston system very closely, and Bagwell was a guy that we really zeroed in on. We did not zero in on the guys that Boston

Trading Daze

Spec Richardson served as Astros general manager from 1967 to 1975 and was known for making some of the worst trades in the history of the franchise.

On December 4, 1968, he traded 31-year-old All-Star pitcher Mike Cuellar to the Baltimore Orioles for Curt Blefary. Cuellar won 143 games in eight seasons with the Orioles, including four seasons of at least 20 wins. He won the 1969 American League Cy Young after going 23–11 with a 2.38 ERA and he went 24–8 with a 3.48 ERA in 1970. Blefary, meanwhile, played one season in Houston before being traded to the New York Yankees.

Rusty Staub, an up-and-coming outfielder/first baseman who was headed for stardom, was traded to the Montreal Expos on January 22, 1969 for Jesus Alou and Donn Clendenon, who refused to report to Houston. The Expos instead sent Jack Billingham, Skip Guinn, and $100,000 to the Astros. Staub became the Expos' first star player and was later traded to the New York Mets, driving in 105 runs in 1975. Staub retired 284 hits shy of 3,000 and was the only major league player to have 500 hits with four different teams, including Houston.

On November 29, 1971, the Astros traded future Hall of Famer Joe Morgan to the Reds. He went to Cincinnati with Ed Armbrister, Billingham, Cesar Geronimo, and Denis Menke in exchange for Tommy Helms, Lee May, and Jimmy Stewart. Morgan was an All-Star all eight seasons in Cincinnati and won the National League MVP in 1975 and 1976, the two years the Big Red Machine won the World Series.

Acquired in one of the most lopsided trades in baseball history, Astros first baseman Jeff Bagwell assumes his famous wide-legged batting stance.

kept throwing at us as potential guys ahead of Bagwell in the system at Triple A."

Wood credits scouts Tom Mooney and Stan Benjamin with insisting the Astros get Bagwell in return for Andersen. Despite Boston's initial unwillingness to part with Bagwell, the Astros stuck to their guns up until the 11th hour. "That was one of those trades that came down to just a little bit before the deadline, and you're holding your breath that nothing [bad] will happen, that the commissioner's office is going to give it an okay," Wood said. "It all came through, and the rest is history."

Bagwell was sent to the instructional league in September of 1990 so the Astros could get a better idea of what they had. "It didn't take us long to realize we had a real nugget there," said Wood, who served as general manager from 1988 to 1993 and also made some other notable trades—good and bad—along the way.

He pulled of a great trade when he sent aging first baseman Glenn Davis to the Baltimore Orioles for pitchers Curt Schilling and Pete Harnisch and outfielder Steve Finley in 1991, but he dealt Schilling away 15 months later for pitcher Jason Grimsley and watched him blossom into one of the best starting pitchers in the game with the Philadelphia Phillies. Schilling went 3–5 with a 3.81 ERA in 56 games for the Astros in 1991. "You'd like to bat 1.000 and never have a bad one," Wood said. "I made a couple of good ones, some that helped the ballclub that people don't think about that are not major deals like a Jeff Bagwell deal or that Glenn Davis deal I was always proud of. I messed that up by letting Schilling go, and once he got with [Phillies pitching coach] Claude Osteen, he became what you hope a guy is going to be when you make a trade with a young player."

30 Cesar Cedeno

If he had been able to stay healthy, outfielder Cesar Cedeno might have been the best Astro of them all. Even in a career that was hampered by injury, Cedeno was still very good, if not great. He's considered, along with Craig Biggio, Jeff Bagwell, Lance Berkman, and Jose Cruz, as one of the five greatest offensive players in Astros history. When Leo Durocher took over as manager of the Astros in 1972, he compared Cedeno to the great Willie Mays. He wasn't the only one to make that comparison.

Cedeno was signed by the Astros at 17 out of the Dominican Republic and made his debut in 1970 at age 19. He was considered one of the best players in the National League by 1972 but didn't quite live up to that potential. He was a flashy player—the kind that you hated if he was in the other dugout but loved if he was on your team. "He was absolutely outstanding," former Astros general manager Tal Smith said. "He was the greatest talent I think the franchise has had. That doesn't mean he made the greatest contribution because obviously Bagwell and Biggio and Berkman and others have played longer and performed very well, but Cedeno—from a talent standpoint—I thought he was destined to be in the Hall of Fame."

Cedeno is the only Astros player to hit for the cycle twice—on August 2, 1972, against the Cincinnati Reds and August 9, 1976. The second one came in a 13–4 victory against the St. Louis Cardinals. He went 4-for-5 with four runs scored and five RBIs that night at Busch Stadium. "Hitting is not an easy task," he said. "It just happens sometimes. I guess you have to be lucky enough. You really can't plan to go up there and hit a double and a triple or a home run for that matter. A single is the easiest thing to do, but they don't always happen. It happened a couple of times for me, but not everybody gets to enjoy that."

The speedy Cedeno was built for the ballparks in the 1970s. The Astroturf and spacious outfields made them a playground for Cedeno, who had a rare combination of speed and power. Fans began referring to the Astrodome as "Cesar's Palace." Cedeno was a true five-tool player during his early days in Houston, leading the team in batting average three times (1971–73), hits twice (1971–72), home runs twice (1974, 1976), and RBIs twice (1970, 1974). He still ranks first on the team's all-time list with 487 stolen bases.

Cedeno's all-around talent allowed him to win five Gold Gloves and appear in the All-Star Game four times as a member of the Astros. He was named the Astros' Most Valuable Player in 1972, but injuries slowed him. He tore his anterior cruciate ligament in 1979 and broke his ankle in Game 3 of the 1980 National League Championship Series against the Philadelphia Phillies and dealt with personal problems throughout his career. He was never the same after the 1980 season but played seven more seasons, finishing with the Reds (1982–85), Cardinals (1985), and Los Angeles Dodgers (1986). Cedeno spent 12 of his 17 seasons in Houston and for his career hit .285 with 2,087 hits, 199 homers, 976 RBIs, and 550 stolen bases. "Cedeno's career started off great, and he just didn't play as long or accomplish as much as I thought he might," Smith said. "He had injuries and other issues but a great talent, very comparable to Willie Mays. Just outstanding in all tools and played with great energy, just very dynamic."

The Astros lost both Cedeno and hard-throwing pitcher J.R. Richard (stroke) during the 1980 season, which may have kept them out of the World Series. They lost in five games to the Phillies in the NLCS with four games going extra innings. "Cedeno at the time was probably one of the best players in the major leagues," former Astros infielder Enos Cabell said.

31 Sunshine Kids

To help celebrate Craig Biggio's induction into the Hall of Fame in the summer of 2015, the Astros chartered a plane to Cooperstown, New York, and allowed Biggio to invite some special guests who otherwise might not have been able to go. Biggio took some of the athletic training staff and clubhouse employees who had helped him when he was playing. He also invited four adults who had overcome cancer as kids and had befriended Biggio during his work with the Sunshine Kids, a nonprofit organization dedicated to children with cancer.

Devin Duncan and Steve Jones, both of whom battled cancer when they were in their teens, were among those invited to the induction ceremony by Biggio. Duncan had known Biggio since she was three years old and diagnosed with leukemia and became involved with the Sunshine Kids. Jones was diagnosed with a brain tumor when he was 15 years old in 1983 and underwent operations and radiation. "All of our kids have a special story and the relationship with Craig is so incredible," said Rita Suchma, director of development of the Sunshine Kids Foundation. "And he's given them so much inspiration and so much hope."

The Sunshine Kids was started by Rhoda Tomasco, a pediatric volunteer at M.D. Anderson Cancer Center in Houston in 1982. Astros reliever Joe Sambito began inviting the kids to Astros games, and years later Larry Andersen was doing it and got Biggio involved. Biggio then served as the national spokesman for the Sunshine Kids for more than a decade as a player and helped the organization raise more than $5 million through golf tournaments and other charity work. Craig's wife, Patty, has been instrumental in supporting the Sunshine Kids as well. "It's a big part of my life," Biggio said. "It's something that I enjoy doing, and I enjoy being around them. It's something that I consider myself very lucky and fortunate to be around them. They're like my family. We've had some good stories and some tough stories. It means everything to me and my family to be involved with them."

Duncan said she squealed when she got the call from the Astros that Biggio had invited her to join him in Cooperstown. "I've always thought of him as such a hero," she said, "and to think that he was interested in me coming along and felt our connection and our relationship was good enough for me to be involved was one of the best feelings ever."

For years Biggio wore a yellow sunshine pin on his cap during batting practice and spring training games throughout his career in honor of the Sunshine Kids. The Astros placed a large replica of the sunshine pin next to his retired No. 7 number high above Minute Maid Park during the summer of 2015. Helping with the Sunshine Kids was fulfilling a promise for Biggio. When he was a two-sport star at Kings Park High School in Long Island, New York, Biggio had a young neighbor, Chris Alben, who died of leukemia. Biggio had visited with him often and became a surrogate big brother to Chris' younger brother after Chris died. Biggio made himself a promise at that time: if he was ever in a position to do charitable work for kids with cancer, he would.

Biggio credits Andersen for bringing attention to the Sunshine Kids when he broke into the major leagues in 1988. He said the older players told him to be selective if he ever decided to jump into charity work. They told him to find something he was passionate about and do it right. The Sunshine Kids were an easy fit. "When Larry was traded for Jeff Bagwell in 1990, I didn't want to see it go away," Biggio said. "It's been an unbelievable relationship since."

32 Joe Niekro

The Astros were built around great pitching in the 1970s and 1980s with hard throwers like Don Wilson, J.R. Richard, and Nolan Ryan dominating in the pitching-friendly confines of the Astrodome. Joe Niekro was a different story. Niekro threw a hard knuckleball, and that made him even more effective when he was in the rotation sandwiched between fireballers Richard and Ryan as he was for part of the 1980 season.

Niekro, or "Knucksie" as he was called by his teammates, pitched half of his 22 years in the big leagues with the Astros, anchoring their rotation from 1975 to 1985. He was the first Astros pitcher to win 20 games in consecutive seasons, winning 21 during his only All-Star season in 1979 and 20 in 1980. His 20th win that season came on the final day of the regular season when he fired a brilliant complete game, six-hitter at Dodger Stadium to beat the Los Angeles Dodgers in a one-game playoff to decide the National League West crown. He won 144 games for the Astros, which was still a club record 30 years after he last appeared in a game in a Houston uniform. It was poetry in motion. "Niekro would pitch eight or nine innings, and nobody would even know he was there," said former teammate Enos Cabell.

Niekro, a native of Martins Ferry, Ohio, and his brother, Hall of Famer Phil Niekro, were tutored in pitching by their father, Phil Sr., a former coal miner who taught them the knuckleball. They combined to win 539 games while both pitching well into their 40s. The early years of Joe's career were nothing special. He pitched for the Chicago Cubs, San Diego Padres, and Detroit Tigers before teaming with his brother in 1973 in Atlanta. It was while he was with his brother that Joe began tinkering with the knuckleball their father had taught them.

The Astros purchased Niekro from the Atlanta Braves for $35,000 in 1975. The knuckleball began to become a weapon, and Niekro established himself in Houston. "Times were different in baseball back then. Joe was 30, 31 when he got to Houston," said Tal Smith, who was the Astros' general manager from 1975 to 1980. "It took him a couple of years until he established himself. In those days prior to the advent of free agency, you had more time, more patience to provide opportunities. That gave Niekro time to perfect the knuckleball, then he produced back-to-back 20-win seasons, and all of the memorable things that happened. He was such a special guy. I never heard anybody who said anything disparaging about him. He always had a smile, a quip. He kept everybody loose in the clubhouse. And he was the consummate winner."

Niekro pitched 22 seasons in the majors before retiring following the 1988 season with a career record of 221–204. "I loved Joe, but his knuckleball he threw really hard," said Alan Ashby, who caught Niekro for much of his career in Houston. "He's the reason for my fingers being the way they are and maybe my psyche being the way it is. He was tough. He was really tough. He had back-to-back years as a 20-game winner. He really had his stuff together."

Niekro died of a brain aneurysm in 2006 at the age of 61.

33 The 2004 Season

The signing of Roger Clemens and Andy Pettitte to an already talented Astros club shot expectations through the roof in 2004. There were All-Stars aplenty in the lineup and pitching rotation, and the excitement for the season was unprecedented. Many picked the Astros to reach the World Series for the first time in their history.

Things went as planned during the first six weeks. The Astros were in first place in late May behind a rotation featuring Clemens, Pettitte, and Roy Oswalt and a stacked lineup that had Craig Biggio, Jeff Bagwell, Lance Berkman, and Jeff Kent. The Astros sputtered through much of the summer, however, and hit the All-Star break with an underachieving record of 44–44. Speculation was rampant manager Jimy Williams would be fired, and Williams was booed loudly when introduced as a National League coach prior to the 2004 All-Star Game at Minute Maid Park. He was replaced the next day by Phil Garner.

Garner was a fiery competitor whose nickname, "Scrap Iron," mirrored how he wanted his teams to play. Still the Astros were floundering in mid-August and out of the division race, 19½ games behind the St. Louis Cardinals. They were six back in the wild-card, so there was hope. But they had to start winning—and quickly. The Astros were in Philadelphia for a series against the Phillies in late August when Garner and general manager Gerry Hunsicker met to have breakfast to discuss the state of the club. Pettitte was pitching with an injured elbow, and things looked bleak. "I said, 'I'll tell you Gerry, it's not going the way I thought it would go,'" Garner said. "'I felt like that I could have us playing better ball now. If it were my money, if I were [owner] Drayton McLane, I would start making changes because it's not working.'" Hunsicker, who turned out to be in his final year as general manager, said he owed it to the team of veterans to play it out. "I really felt we had the horses to win," he said. "Time was ticking. Time was running out."

The day Hunsicker and Garner met turned out to be a momentum-changer. The Astros beat the Phillies 9–8 with Clemens hitting a two-run single in a six-run fourth inning. "That was the start of the run we had," Garner said. In a particularly contentious game against the Chicago Cubs a week later, five-tool outfielder Carlos Beltran—a major midseason acquisition—a hit in the knee by a pitch and had to leave the game. Later in the inning with the bases loaded, a pitch whizzed past Berkman's head, forcing him to the ground in "pain." He was given first base, even though it didn't look like he had been struck by the ball. "He should get an Oscar," Cubs manager Dusty Baker bristled.

The Astros followed with three straight singles for a five-run inning to take control of the game, and reliever Dan Wheeler— acquired in a trade two days earlier—infamously made his Astros debut in the bottom of the inning and immediately bought into Garner's hard-nosed culture. "I said, 'Danny, I'm Phil Garner, it's nice to meet you. By the way, get the first two outs in the ninth and quick as you can and drill the last guy,'" Garner said. "It turned out to be Derek Lee, the biggest son of a bitch on the team. He drills Derek Lee in the back. To be honest with you, I think that made Danny Wheeler. Instantly he was a favorite of the team. He pitched brilliant ball for us. It all started coming together."

The Astros went 36–10 down the stretch and clinched the NL wild-card on the final day of the season. They advanced to the play-offs and beat the Atlanta Braves in five games for their first playoff series win. The Cardinals beat the Astros in seven games in the National League Championship Series, but the Astros had turned Houston into a baseball city.

34 Roy Oswalt

It was supposed to be only a cameo. Astros pitching prospect Roy Oswalt was pitching well at Class A Kissimmee of the Florida State League in 2000 when he was called up to Double A Round Rock to make a spot start. "They called me up and said, 'You're going to pitch one game and you're going back to A ball,'" said Oswalt, who even had been given a return plane ticket. Oswalt only packed enough clothes to stay one night.

But Oswalt, a hard thrower despite his smaller stature, made the most of what was supposed to be a one-time opportunity. He struck out 15 batters and dazzled Express manager Jackie Moore, as well as Hall of Fame pitcher Nolan Ryan, who owned the Round Rock club and was at the game. "That night, I'm thinking I might just be able to stay up here," Oswalt said.

Still, he went to bed planning on rejoining Kissimmee the next day. Before he could get on the plane the next morning, he got a phone call informing him he was going to stay in Round Rock for a while. "I didn't know this at the time, but Nolan had actually called [farm director Tim] Purpura up there and said, 'This guy needs to be here,'" Oswalt said. "'He's pitched just as well as anybody we had.' He kind of stuck his neck out for me, and everything kind of took off."

Oswalt went 11–4 with a 1.94 ERA that year for Round Rock and was pitching in the big leagues a year later at 23 years old, going 14–3 with a 2.73 ERA for the Astros. Oswalt had a sharp, high-arcing curveball and worked fast. He won 19 games in 2002, beginning a seven-year run in which he was one of the best starting pitchers in baseball. Not bad for a kid who was drafted in the 23rd round out of Holmes Community College in 1996. Astros scout

James Farrar followed him throughout the summer before signing him for $500,000.

Oswalt won 20 games in 2004 and 2005 in a rotation that included Roger Clemens and Andy Pettitte, helping the Astros reach the playoffs. "When those guys came over, it was all about Roger and Andy," Oswalt said. "They had played for the Yankees for a big-market team for a long time and they had been to the World Series and stuff like that. I had it in my mind they weren't going to beat me. I took that all through life. Somebody give me a challenge, I'm going to try to come out on the other side better."

Bulldozed

It was only a few hours before the biggest start of his career, and Roy Oswalt was sitting at his locker in old Busch Stadium with a towel over his head. It was Game 6 of the 2005 National League Championship Series, and Oswalt was getting his mind right. Astros owner Drayton McLane made his way to the clubhouse and tried to offer encouraging words to Oswalt. "He wasn't a big talker," McLane said. "I started to give him a real pep talk, saying, 'We had to win this game because we lost it under this situation last year.' He didn't move. He didn't acknowledge I was there. I thought, *I need to think of something quickly* and I thought of the bulldozer. I said, 'Roy, if you win this game, I'll buy you a brand new Caterpillar bulldozer.' He jumped straight up and threw the towel off his head and said, 'You've got a deal!'"

Oswalt pitched seven strong innings to lead the Astros to a 5–1 win and into the World Series for the first time in their history. Oswalt, who had 40 acres of land near Weir, Mississippi, had told McLane sometime earlier he wished he had a bulldozer to help his father, a logger, remove tree stumps on the land. A few weeks later, McLane delivered a yellow Caterpillar D6 bulldozer at a price tag of $230,000. "I remember about the sixth or seventh inning, I was walking off the field thinking, *I just won a bulldozer*," Oswalt said. "I told him after the game, 'Hey, it doesn't matter what color or what size. Just call me when I need to pick it up.'"

Part of a great 2005 pitching staff, Roy Oswalt delivers a pitch against the Chicago White Sox in the first inning of Game 3 of the World Series.

He learned the value of hard work growing up in Mississippi as the son of a Vietnam War veteran and logger. "A lot of people get different compliments here and there, but my main goal coming into this as a player is when they talk about you is, 'He left everything out on the field,'" Oswalt said. "I always did that. I didn't go into a game thinking I was going to get beat. I always went into a game wondering how bad we were going to win. I was kind of raised that way. You take that all the way through life and apply it to everything."

Oswalt quickly garnered the reputation for his competitiveness and pitched in some huge games for the Astros, winning arguably the biggest game in franchise history. Oswalt held the St. Louis Cardinals to one run in seven innings to win Game 6 of the 2005 National League Championship and send the Astros into the World Series.

Oswalt won 143 games in 10 years with the Astros and was one win shy of Larry Dierker's club record for wins before he asked to be traded halfway through the 2010 season. Oswalt's trade triggered a massive rebuilding effort for the Astros, who didn't return to contention until the 2015 season.

35 Hatcher's Game 6 Home Run

With the Astros trailing by a run during the top of the 14th inning of Game 6 of the 1986 National League Championship Series, Houston manager Hal Lanier told outfielder Billy Hatcher to be ready to bunt if Bill Doran reached base. But Doran struck out against New York Mets pitcher Jesse Orosco, leaving the Astros two outs from elimination. The tension couldn't have been any higher as Hatcher strolled to the plate.

As Hatcher focused in on his upcoming at-bat, he heard a voice. "Right beside the dugout, there was this lady that was with a little girl," Hatcher said. "I can't remember how old she was, but she said, 'It's all right, Billy's going to hit a home run.' I remember her saying that, and then when I hit the home run, I was running around the bases saying, 'She knew this was going to happen before it happened.' It was unreal. It was an out-of-body experience."

Hatcher's game-tying home run was one of the biggest homers in Astros history. He swatted a high fly ball down the left-field line that struck the foul pole about halfway up, sending the crowd of 45,718 fans into a frenzy. Hatcher ran backward to first base as he watched the ball sail down the line and over the fence to tie the game—one of the greatest contests in playoff history. "It was unreal," Hatcher said. "Looking back on it, I was running around the bases, and it was so loud you couldn't hear yourself think. It was that loud. I don't think my feet hit the ground. It was a special moment."

The exhilaration and good vibes didn't last too much longer for the Astros, who watched the Mets score three times in the 16th inning to take a 7–4 lead. The Astros rallied for a pair on the bottom of the 16th, including an RBI single by Hatcher, but

Put a Cork in It

Billy Hatcher provided one of the best moments in franchise history with his dramatic 14th inning home run off the foul pole in Game 6 of the 1986 National League Championship Series in Houston. The hit tied the game, but the Astros lost 7–6 in 16 innings and were eliminated. Hatcher, acquired by the Astros from the Chicago Cubs on December 16, 1985, for Jerry Mumphrey, put together a terrific year in 1987 in his second full year majors, but it wasn't without controversy.

Hatcher received a 10-day suspension after he was caught with a corked bat on August 31, 1987. He was ejected in the fourth inning of the game after the bat he was swinging split in two, revealing it had been corked. Umpire crew chief John McSherry said the bat contained three to four inches of cork. Hatcher told reporters after the game all his regular bats were broken, so he unknowingly grabbed the corked bat. He said the bat was the one used by Astros pitchers in pregame batting practice.

It had a No. 45—Dave Smith's number—on the knob. "I don't know how it got in the bat rack," Smith said. "Maybe a bat boy or someone accidentally brought it out."

Orosco struck out Kevin Bass swinging to end the game, series, and send Houston to another heartbreaking playoff loss. "We should have won," Hatcher said. "It wasn't just that one game; I think it was the whole series. That was probably one of the best series in baseball ever. Both teams left everything they had out on the field. There was no second-guessing anything that you did because you left everything you had out there on the field. It was two good teams going at each other, and they ended up being World [Series] champions."

October has a way of making heroes out of the most unlikely players, and Hatcher certainly fit that mold. He had some speed and a little pop and wound up pushing his way into the starting lineup for much of the second half of the year. He batted .258 with six homers, 36 RBIs, and 38 steals that season, which didn't include the three he had in the NLCS against the Mets. "They couldn't throw me out," he said. "I was trying to get on base [in the 14th], and Jesse Orosco threw me a pitch inside, where I like the ball, and I hit it pretty good. I never tried to hit a home run. Whether it was a base hit or a double, I was trying to hit the ball hard and run."

More than a quarter century after his iconic homer, Hatcher still gets reminded about his dramatic shot, even if it didn't win the game. It's revered in Houston much the same way Carlton Fisk's homer off the left-field foul pole in the 12th inning of Game 6 of the 1975 World Series is remembered, and both ultimately came in playoff series that were lost by the home team. Still, it's a moment for which Hatcher will be remembered forever. "That was a special time for me, a special moment," he said. "When I start thinking about that '86 team, I'm still friends with a lot of those guys. I won a World Series with Cincinnati in 1990 when I got traded, and that was special for me. But I never played with a group of players that went out every single day and played hard liked that. It was every day."

36 Visit the Hall of Fame

The National Baseball Hall of Fame is not an easy place to reach, though that didn't stop thousands of orange-clad Astros fans from filling the streets of Cooperstown, New York, when Craig Biggio was inducted into the Hall in 2015. Cooperstown and its idyllic Main Street and shops are a couple of flights and at least a 90-minute drive from Houston, but it's certainly worth the trip.

Biggio became the first player wearing an Astros uniform to be inducted into the Hall, but a stroll through the museum will reveal several Astros artifacts. The curators at the Hall change the displays frequently, so Astros items that are on display one year might not be there the next. Some artifacts from the team's greatest moments, though, are at the Hall of Fame.

One of the greatest moments in team history came on October 9, 2005, when Chris Burke hit a walk-off homer in the 18th inning to beat the Atlanta Braves in Game 4 of the National League Division Series, ending the longest postseason game in history. The home run ball is in the Hall of Fame and was donated by the Astros and fan Shaun Dean, who not only caught Burke's ball but Lance Berkman's grand slam earlier in that game.

Hall of Famer Nolan Ryan, who played nine of his 27 seasons in Houston, has several items in Cooperstown, including some from his days with the Astros like the cap he wore when he broke Walter Johnson's all-time strikeout record on April 27, 1983, and the cap he wore when he threw his record-breaking fifth no-hitter on September 26, 1981. The only pitcher to lose a no-hitter, Ken Johnson of the Colt .45s, also has the cap he wore when two errors made him the losing pitcher in a 1–0 defeat to the Cincinnati Reds on April 23, 1964.

Among the other milestone Astros items in the Hall: the bat used by Jeff Kent to break Ryne Sandberg's record for homers by a second baseman (October 2, 2004) and the No. 12 jersey worn by catcher Ivan "Pudge" Rodriguez when he caught his 2,227th career game on June 17, 2009, breaking Carlton Fisk's all-time record.

Other Astros Items in the Hall of Fame

- The cap worn by Don Wilson when he threw his no-hitter on June 18, 1967, and the cap he wore for his second no-hitter on May 1, 1969.
- The shoes worn by slugger Bob Watson when he scored baseball's millionth run on May 4, 1975.
- An official game ball signed by the 1986 National League All-Star team from the year the game was held at the Astrodome for the final time.
- Caps worn by Jim Deshaies when he struck out the first eight batters he faced on September 23, 1986, and by Mike Scott during his division-clinching no-hitter two days later.
- A ticket to the final game at the Astrodome, October 3, 1999, and a ticket and ball from the first game at Enron Field, April 7, 2000.
- A jersey worn by Carlos Beltran during the 2004 postseason when he tied a major league record by hitting eight homers in a single postseason.
- The jersey worn by Jeff Bagwell during the final game of the 2005 World Series, which was Bagwell's final game, and the spikes worn by Biggio during the 2005 World Series.
- The bat, jersey, cap, and gloves worn by Biggio when he recorded his 3,000th hit on June 28, 2007 were all sent to Cooperstown.
- The space helmet worn by an Astros "Earthman" groundskeeper. Originally designed in the early 1960s to keep the space theme, astronaut suits and helmets were worn by the groundskeepers. Almost everyone on staff at the Astrodome had some special space-related costume. Some of these were featured during a throwback game at the 45th anniversary of the "Astros" in 2010.

The early days of the franchise's history and the opening of the Astrodome produced several artifacts for the Hall, though many aren't on display. The first baseball thrown out in the Astrodome in 1965, the ticket to the first exhibition game against the New York Yankees at the Astrodome, and a sample of Astroturf are in the Hall. The first regular-season game ball and a 1965 ball signed by the Astros and nine astronauts are also in Cooperstown.

37 Pettitte, Clemens Come Home

The signing of pitchers Andy Pettitte and Roger Clemens prior to the 2004 season not only gave the Astros some World Series expectations, but it cast a New York-type spotlight on a Houston franchise that had yet to win a playoff series in its 40-year history. Things were supposed to change now. Pettitte and Clemens, friends who were the anchors of the New York Yankees rotation, joined an Astros team that already had major star power in Craig Biggio, Jeff Bagwell, Lance Berkman, and Jeff Kent. Adding Pettitte and Clemens to Roy Oswalt in the rotation made the Astros the favorites to win the National League.

Pettitte grew up and lived in the blue-collar Houston suburb of Deer Park when he befriended Astros owner Drayton McLane at the annual Houston Baseball Dinner in the 1990s. Pettitte and McLane would periodically have lunch, and when Pettitte hit the free agent market after the 2003 season, McLane called him to gauge his interest in pitching at home. "He had said he missed his family, being in New York for six or seven months a year," McLane said. "So I just approached him and [agents] Alan and

Randy Hendricks and just started talking to him when he became a free agent and worked with them really intensely." Pettitte and the Astros reached a three-year, $31.5-million deal on December 16, 2003. Pettitte wore No. 21 in honor of Clemens, who had worn the number with the Boston Red Sox and Toronto Blue Jays.

Astros general manager Gerry Hunsicker said landing Pettitte was one of the most unusual acquisitions he had ever been involved with because of the dynamics. Pettitte was from the area, but the Astros had to compete against the Yankees and didn't think they had a chance of signing him. "As the discussions progressed, it appeared to us more and more that Andy really started to think seriously about staying at home, playing for the hometown team," Hunsicker said. "He liked what we were doing and the team that he would be joining, and at that point for the first time, we thought we had a fighting chance…When it happened, of course, it stimulated Roger."

Clemens had retired following the 2003 season with the Yankees, but the talk in Houston was about a comeback. Two days before Christmas, McLane and his wife paid a visit to the Clemens home in the Memorial area of Houston and gave them a small glass baseball glove ornament as a gift. They started talking. "It was complicated because he had fully retired, and we persuaded him to come back," McLane said. "That was fun to do." Clemens signed with the Astros on January 19, 2004, igniting excitement throughout Houston.

The Astros—and Pettitte—got off to a poor start in 2004. Pettitte's elbow deteriorated, and he finally decided to have surgery in August. Pettitte had given up on punishing himself for a playoff run that wasn't happening for the floundering Astros. Clemens, meanwhile, started the All-Star Game in Houston in 2004—18 years after he started for the American League in the Astrodome— and finished 18–4 with a 2.98 ERA to win his seventh and final Cy Young. The Astros lost in seven games in the National League Championship Series to St. Louis Cardinals.

Mike Hampton

The only Astros lefty to win 20 games prior to Dallas Keuchel doing it in his final start of the 2015 regular season was Mike Hampton, a bulldog competitor who won 22 games in 1999. Hampton came to the Astros in one of the best trades in club history. They acquired him from the Seattle Mariners in 1993 for outfielder Eric Anthony, who never quite lived up to his power potential.

Hampton, who stood only 5'10", spent seven years with the Astros and appeared in 216 games, making 172 starts. He was 76–50 with a 3.59 ERA and was second in the Cy Young voting in 1999, but he was traded to the New York Mets in the offseason and cashed in big time later in his career with a $105 million deal with the Colorado Rockies. Hampton was a great athlete, which helped him become one of the best fielders in the game as well as a good hitter for a pitcher.

"I was here in '97 and '98, and '98 to me was the year he really turned it around," former Astros catcher Brad Ausmus said. "He kind of got off to a mediocre start and really took off the last half of the season and became one of the better lefties in the game. He's one of my favorite pitchers I ever caught and one of the better teammates I've been around."

The Astros convinced Clemens to return for another season in 2005, signing him for $18,000,022. Clemens went 13–8 with a 1.87 ERA. Pettitte got off to a poor start before catching fire. He went 14–3 with a 4.20 ERA in his final 20 starts. With Oswalt, Pettitte, and Clemens leading the way, the Astros won the National League pennant and were swept in four games in the World Series by the Chicago White Sox.

Clemens' final year in Houston came with a twist. He came out of retirement in May on a pro-rated $22 million agreement, but he didn't make his first start until June 22. As part of the agreement, he was allowed to skip series on the road in which he wasn't pitching. It was an arrangement only he could get away with. He went 7–6 with a 2.30 ERA in 19 starts before coming out of retirement for a final time and finishing his career with the Yankees in 2007. Pettitte, meanwhile, went 15–9 with a 4.05 ERA for the Astros in 2006 before rejoining Clemens in the Bronx and pitching the final six years of his career.

Some of Pettitte's Houston teammates, including Berkman and Chris Burke, said losing Pettitte to the Yankees sent the Astros on a downward spiral. "The entire time he's gone, the Yankees never won a playoff series, and we got to the NLCS and the World Series while he's with us," Burke said. "Then he goes back to the Yankees, and they win another World Series. I don't consider that coincidence at all."

38 Astrodome Scoreboard Dazzles

The massive video screens and fancy graphics you get with today's ballpark scoreboards have nothing on the Astrodome. With 40,000 lights that spanned nearly 500 feet along the wall above center field, the scoreboard was like none before it and none since. If you went to the Astrodome in its heyday, the scoreboard was as much of an attraction as the air-conditioning, cushioned seats, and the players.

The Astrodome scoreboard was about more than keeping score, though there was plenty of space for that. It was gaudy and wonderful with snorting bulls, blazing cowboy pistols, and fireworks going off when the Astros hit a home run. That sequence, known as the Home Run Spectacular, took 40 seconds to complete, and you couldn't take your eyes off of it.

The late Jack Foster, who was owner and president of Fair Play Scoreboards in Des Moines, Iowa, worked with Astros owner and Astrodome visionary Roy Hofheinz to design the scoreboard in 1964. Hofheinz didn't do much that wasn't flamboyant, and so when Foster came to the Judge with his first scoreboard model, he was met with disapproval. "He looked around the room and said: 'Vanilla!'" Foster said in 1989. "'I ordered strawberry, and you brought me vanilla. We need some excitement in here. I want this to be most explosive. Go back and come again.'"

Foster came back with the scenes for the Home Run Spectacular on cards and showed them to Hofheinz, who said, "How much?" Foster told him it would cost $2.1 million, and it soon became a reality.

The Home Run Spectacular had four sequences.

- When a home run was hit by an Astros player, a lighted Astrodome appeared to the left of the board. A baseball exploded through the roof and traveled to the right across the two large message boards before crashing into a large, exploding baseball with the words, "Home Run" on it.
- Then one cowboy on each side of the scoreboard shot off guns into the air and ground, while the bullets ricocheted back and forth.
- Snorting bulls then appeared on each side of the scoreboard with the Texas flag and the United States flag being unfurled from their horns. A cowboy on a horse chased a steer on the left side of the board before successfully roping him on the right side.
- Finally, multicolored fireworks filled the entire area in a display that was supposed to last a total of 40 seconds, giving the batter enough time to round the bases.

"That was Hofheinz," longtime Astros executive Tal Smith said. "If it had been up to most people, they would have had a very nice, modern, up-to-date scoreboard at that time, but it wouldn't have had the sizzle and the distinctiveness that the one in the Dome did."

Astros first baseman Glenn Davis was the last player to touch off the scoreboard with a ninth-inning home run off the Cincinnati Reds' Tom Browning on September 6, 1988. The scoreboard lit up for the last time following the game with a message that read, "Thanks for the memories." It was removed to accommodate another 10,000 seats that were being added to satisfy the NFL's Houston Oilers. "To me, losing the scoreboard was the writing on the wall," former Astros pitcher Larry Dierker said. "The Dome didn't feel like a ballpark without it."

39 Jeff Kent's Walk-Off Home Run

At the time, it went down as one of the biggest home runs in the history of the Astros, and for the man who provided the moment—second baseman Jeff Kent—it was a memory of a lifetime. Kent's three-run home run off Jason Isringhausen in the bottom of the ninth rocked Minute Maid Park and sent the Astros to a 3–0 win against the St. Louis Cardinals in Game 5 of the 2004 National League Championship Series. The Astros took a 3–2 series lead over the Cardinals before losing Games 6 and 7 in St. Louis. Still, Kent's walk-off homer remains an indelible image in Astros lore. "There were pictures of me coming from third base to home plate, and I don't know if I've ever been so excited in my whole baseball career, even in the World Series [with the San Francisco Giants in 2002]," Kent said. "I guess I got ahead of myself because I thought we were going to win and go to the World Series. We didn't, and it was humbling knowing we lost against St. Louis a few days later."

Kent, the former National League Most Valuable Player with the Giants, came to the Astros on a two-year deal to play second base, which meant franchise icon Craig Biggio had to learn how to play the outfield. The hard-nosed Kent produced in his two years in Houston, hitting .297 with 22 homers and 93 RBIs in 2003 and .289 with 27 homers and 107 RBIs in 2004, making the All-Star Game that year in Houston. Kent helped the Astros win their first playoff series in history, beating the Atlanta Braves in five games in the NL Division Series in 2004. In their first NLCS appearance since 1986, the Astros lost the first two games in St. Louis before returning to Minute Maid Park to even up the series at two games apiece. Game 5 in Houston proved to be a masterpiece.

Cardinals starter Woody Williams, a Houston native, threw seven scoreless innings and allowed one hit, and bulldog Astros starter Brandon Backe tossed eight scoreless innings and allowed one hit. Each walked two batters and struck out four. Facing Isringhausen to start the ninth, Carlos Beltran singled and stole second base with one out. The Cardinals intentionally walked Lance Berkman to face Kent, who clubbed the first pitch he saw high over the left-field wall for the game winner. The picture of Kent approaching home plate with a huge smile on his face is one of the most unforgettable images of the Astros' magical playoff runs in 2004 and '05. "I was thinking, *Drive the ball deep*," Kent said. "I knew I was going to get something good early in the count. They had walked Berkman in front of me, and I had been used to that because they would walk Barry Bonds a lot of times in front of me, too, [with the Giants]."

Kent wasn't a warm and fuzzy guy with the media or his team-mates during his time in Houston, but he genuinely enjoyed the game and the fans. He showed some rare on-field emotions after he

Jeff Kent celebrates his walk-off, three-run home run in the bottom of the ninth inning to defeat the St. Louis Cardinals 3–0 in Game 5 of the 2004 NLCS.

hit the home run, throwing his helmet into the air between third base and home plate with a huge smile on his face as he waited for his teammates to mob him at home plate.

"It happened way too fast," he said. "We were a pretty good team. The team went to the World Series the year after I left, and I was pretty bitter about that. The time I had in Houston, albeit short, was pretty great. I'm grateful for the time I had playing in the middle of the country. The people and the fans were great. They were my kind of people. I loved every minute of it."

40 John McMullen

Dr. John McMullen's early moves as owner earned him some instant popularity with Astros fans. He bought the team on May 10, 1979, from GE Credit/Ford Motor Credit when the Astros looked like they were going to run away with the National League West, and after Houston collapsed and missed the playoffs, he signed hometown hero Nolan Ryan and two-time National League Most Valuable Player and former Colt .45 second baseman Joe Morgan. The Astros won the division and made their first playoff appearance in 1980 and appeared to be poised for a few years of playoff runs.

But when McMullen wanted Ryan to take a pay cut after the 1988 season and Ryan instead signed with the cross-state Texas Rangers—of all teams—the fans turned on McMullen. During a game in 1989, two fans holding signs critical of McMullen were booted from the Astrodome. Ryan went on to throw two more no-hitters and record his 5,000[th] strikeout and 300th win with the Rangers. McMullen sold the club to Drayton McLane for $117 million in 1992 and was hardly heard from again in Houston.

Former Astros general manager Tal Smith, who was fired by McMullen after the 1980 season, said McMullen could be difficult. "Obviously, in 1980 we had a pretty good year and we lost the LCS," Smith said. "I had a year remaining on my contract, and he decided that was not a relationship he wanted to continue, and that was the parting of our ways. That caused quite an uproar among the rest of his partners here in Houston."

Bill Wood, who was hired by the Astros in 1976 and served as general manager from 1988 to 1993, said McMullen was demanding, but he had some common sense to most of his thought process. McMullen, who also owned the New Jersey Devils of the National Hockey League, didn't have much of a baseball background. So if he came up with a bad idea, Wood could usually talk him out of it. "I had to call him at home every night after the ballgame if we were on the West Coast," Wood said. "He didn't stay up for the games. [He lived in New York and had offices in the World Trade Center,] so I had to call him when the game was over and wake him up and tell him if we won or lost. He was into the club. He wanted the club to win, but there was a business side that always factored in."

The Astros didn't spend a lot of money in free agency during McMullen's ownership, and Wood said there was a time he talked McMullen out of cutting expenses in scouting and player development, too. "We were able to change his mind on that," Wood said. "I couldn't change his mind on Nolan Ryan, and that one, I thought, for the longest time was going to be on his grave marker."

Hall of Fame second baseman Craig Biggio, who was drafted in the first round in 1987 out of Seton Hall University in New Jersey, had a strong friendship with McMullen. "He meant a lot to me," he said. "He was my owner, my boss. I would go to the hockey games when I was back on the East Coast in the winter time. I really got to know Mac at a different level and from the golf tournaments he used to have. He'd get Joe Morgan, Mike Scott, Enos Cabell, and all of the young guys, and we would go on a golf trip in in the winter time. To Mac, it was about the camaraderie of being around the guys. That's what he loved."

McMullen, a New Jersey native, graduated from the Naval Academy in 1940 and rose to the rank of commander during a 15-year naval career. He received a master's degree in naval architecture and engineering from MIT and a doctorate in mechanical engineering from the Swiss Federal Institute of Technology in Zurich. In 1959 he founded John J. McMullen Associates, an international firm of naval architects and marine engineers known for its innovations in commercial and naval ship design. In 1972 he acquired Norton Lilly International, a shipping agency. McMullen purchased a share of the New York Yankees in 1974 and quipped, "There is nothing quite so limited as being a limited partner of George Steinbrenner's."

41 26-Game Road Trip

The 1992 Astros began the season as anything but road warriors. They lost 27 of their first 40 games away from the Astrodome, which helped spread dread among the field staff and players, as they knew they had to play 26 consecutive road games in a span of 28 days in the middle of that summer. The Republican National Convention was taking over the Astrodome, forcing the road-weary Astros to pack their bags for a month. "We weren't real excited about it," manager Art Howe said. "We weren't really playing well on the road at all."

That year's team had a promising young core that included slugger Jeff Bagwell, who won the National League Rookie of the Year in 1991, future Hall of Fame second baseman Craig Biggio, future NL Most Valuable Player Ken Caminiti, and up-and-coming stars Luis Gonzalez, Steve Finley, and Darryl Kile. The road trip, which began July 27 in Atlanta, included stops in Cincinnati, Los Angeles, San Diego, San Francisco, Chicago, St. Louis, and Philadelphia. There were only two off days in that span, and they spent one of those in Houston catching up on laundry. The trip was set to cover 9,186 miles, and the young Astros were going to find out how resilient they are. "I thought it was unfair," general manager Bill Wood said. "It was a huge hurdle for the ballclub to overcome. I was concerned about everybody because, as the general manager, you want to do the job as best you can and now comes this [road trip]. I remember thinking going into the road trip anything could happen, but I was pleased with the progress we were making at that point. We had a young ballclub."

The trip began with the Astros winning two of three at the Atlanta Braves, who were just beginning to become a dynasty in the National League East. Wood took some validation from a dugout conversation with Braves manager Bobby Cox, who told Wood, "I really like your players and the direction you're going." Wood was pleased and noted, "All of a sudden, you say, 'Alright, somebody on another ballclub recognizes what we're trying to do and maybe we're on the right track.' I'm seeing with my own eyes these young players and they have ceilings and are going to improve. We think we're going in the right direction, and now you're hearing this from people you respect in the game."

From Atlanta the Astros came out of an off day and lost three of four games at the Cincinnati Reds, split a pair at the Los Angeles Dodgers, were swept in four games at the San Diego Padres, took two of three at the San Francisco Giants, and split a four-game series at Wrigley Field before taking a day off in Houston. They finished up the trip by losing two of three in St. Louis to the Cardinals before sweeping the Philadelphia Phillies at Veteran Stadium to finish a respectable 12–14 on the trip. "We had 15 rookie or sophomores, a bunch of young guys, and the trip really wasn't that bad," Biggio said. "The way they scheduled the games, a lot of times you bounce around, and the travel doesn't make any sense, but the league looked at it and really took care of us...We had a good time with it. That's part of the bonding. We were so young the year before and now we're all a bit older and we got along. To go on a 26-game road trip, it was fun. We were like, 'Let's have a good time with it.' There was nothing we could do about it."

The Astros went 33–17 to finish the season in 1992, including winning nine of their final 15 games on the road after the month-long road trip. They finished .500 and had only one losing season in the next 14. "Realizing that we were going to be on the road so much, I wasn't looking forward to it," Howe said. "As it turned out, it was a blessing. The guys learned how to win on the road... It really helped us get over the hump as far as playing on the road and learning how to get it done."

42 22-Inning Game

As far as walk-off victories go, the celebration was quite tame compared to today's standards. Maybe that's because the Astros were too tired to jump up and down in a huddle and drench each other with buckets of Gatorade. After Bill Doran slapped home plate to score the winning run in the 22nd inning of a marathon game in the Astrodome against the Los Angeles Dodgers that began on June 3, 1989 and ended on June 4, Astros manager Art Howe ran out to hug Doran at the plate. After seven hours and 14 minutes, everyone was just glad the game was over.

The game, which ended at 2:50 AM on a Sunday, was the longest in terms of time in the history of the Astros and the Dodgers and was the longest night game in National League history. Astros shortstop Rafael Ramirez delivered the game-winning hit with a line-drive single to right field that caromed off the glove of Dodgers lefty pitcher Fernando Valenzeula, who was playing first base. Doran scored from second, tripping over catcher Mike Scioscia, who couldn't handle the throw. Unsure whether he touched home plate, Doran stretched out on his stomach and slapped it with his left hand and was called safe by umpire Fred Brocklander. The Astros won 5–4. "I was really too tired to argue with Fred," Scioscia said. "Fred said he touched the plate. There was so much confusion at the time I didn't have the angle to see."

Legendary Dodgers broadcaster Vin Scully had worked NBC's *Game of the Week* earlier that day in St. Louis, which went 10 innings, prior to flying to Houston for the Dodgers-Astros game. He arrived during the national anthem. Scully announced 19 of the 22 innings because broadcast partner Don Drysdale had laryngitis.

The only Astros players who didn't get on the field were injured outfielder Kevin Bass and pitchers Bob Forsch and Mike Scott. Jim Clancy, a starting pitcher, threw the final five innings for the Astros. Dodgers manager Tommy Lasorda, meanwhile, played every eligible player save for Tim Belcher, who was scheduled to start Sunday. That included Dodgers ace Orel Hershiser, who came on in relief and struck out eight batters in seven scoreless innings. Jeff Hamilton, a third baseman, was on the mound when the game ended after replacing Hershiser in the 21st.

Hamilton, a pitcher in high school, was hitting 92 mph on the radar gun and sent the Astros down 1-2-3 in the 21st inning. After Doran singled to start the 22nd, Hamilton got Glenn Davis to ground out and struck out Ken Caminiti, who broke his bat over his leg in frustration. "There was no backing down," Doran said. "That just wasn't an option." Ramirez finally became the hero.

Sixteen pitchers threw 643 pitches, and 12 dozen baseballs were used. Mike Evans, a former Dodgers employee, watched the first inning of the game in Honolulu, Hawaii, boarded a plane and flew to Los Angeles and watched the rest of the game on television there.

Less than 11 hours after the game ended, the two teams were back on the field for a Sunday matinee. The Astros beat the Dodgers 7–6 in 13 innings in a game that took four hours, 17 minutes, giving the Astros 10 wins in a row. The Astros were down by six runs early before Louie Meadows hit a pinch-hit grand slam in the fifth inning to cut the lead to one. The Astros tied the game in the bottom of the ninth on a Craig Biggio home run. "Don't tell me!" Scully screamed into the microphone to the listeners back in California. Scott not only pitched one inning in relief to win the game, but he also lifted a sac fly to center in the bottom of the 13th to score Ramirez with the winning run. "We won two extra-inning games and played 35 innings," Howe said. "It was unbelievable."

43 Jose Cruz

You could introduce Jose Cruz before a crowd of Astros fans today, and they would burst out the familiar "Cruuuuuuuzzzzz" chant that helped define his career. One of the most popular players and figures in franchise history, Cruz was named the team's Most Valuable Player four times (1977, 1980, 1983–84) by the Houston Chapter of the Baseball Writers' Association of America and is the only person to be in uniform for the first nine of the Astros' playoff appearances as a player or coach. His No. 25 was retired in 1992.

Cruz, known by those around him as "Cheo," played 19 seasons in the big leagues, and his best years occurred in Houston (1975–87). He retired with 2,251 career hits, 165 homers, 1,077 RBIs, and 317 stolen bases and still holds the Astros' career record for triples (80). Only Craig Biggio and Jeff Bagwell have more hits in an Astros uniform than Cruz. "He is one of the most underrated, underappreciated players in the history of the game," former teammate Bill Doran said. "Not by his teammates. We all knew. There wasn't a better hitter, a better teammate. There wasn't a better guy in baseball than Jose."

Cruz was born in Arroyo, Puerto Rico, and was signed by the St. Louis Cardinals at 19 years old. He reached the big leagues in 1970 as the first of three brothers to play Major League Baseball. Hector, an outfielder/first baseman, played nine years with the Cardinals, Chicago Cubs, San Francisco Giants, and Cincinnati Reds, and Tommy got a cup of coffee with the Cardinals (1973) and Chicago White Sox (1977). The Astros purchased Cruz's contract on October 24, 1974, and when Bob Watson took over first base for the traded outfielder Lee May, a spot opened for Cruz. He established himself as one of the top hitters on the team in 1977 by batting .299 with 17 homers, 87 RBIs, and 44 stolen bases. He kept up that level of production for nearly a decade, hitting .300 or better five times, making two All-Star teams, and leading the league in hits in 1983.

When Cruz was signed by the New York Yankees in 1988, he was the Astros' all-time leader in games played, hits, at-bats, RBIs, and total bases. He was second in runs scored, doubles, extra-base hits, stolen bases, and walks. "To tell you the truth," he said. "Everything happened to me when I got traded to Houston. This is where I made my home, raised my family. This is the best for me because the fans treated me so good here that I decided to stay here forever. I had some good years here."

Cruz was a left-handed pull hitter when he joined the Astros. He overheard a conversation one day when Pete Rose was telling Rusty Staub he needed to learn to use all fields. That made sense to Cruz. Playing in the spacious Astrodome, he realized he could do more damage if he could spray the ball around the field. "I listened because I wanted to spend a long time in the big leagues," he said.

Outfielder Terry Puhl hit in the same group with Cruz during batting practice and saw firsthand the work Cruz put in to become an all-around hitter. "He's the most dangerous hitter of my era for the Astros, no question about it," Puhl said. "He used to say, 'Give me a bat, Give me any bat.' He'd say, 'It's not the arrow, it's the Indian.' I gave him a fungo and I saw him take an at-bat against Steve Carlton and hit a double off the wall."

It was former Astrodome public address announcer J. Fred Duckett who took Cruz's popularity to another level in Houston. His exaggerated pronunciation of his last name— "Cruuuuuuuzzzzz"— became a trademark. Cruz embraced it. "The first time I heard that, you cannot tell if they were booing me or rooting for me," he said. "I realized in time, when I listened to that, it was good for me."

Larry Dierker brought Cruz back into the fold when he became manager of the Astros in 1997. Cruz served as first-base coach from 1997 to 2009. That gave him a chance to spend a few months in the majors with his oldest son, Jose Cruz Jr., a 12-year big leaguer who finished his career with 38 games with the Astros in 2008. "I'm a pretty lucky guy," Cruz said. "I'll always be proud to be in this organization because this is the best thing that ever happened to me and my family."

44 The Toy Cannon

Jimmy Wynn was a 5'9" power hitter who played in one of the most pitching-friendly ballparks in history. In the early days of the Astrodome, the dimensions weren't kind to hitters. It was 340 feet to left, 406 feet to center, and 330 feet to right. The power alleys were 375 feet. That's what made the accomplishments of Wynn so amazing. He walloped 291 home runs in his 15-year career, including 223 with the Astros that stood as a club record until Jeff Bagwell passed him in 1999. While playing his home games in the Astrodome, he hit 121 of his 214 homers in that span (1965–1973) on the road, so he wasn't about to let the Eighth Wonder of the World tame his power. "I'm a little bigger than him and I had some strength and I would have to stand on second base to hit a ball that far," former teammate Norm Miller said. "Jimmy never hit a cheap home run."

James Sherman Wynn was born on March 12, 1942, in Cincinnati, growing up not far from Crosley Field, home of the Reds. His father, Joe Wynn, taught him how to play baseball and coached him in Little League. In his autobiography entitled *Toy Cannon*, Wynn said his dad would tell him, "Jimmy, if you want to drive a Chevy someday, you will need to become really good at hitting singles. If on the other hand, you hope to drive a Cadillac in the future, you will need to become very good at hitting home runs."

Wynn lived so close to Crosley Field that some of the Reds players had to come down his street on the way to the ballpark. He got to know some of the players, who heard about Wynn's growing promise as a prospect himself. One day Vada Pinson stopped at his house driving Frank Robinson's white Thunderbird convertible and took him to the ballpark for a tour. He got to meet all the players, and Robinson even gave him a baseball glove.

In high school Wynn played against Pete Rose in baseball and Roger Staubach in football. Wynn lined up a tryout at Crosley Field and was offered a contract out of high school, but his mom wanted him to attend college. He played at Central State in Ohio and two years later signed with the Reds at 19 years old for a $500

Upper-Deck Shots

Astros teammates Doug Rader and Jimmy Wynn both hit home runs into the upper deck of the Astrodome within a few days of each other in 1970. Getting the ball over the fence in the Astrodome in those days was hard enough, but hitting one into the gold seats of the upper deck? That took a mammoth clout.

Rader, a defensive whiz who won five consecutive Gold Gloves at third base for the Astros, blasted a shot into the upper deck's left-field seats during an exhibition against the New York Yankees on April 3, 1970. It landed six rows up, hitting an empty chair. He was the first player to reach that portion of the stadium.

Wynn, the Astros' first great slugger, went upper deck on April 12 just a few sections over from Rader's blast. Wynn unbelievably hit a knuckleball off the bat of Hall of Famer Phil Niekro. The home runs were hit in the days before homers were measured, but it's safe to say those balls traveled at least 430 feet.

Both seats were later marked with the date of the home runs and images of the players' nicknames. Rader was known as the "Red Rooster," and the head of a red rooster was painted on the back of the seat. Wynn, of course, was known as "Toy Cannon," and a cannon blasting a cannonball was on the back of the seat he hit.

On May 17, 1990, Eric Anthony became one of the few to homer into the upper deck in right field when he hit a mammoth blast off Mike Bielecki that was measured at 410 feet. "Whoever measured that ball must have been sleeping," Astros manager Art Howe told reporters. "That was hit least 500 feet, and it was still going up."

bonus and a $375 monthly salary. That was 15 years after Jackie Robinson broke the sport's color barrier and about a decade after Hank Aaron, Willie Mays, and others helped clear a path for all the black players who followed. Wynn experienced racism in the minor leagues and would call home to his dad. "My father told me that I would run into things like that," he said. "He told me to discuss it with him. That's exactly what I did. By doing that, it made me a much better person."

Despite putting up great numbers in the Florida State League for Tampa in 1962, Wynn was left unprotected by the Reds and taken by the expansion Colt .45s in the 1962 draft. He made his major league debut a year later and smashed 22 homers in 1965, the first year of the Astros. He was an All-Star in 1967 when he hit .249 with 37 homers and 107 RBIs. On June 10 of that year at Crosley Field—blocks from where he grew up—Wynn hit a mammoth homer in the eighth inning that cleared the 58-foot scoreboard in left-center field and landed on I-75 outside the stadium. Five days later in the Astrodome, Wynn became the first Astros player to hit three homers in a game. "He hit balls so far it was remarkable," Miller said. "He's the greatest guy in the world and pound for pound could hit the ball farther than anybody I've seen in my life."

Wynn, an All-Star with the Los Angeles Dodgers in 1974 and 1975, played 11 seasons for the Astros and was one of the franchise's first stars, earning the nickname "Toy Cannon" by newspaper reporter John Wilson. "The Astros have been my life," Wynn said. "They gave me an opportunity to bring my skills out. It gave me a chance to realize my dream."

45 Tal Smith

Tal Smith has witnessed nearly every key moment in the history of the Houston baseball franchise. From the birth of the Colt .45s in 1962, to the opening of the Astrodome three years later, to an incredible run of six playoff appearances in nine years (1997–2005), Smith was there. He worked for the Astros on and off for 35 years, serving in different capacities since Houston was awarded a National League franchise in 1960. He spent his final 17 years with the club as president of baseball operations but was a successful general manager in the late 1970s.

A native of Framingham, Massachusetts, Smith dabbled in radio broadcasting while a student at Duke University. He spent a summer as an editorial assistant for *The Sporting News* in St. Louis. After he graduated he served for two years as an officer in the Air Force and briefly worked as a newspaper reporter for the *Cape Cod Standard-Times*. Along the way he had written Cincinnati Reds general manager Gabe Paul about a position with the club, which led to Smith's first baseball gig. In 1957 Paul hired him as an administrative assistant in the Reds' player development department.

In Cincinnati, Smith worked his way up in scouting and player development. When Paul was hired by Judge Hofheinz to help get the city's expansion franchise up and running in 1960, Smith came along as assistant general manager. "You start from scratch, and that's sort of fun because, if there are mistakes made, they're yours and not somebody's that you inherited," Smith said. When Paul took a job with the Cleveland Indians less than a year later, Smith was going to follow him before Hofheinz asked him to stay and oversee the construction of the Astrodome. "[Gabe] said, 'This sounds like a unique opportunity. Why don't you give it a try? If it doesn't work, you still have a home here if you need it,'" Smith said. "So I accepted, and it was just a fascinating experience."

Smith helped oversee the construction of the Dome, handling its famous grass issues from April 1963 to December 1965. "You had to pore over plans and specs," Smith said. "Things like signage; designation of the levels; the ticketing; aisle designation, which way are you going to go—odd or even; the hardware; which way will the doors open; clubhouses; all kind of things."

He was named vice president and director of player personnel in 1965 and in 1972 he switched hats to oversee the Astrodome-Astrohall stadium corporation. Paul, meanwhile, went to the New York Yankees in 1973 and persuaded Smith to join him as the executive vice president. He didn't stay long in the Bronx. The Astros went through a reorganization soon after Smith left, and he was asked to return as the club's GM in 1975.

Slowly rebuilding the club, the Astros finally broke through in 1980 and made the playoffs for the first time by winning the National League West. They lost to the Philadelphia Phillies in five memorable games in the National League Championship Series, and Smith had a falling out with Astros owner John McMullen and was fired. That began a stretch of 13 years away from the Astros.

He started Tal Smith Enterprises, which provided consultation to major league clubs on matters such as salary arbitration, the financial appraisal of franchises, and expert testimony in sports-related litigation. The firm blossomed, and Smith eventually provided consulting services to nearly all 30 major league clubs. "I wanted to stay in Houston and I thought there was a niche for the way the game had grown," Smith said. "We could really be a benefit to clubs in contract negotiations and salary arbitration and things like that. There were a lot of specialized areas that could be handled by somebody on a short-term basis instead of trying to staff for them on a permanent basis."

Smith was hired by Drayton McLane to do consulting work when McLane was considering buying the Astros in 1993. Impressed with his knowledge of the franchise, of Houston, and baseball in general, McLane talked Smith into another return to the organization in 1994—this time as club president. He stayed through the end of the 2011 season. "I've seen Houston grow, prosper, and change, and we just love it from a baseball stand-point," he said.

46 Jim Deshaies Strikes Out the First Eight Batters

For a team with so much pitching history, the Astros had perhaps their three greatest consecutive pitching performances late in the 1986 season—capped by Mike Scott becoming the only pitcher to throw a no-hitter in a clinching situation. He dominated the San Francisco Giants in memorable fashion to lock down the National League West title. Scott's gem came one day after Hall of Famer Nolan Ryan struck out 12 batters in eight scoreless innings, allow-ing just one hit in a 6–0 win against the Giants, pushing the Astros to within a game of clinching a playoff spot. Ryan's performance, however, came on the heels of a record-breaking outing by rookie left-hander Jim Deshaies.

Deshaies, who the Astros had acquired from the New York Yankees in the Joe Niekro deal a year earlier, had no idea when he took the mound against the Los Angeles Dodgers on September 23, 1986, in the Astrodome that he was about to set the stage for Ryan and Scott, as well as put himself in the record books. A lefty who didn't throw particularly hard, Deshaies set a modern-day major league record when he struck out the first eight batters he faced. "The bottom line is I had hair back then and I could run from home to first base without needing a ventilator," joked Deshaies, who was a longtime broadcaster for the Astros before joining the Chicago Cubs. "That was a long time ago."

The Astros and Dodgers had struck up quite a rivalry in the '86 season with bombastic Dodgers manager Tommy Lasorda at one point proclaiming the Astros were simply renting first place. Of course, the Astros spent 149 days atop the NL West standings that season, so they were renting to own. The Dodgers finished in fifth place—23 games behind the surprising Astros—and were more bark than bite.

Deshaies, then 26, was en route to winning 12 games in his first full season in the major leagues. He was pitching for the first time that Tuesday in nearly two weeks and felt strong coming out of the bullpen before the game, which wasn't always the case for him. "I was terrible at the start of games," Deshaies said. "The team was always holding its breath until I could get through the first couple of innings, and I picked up steam as I went along."

Deshaies started the game by striking out Steve Sax, Reggie Williams, and Enos Cabell in the first inning. Pedro Guerrero, Alex Trevino, and Jeff Hamilton all whiffed in the second, and when Dave Anderson became his seventh consecutive strikeout victim to start the third inning, Deshaies began to hear the crowd buzz. "After I got the seventh, I get the ball back and I was rubbing it up and I hear a secondary ovation," he said. "I kind of turned around and look at the scoreboard and they put a message saying, 'Jim Deshaies has just tied the modern record for most strikeouts to start a game with seven.' That was the first time I got wind of something was going on."

Deshaies broke the record by striking out Jose Gonzalez to bring up the ninth spot in the order, which would have been pitcher Dennis Powell had Lasorda not decided he had seen enough strikeouts and sent Larry See to pinch hit for him. See popped out to end the streak. "At that time, you're so caught up in what you're doing and you don't second-guess what's going on," Deshaies said. "It didn't cross my mind it was out of the ordinary or to question his motives. I really felt I should have gotten the ninth one. I had him 2–2, I believe. When you're pitching and in a zone like that, you can almost foresee results if you make a certain pitch."

Deshaies struck out only two batters the rest of the way but pitched the entire nine innings in the 4–0 victory for the first of his six career shutouts. He only had a day to revel in his feat before Ryan dominated the Giants the next day. Deshaies was in the clubhouse after Ryan's game and was shaving while wise-cracking with catcher Alan Ashby. "I joked and said, 'Everything that Nolan's done in the game, and you think he could have let me be the guy for more than 24 hours?' I was just having fun with it," Deshaies said. "Ash says, 'Well, I've got a feeling Scotty's going to come out tomorrow and show you both up.'"

Scott did just that on September 25, 1986, providing one of the signature moments in franchise history. He struck out 13 batters as the Astros clinched the division title with a 2–0 win in the Astrodome. "It's kind of fun to be lumped with that three-game sequence—a two-hitter, one-hitter, and no-hitter," Deshaies said.

47 Art Howe

It was the biggest game in the history of the Astros at the time, and Art Howe rose to the occasion. The Astros had blown a shot to win the 1980 National League West title by getting swept by the Los Angeles Dodgers in the final three games of the regular season, setting up a winner-take-all tiebreaker to determine the division title at Dodger Stadium. Howe went 3-for-5 with a two-run homer and four RBIs to lead the Astros to a 7–1 win, cementing his place as a hero.

The soft-spoken Howe wound up spending seven seasons in Houston, playing all over the infield and later became the first former Astros player to manage the club. As a manager he took over an aging team that was being disassembled in 1989 and led the Astros into a new era that included Craig Biggio, Jeff Bagwell, Luis Gonzalez, and Darryl Kile. He was fired at the end of the 1993 season but wound up managing the Oakland A's (1996–2002) and the New York Mets (2003–04) with some success. "I helped rebuild two or three organizations," Howe said. "I handled the club real well. Players liked playing for me, and I feel like I put our players in the best position to be successful. As a manager that's your job. I'm kind of surprised I haven't gotten another opportunity."

Howe grew up in Pittsburgh and attended the University of Wyoming. After finishing school he went to work at Westinghouse Telecomputer Center. A year and a half later, he went to a Pirates tryout camp in Pittsburgh and was signed. Howe was a part-time player in Pittsburgh for a pair of seasons before being traded to Houston in exchange for Tommy Helms. The Astros were a club on the rise when Howe came aboard, and he became a huge part of their success. He hit .283 with 10 homers and 46 RBIs in 1980, helping a talented Astros team win the NL West. "I was very excited about [coming to Houston] because when I was in Pittsburgh I was playing behind Richie Hebner and I wasn't getting much of an opportunity to play at all," he said. "I knew going to Houston I'd have a much better opportunity. I was excited about that, and as it turned out, it worked out really well for me."

Howe played through several injuries with the Astros, including a broken jaw suffered in 1978 when he was struck by a pitch from Scott Sanderson of the Montreal Expos. He set a team record with a 23-game hitting streak in May 1981, batting .460 during the streak. He missed the entire 1983 season, following ankle and elbow surgery and signed with the St. Louis Cardinals, where he finished his career. He hit .269 with 39 homers and 266 RBIs with the Astros. "We were very fortunate to pick up Art," former general manager Tal Smith said. "You take over a club that finished 43½ games out and you have to start making adjustments, and we did with a number of veteran players. One of those was Tommy Helms, who the Astros had acquired in the ill-fated Joe Morgan deal from Cincinnati…Art came here, and it took him a while to become established, but he certainly did and became a key component and a great contributor in the 1979 and 1980 clubs and went on to have a very fine career. A true gentleman in every respect."

Howe joined Bobby Valentine's staff with the Texas Rangers shortly after he retired and after three seasons was hired by the Astros to manage, taking over for Hal Lanier. In 14 years as a big league manager, Howe nearly broke even (1,129–1,137) and won a pair of division titles with the A's in 2000 and 2002. But it was in Houston where he got his first managerial job. "I knew a lot of the players on the team," he said. "Mike Scott was still on the team. I had actually played with Mike before I left, Terry Puhl, and Alan Ashby, guys that were my teammates, so it was really a dream come true to be able to come back here to Houston and get my first managing shot. I totally enjoyed it."

48 Lima Time

Jose Lima was perhaps the most unheralded players of the nine that were swapped between the Astros and Detroit Tigers on December 10, 1996. The Tigers sent catcher Brad Ausmus, pitchers Trever Miller and C.J. Nitkowski, slugger Daryle Ward, and Lima to the Astros for pitchers Doug Brocail, Todd Jones, outfielder Brian Hunter, and shortstop Orlando Miller and cash. "That was one of the crazier acquisitions we ended up making," former Astros general manager Gerry Hunsicker said.

Lima, a 24-year-old right-handed pitcher, had posted a 6.24 ERA in 57 career games (20 starts) with the Tigers and certainly gave no indication of the brief success he was going to have in Houston. He pitched in the bullpen for the Astros in 1997 (and not very well) before putting up a pair of improbable seasons, going 16–8 with a 3.70 ERA in 1998 and 21–10 in 1999 while making the National League All-Star team. He did it with passion and flare the nondescript Astros weren't used to seeing, and the fans enjoyed every moment. The charismatic Lima signed countless autographs for fans, threw souvenirs into the stands, danced at the drop of a hat, and even sang in a commercial for the local Tex-Mex restaurant chain, Casa Ole. He even had his own salsa CD and own slogan: "Believe it!"

Lima Time was taking over Houston. "Lima, more than any player I've ever been around, loved life," Hunsicker said. "He came to the ballpark with a smile on his face every day and when he got between the lines he was a fierce competitor. He hated to lose, but the next day, he had that smile on his face. He kept the clubhouse loose and obviously for a few years became one of the best starting pitchers in the game."

Lima didn't have great stuff or throw particularly hard. He had a great change-up, which was a swing-and-miss pitch, even when hitters knew it was coming. He mysteriously lost it later in his career and started hanging more pitches. He pitched down in the zone and benefitted from the spacious Astrodome, where long fly balls could be given up without usually leaving the park. And once Lima started to have success and Lima Time grew into a cult following, he became emboldened. "He had confidence bordering on overconfidence," manager Larry Dierker said. "He never really changed. He just challenged everybody and got away with a lot, and really, to be honest, those years at the Dome, I was scratching my head saying, *How is he doing this? His stuff isn't that good, and they're getting great swings at him, and he's not giving up very many runs and he's pitching seven, eight, nine innings and he's laughing and jumping over the foul lines and having a great time and putting the whole team in a good mood.*"

Hall of Fame second baseman Craig Biggio, a hard-nosed baseball player, admitted Lima's antics would have rubbed him the wrong way had he not been on the Astros. "He was the guy on the top step of the dugout for every single guy and wanted every guy to be successful, along with himself," he said. "He was good energy. He was positive energy and he was good for the team and he was good for the city. God bless him. He's not here anymore, but he was a fun teammate."

Lima gave up a record 48 home runs after the team moved out of the Astrodome in 2000 and went 7–16 in 33 starts. The Astros traded him back to the Tigers midway through the 2001 season for Dave Mlicki, and he bounced around after that. He went 13–5 with the Los Angeles Dodgers in 2004 and finished up with four bad starts with the New York Mets in 2006. Lima died of a heart attack on May 23, 2010, at 37 years old.

49 Three Consecutive No. 1 Picks

Having the No. 1 overall pick in a draft isn't something any team wants to experience—for obvious reasons. That means you've been, well, the worst team in the league. That means you have a long way to go before you can get competitive again and likely have a frustrated fanbase. The Astros found this out all too well when they—dare we say?—earned the No. 1 overall pick in an unprecedented three consecutive years from 2012 to 2014 after having the worst record in the league the three previous years.

Only a few years removed from a World Series berth, the team began rebuilding during the 2010 season when they traded away franchise icons Lance Berkman and Roy Oswalt. The next year, up-and-coming players Hunter Pence and Michael Bourn were dealt as the rebuild efforts kicked into gear. Jim Crane bought the club from Drayton McLane following the 2011 season and hired general manager Jeff Luhnow to take the rebuilding process to the next level, stripping down the payroll. Any veteran player with any value was traded for prospects as Luhnow tried to replenish a weak farm system. It was a tough pill to swallow. The Astros lost 106 games in 2011, 107 games in 2012, and a franchise-record 111 games, including 15 in a row to end the season, in their first year in the American League in 2013. Their reward? The No. 1 pick in the draft three years running. "When you have that opportunity, you realize it's an opportunity to select the best player in the draft class and you don't have to worry about what everybody else is doing," Luhnow said. "But it does put a lot of pressure on you as an organization to make the right move and get a guy who can help."

When the Astros picked first overall in 2012, it was their first time doing so in 20 years, when the team famously passed on Michigan high schooler Derek Jeter at No. 1 and took Cal-State Fullerton third baseman Phil Nevin. Luhnow, who helped the Cardinals build a strong farm system while he was in charge of player development in St. Louis, took 17-year-old Puerto Rican shortstop Carlos Correa with the top pick in 2012, a pick that was considered somewhat of a stretch. Under the new collective bargaining agreement, the Astros had the most money to spend in the draft bonus pool and signed Correa for $4.8 million, well below the recommended slot value for the pick ($7.2 million). The Astros used the savings to sign right-handed pitcher Lance McCullers Jr., who they took with the 41st overall pick, even though he was committed to Florida. "That first go-round was very successful because, not only did we draft who we thought was the best player," Luhnow said, "but we also happened to get value that allowed us to get another player that we considered to be first-round talent."

In 2013 the Astros took polished Stanford senior right-hander Mark Appel with the No. 1 pick, bypassing slugger Kris Bryant, who went No. 2 to the Cubs. Appel's pro career started slowly, while Bryant burst onto the scene for the Cubs in 2015 and won National League Rookie of the Year. (Appel was dealt to the Philadelphia Phillies in a seven-player trade on December 13, 2015.) The 2014 draft saw the Astros attempt to get creative with their draft pool again, taking San Diego high school lefty Brady Aiken with the No. 1 pick. "A lot of our senior scouts agree this is the best high school left-hander that they've scouted," scouting director Mike Elias said on draft day. The Astros were hoping to sign Aiken below the pick value and in turn sign prep right-hander

Jacob Nix and prep outfielder Mac Marshall—two highly touted players who slipped in the draft because they were considered likely college commits.

Nix initially had an agreement in place with the Astros and traveled to Houston for a physical exam. Aiken's original $6.5 million offer was withdrawn because Aiken's physical exam revealed what the club cited as some issues with his pitching elbow. They later offered Aiken a $5 million deal, but he declined, and Nix wound up without an offer of his own due to the reduced pool of signing bonus money. Rather than exceed the dollars allotted for Nix's draft slot and get penalized by the forfeiture of future draft choices, the Astros wound up not signing Nix either.

The Astros got a compensation pick in the 2015 draft for not signing Aiken, who eventually had Tommy John surgery, and took LSU shortstop Alex Bregman with the No. 2 overall pick, a result that pleased the Houston front office in the wake of the Aiken mess. "All in all, I think it was a good opportunity to replenish your farm system very quickly by taking the top player in the draft, and we had that opportunity," Luhnow said. "To have it three times in a row put us in a position where we can even be talking about playoff appearances in 2015, as opposed to having to wait to 2017, '18, or '19."

50 Rainbow Jerseys

They were colorful, gaudy, and unmistakable. And to most Astros fans growing up in the 1970s and 1980s, they were glorious. The Astros rainbow uniforms, which they wore from 1975 to 1986, made the Astros stand out from their opposition in a blend of yellow, orange, and red horizontal stripes. Some of the team's greatest moments came wearing the rainbow tops. Who can forget Nolan Ryan's teammates lifting him into the air after he recorded his record-breaking fifth no-hitter? And who can forget Glenn Davis stepping on first base for the final out of Mike Scott's no-hitter, which clinched the 1986 National League West crown?

The rainbow uniforms were some of the most iconic of the 1970s and 1980s. "My first experience with them," longtime outfielder Terry Puhl said, "was when I came up from Triple A to Houston and I came walking in, and at that time, we wore them at home and on the road. That was the only uniform that we had. I loved them, I really did. I still have one of them at home. It was the first major league uniform I ever wore. To me, it was fabulous."

The uniforms of the 1970s began drifting away from some of the traditional gray road flannel jerseys that endured for decades as some teams jumped into the funky 1970s with both feet by donning polyester tops bursting with color. The Oakland A's ditched button-up jerseys for pullovers and used lots of green and gold. Judge Hofheinz always had an eye for something splashy and asked advertising firm McCann-Erickson to come up with something to replace the shooting star logo the team had worn on its home uniforms since it moved into the Astrodome in 1965. The rainbow pullover jerseys, which were worn at home and on the road from 1975 to '79 and only at home from 1980 to '86, made the Astros unique. "It was criticized by some, but it was really loved here in Houston," longtime Astros executive Tal Smith said. "It helped set the club apart, helped establish its identity. That's all positive."

The early versions of the rainbow jerseys featured the players' jersey numbers in a white circular patch on the back that former Astros slugger Bob Watson likened to a bull's-eye. The Astros also had the uniform numbers on the front of the pant legs at the time. "I didn't like those," Watson said. "When they first started wearing them, the number on your back was in a white circle like a bull's-eye. And then they had the number on your leg, on your pants. That was unusual. The rainbow colors kind of grew on you. When they first did it, I went 'You've got be kidding me!' We were a Sherwin-Williams color wheel or something. The thing was that was the era of all the weird uniforms from the Cleveland Indians

Sporting the infamous rainbow jersey, Astros pitcher Nolan Ryan acknowledges the crowd after throwing his fifth career no-hitter.

wearing all red, the Pirates wore all black, and I think the one that I really wouldn't have liked—the Chicago White Sox wore shorts—and all that kind of stuff. I know they were trying to do something nontraditional, and the rainbows were definitely nontraditional."

The Astros changed uniforms in 1987 and had the rainbows only on their sleeves. In 1994 they changed uniforms again and ditched the rainbow pattern before reaching back into their heritage and bringing them back on the side of their batting practice alternate jersey beginning in 2013. But you can go to any Astros game—home or road—to this day and still see fans wearing the rainbow top in the stands.

51 Enos Cabell

Thirty years after he played his final game for the Astros, Enos Cabell could still be found on several of the club's all-time hitting record charts. A larger-than-life personality who was quick to crack a joke and give you the straight answer—whether you liked it or not—Cabell was also one of the more underrated players in Astros history.

Cabell played eight of his 15 big league seasons in two stints with the Astros, helping to anchor the lineup and provide veteran leadership during the Astros' first rise to prominence in the late 1970s. A corner infielder who also played some outfield, "Big E"—he stood 6'4" and weighed 170 pounds—batted .281 with 1,124 hits, 45 homers, 405 RBIs, and 191 steals during his time in Houston (1975–80, 1984–85). "One of my all-time favorites," said Tal Smith, who served as general manager during most of

Cabell's playing days. "He was really one of our leaders, the sort of guy you'd want in the foxhole with you because he'd find a way to survive."

Cabell grew up in Compton, California, and was signed as an amateur free agent by the Baltimore Orioles in 1968. He was traded to the Astros following the 1974 season for Lee May and quickly became entrenched in Houston. In 1978 he was named the team's MVP after setting club records in at-bats (660) and games (162) and tallying a then-record 195 hits, which ranked third in the National League. "I had a lot of great years here," Cabell said. "We had a lot of great people come through…You get older, the memories get better, and the lies get bigger."

Cabell's father, Enos Sr., wanted to be a professional baseball player but never got an opportunity because of his race, Cabell said. While in the Army, Enos Sr. played against Jackie Robinson and was a pretty good player. His father, who spent 27 years in the Army, passed away in 2000, which meant he got to see all of his son's career. That was a source of pride for both of them. "I kind of lived his dream," Cabell said. "There would be 40,000 people in the stands, and all I could hear was my father yelling at me. If I was doing something bad or wasn't getting any hits, I could hear him over 40,000 people. That was pretty good." Cabell was a better basketball player than baseball player when he was in high school and college, so he relied on his dad to teach him about baseball. "He umpired and coached," Cabell said. "He knew the game frontwards and backward, and when I started playing, I was probably one of the smarter guys on the baseball team."

When Cabell arrived in Houston prior to the 1975 season, the Astros had just added outfielder Jose Cruz and pitcher Joe Niekro and were on an upward trend. The younger players were coming, and the Astros found themselves in a pennant race for the first time in 1979 before winning the NL West in 1980. Cabell was traded to the San Francisco Giants after the 1980 season for Bob Knepper and wound up signing back with Houston prior to the 1984 season after two years in Detroit. "I hated it there," he said about the Motor City. On July 10, 1985, he was sent to his hometown Los Angeles Dodgers, where he finished his career. Cabell kept his home in Houston and returned to the Astros about 20 years later to work in the front office. "I never thought I'd play 15 years," Cabell said. "I wasn't drafted. I signed as a free agent and was 6'5" and I was 155, 165 pounds and I was a second baseman when I started. If you see all of that stuff and you see what my career went from there, it's pretty amazing. I wasn't thought of as being a very good player and I ended up being a pretty good player."

And he never lost his sense of humor. "I got 1,800 hits," he said. "I tell the guys in the clubhouse, 'Ain't nobody in here has 1,800.' I said, 'The only ones that can talk to me is [Craig] Biggio and [Jeff] Bagwell.'"

52 Trading for Carlos Beltran

Adding one of baseball's up-and-coming young players to a team already with star power in every corner of the clubhouse injected the Astros with optimism. Outfielder Carlos Beltran had already established himself as a player on the rise, winning the American League Rookie of the Year with the Kansas City Royals in 1999. In his first six seasons, he was a .288 hitter with 108 homers, 465 RBIs, and 150 stolen bases. The 27-year-old All-Star was set to become a free agent at the end of the year, and the Royals knew they were not going to be able to sign him.

The Astros, off to a slow start in 2004, were in the midst of beating the Pittsburgh Pirates with Roger Clemens on the mound on June 24 when general manager Gerry Hunsicker called reporters to the back of the press box and announced a major trade. The Astros had acquired Beltran from the Royals as part of a three-way deal that sent closer Octavio Dotel to the Oakland A's and catching prospect John Buck to Kansas City. "The Beltran deal was one of the more exciting trades that I was involved with," Hunsicker said. "He obviously was a very talented player, and being in Kansas City, maybe people in Houston didn't realize how talented he was. But if you were a baseball person, you knew he was a special player."

Beltran, a dynamic switch-hitter from Puerto Rico, played 90 games with the Astros, batting .258 with 23 home runs, 53 RBIs, and 28 stolen bases while representing them in the All-Star Game. The Astros rallied furiously in the final two months of the season, going 36–10 down the stretch to win the National League wild-card on the final day of the regular season. Beltran was going to get his first taste of the postseason, and a legend was about to be born. "Never did I dream or could have dreamt that Beltran would make the impact he did," Hunsicker said. "His postseason run that year was legendary, still is."

Beltran tied Barry Bonds' single postseason record by hitting eight home runs. He hit two home runs in Game 5 of the National League Division Series against the Atlanta Braves and then hit one homer in each of the first four games of the National League Championship Series against the St. Louis Cardinals, including the game-winner in Game 4. He set a record by hitting a homer in five consecutive postseason games. "There's some guys who wear a Superman shirt, but he was Superman," teammate Craig Biggio said. "Every ball he hit was hard. Every out he made was hard. It was one of the most incredible hitting experiences I've seen in my life."

The Astros were outbid by the New York Mets to retain Beltran in the offseason during negotiations that went down to the wire. He signed a seven-year, $119-million contract to join the Mets. Astros owner Drayton McLane spearheaded the negotiations, but the deal fell through because the Astros wouldn't give Beltran the full no-trade clause he got with New York. The Astros had offered $108 million over seven years and a limited no-trade clause. His departure left a bitter taste in the mouths of Astros fans. Beltran was routinely booed loudly by the fans when he returned to Minute Maid Park—even after the club moved to the American League and Beltran was with the New York Yankees more than a decade later.

Beltran made five All-Star teams with the Mets, winning three Gold Gloves. He also was a two-time All-Star with the Cardinals in 2012 and 2013. His postseason performances remained legendary, earning him the nickname "Senor Octobre." He hit three homers for the Mets in the 2006 NLCS. For the Cardinals he hit two in the 2012 NLDS, one in the 2012 NLCS, and two in the 2013 NLDS. All in all, he has an astounding 16 homers and 40 RBIs in 52 playoff games.

53 J.R. Richard

Ask anyone who played for the Astros in 1980, and they will tell you the same thing. Had hard-throwing pitcher J.R. Richard not suffered a stroke midway through that season, the Astros would have won the World Series. Hell, they nearly got there without him anyway, losing in five heartbreaking games to the Philadelphia Phillies in the National League Championship Series. They all say

Richard would have made the difference that would have pushed the Astros over the top. And that is hard to argue. "He was the best pitcher in baseball," former general manager Tal Smith said. "If I had one game I had to win, my choices would be either J.R. or Bob Gibson. J.R. was absolutely dominating. He was unhittable."

James Rodney Richard grew up in a small town in northern Louisiana and spent most of his time outdoors fishing and hunting for rabbits and birds. He also liked to throw rocks at some of the animals he encountered. He didn't hit many, but he started to develop some shoulder strength. Richard's mother wanted her kids to play outside, and J.R. could be found playing baseball on the sandlot. He grew bigger and stronger than other kids his age and was 6'8" and 220 pounds by the time he finished high school. Richard was a three-sport star at Lincoln High School in Ruston, Louisiana, but he dominated in baseball with his power fastball. He was 11–0 with a 0.00 ERA his senior year.

Richard was a hot commodity in the 1969 draft and was taken by the Astros with the second pick and signed to a six-figure bonus. He struggled with control in the minors before making a memorable major league debut. On September 5, 1971, in San Francisco, he struck out 15 Giants in a complete-game win. Richard bounced between the minors and majors the next three years before making the rotation in 1975, going 12–10 with a 4.39 ERA. He won 20 games in 1976 and established himself as one of the most intimidating arms in the game with his size and 100-mph fastball. He won 18 games in each of the next three years, striking out 303 in 1978 and 313 in 1979 for a couple of top five Cy Young finishes. "Playing first base, when guys would get on base somehow, they would come down to first base and say, 'Gee whiz, he is so uncomfortable to hit off of,'" teammate Bob Watson said.

The Astros signed Nolan Ryan prior to the 1980 season, giving Houston a scary rotation that included Ryan, Richard, and Joe

Niekro. Richard began the year 10–4 with a 1.90 ERA in 17 starts and started the All-Star Game in Los Angeles. "When he got on the mound, he was so big and threw so hard and had such a devastating slider that right-handed hitters found it very intimidating to hit off of him," Ryan said.

But Richard would pitch in only one more game in his career. Throughout the 1980 season, he complained of discomfort in his shoulder and forearm and went on the disabled list. He was criticized in the media for pouting and being jealous of Ryan's larger contract, especially after repeated medical tests showed no problems. Tragically, Richard suffered a stroke while playing catch on the Astrodome floor on July 30, 1980, and nearly died. "He went to almost where he was a kid again," friend and teammate Enos Cabell said. "He couldn't button his shirt. You had a guy 6'8" and 275 pounds and a hell of an athlete, and he can't button his shirt."

Richard attempted a comeback in 1981, but the toll the stroke took on his body was too much. He was released in 1984, and his life spiraled downward to the point he was homeless at one point. He later became a minister and counselor. "The stroke was devastating," Cabell said. "If he wasn't so big and strong, he probably would have died. It's a tribute to him. At that time he was one of the leaders on our team, and when he pitched, we knew we were going to win. They weren't going to beat us. It was devastating for the franchise, too, because it put us back. In '81 we got to the playoffs, but it was a few years before they won again. If J.R. would have been there, he would be in the Hall of Fame."

54 Notable Announcers

For all the great talent the Astros have had on the field during their history, they've had some pretty impressive voices behind the microphone as well. Two announcers that spent a big portion of their careers in Houston—Gene Elston and Milo Hamilton— have won the Ford C. Frick given annually to a broadcaster by the National Baseball Hall of Fame for the best contributions in baseball. Even Harry Kalas, the legendary voice best known for serving as a narrator for NFL Films and for his 29 years with the Philadelphia Phillies, began his major league career with the Astros in 1965, working with Elston and Loel Passe. He called the first game in Astros history on April 12, 1965, and was hired by the Phillies in 1971.

Here are some of the most recognizable voices in Astros history:

Gene Elston

Elston was the lead voice of the Astros from the beginning, starting in 1962 when the franchise was still called the Colt .45s and ending after the 1986 season, when the Astros captured the National League West. He called 11 no-hitters, including Nolan Ryan's fifth and Mike Scott's that clinched the NL West title on September 25, 1986. Also among his broadcasting feats was Eddie Mathews' 500th home run.

Elston died on September 5, 2015. "Gene worked in the era that radio brought the game into our cars and into our homes," Ryan said. "As a kid growing up in Texas, my connection to Major League Baseball was through Gene and his radio partners. It was a big part of my life. It was a great experience for me to be around

Gene when I came to Houston as a player. He had a real passion and commitment to baseball."

Milo Hamilton

Hamilton, who received the Frick Award in 1992, retired following the 2012 season, ending a chapter of a career that's spanned 67 years, including more than 50 in the major leagues. He spent 28 years calling Astros games after beginning his career in 1953 with the St. Louis Browns. He later worked for the St. Louis Cardinals (1954), Chicago Cubs (1955–57, 1980–84), Chicago White Sox (1961–65), Atlanta Braves (1966–74), and Pittsburgh Pirates (1975–79). He famously called Hank Aaron's record-breaking 715th home run in 1974 and he served as play-by-play announcer for the 1979 World Series champion Pirates. He also called 11 no-hitters, Ryan's 4,000th strikeout in 1985, and Barry Bonds' 70th home run in 2001 and was known for saying "Holy Toledo!"

He died on September 17, 2015. "For me Milo was part poet and part P.T. Barnum," said former Astros player and manager Phil Garner, who was dubbed "Scrap Iron" by Hamilton. "He was a great ringmaster and he loved painting the prose of baseball. He had a special talent. I have wonderful memories of Milo off the field as well from our hunting trips. He was an absolute treasure."

Larry Dierker

Dierker, the Astros' first 20-game winner, won 139 games in his 14-year career as a pitcher before serving as a cerebral color commentator on Astros' radio and television broadcasts from 1979 to 1996, working alongside Hamilton, who dubbed him "the Wrangler." The Astros plucked him from the broadcast booth in 1997 to manage the team, and he won four division titles in five years, cementing his place as one of the most important figures in franchise history.

Bill Brown

One of the most steady voices the Astros have ever had, Brown began calling Astros games in 1987 as the club's primary play-by-play voice on television. A true professional, Brown's even-tempered style made him a fan favorite. Brown spent one year with Home Sports Entertainment (HSE) in Pittsburgh, and worked as the television voice of the Cincinnati Reds from 1976 to 1982.

Alan Ashby

A catcher who spent 11 of his 17 big league seasons in Houston, Ashby worked as the team's color analyst from 1998 to 2006 alongside Hamilton. He spent six seasons (2007–2012) calling games on radio and TV for the Toronto Blue Jays before returning to Houston as the primary color analyst and occasional play-by-play voice on TV in 2013.

Jim Deshaies

One of the most popular announcers in club history, Deshaies settled nicely into the role as television color reporter following his playing career, most of which was spent with the Astros. The witty Deshaies was a fixture in the booth with the Astros from 1997 to 2012, when he took an offer to join WGN and provide color commentary at Cubs games. Deshaies' easygoing style and quick wit made him a fan favorite on the Houston airwaves, and he and Brown made a terrific team.

Rene Cardenas

Cardenas, a native of Nicaragua, started his professional baseball broadcast career with the Los Angeles Dodgers in 1958, becoming one of the first members of a Spanish radio broadcast team in baseball history. Cardenas further made history as a pioneer by becoming the first Spanish radio broadcaster to call a World Series

(1959) and an All-Star Game (1961). Cardenas was brought into the Houston organization by Judge Hofheinz in 1962 as the director of the Spanish division for the Colt .45s and stayed with the Astros through 1975.

Loel Passe

Passe made the transition from the minor league announcer for the Houston Buffs to the big league Colt .45s in 1962. He was part of Houston's original broadcast team and called Colt .45s/Astros games for 15 seasons. Passe, who died in 1997 at 82, was known for his homey "Hot ziggity dog" and "sassafras tea" catchphrases.

Chris Burke's Walk-Off Home Run

Having produced perhaps the greatest moment in the history of the Astros, second baseman Chris Burke has embraced his place in franchise lore. Burke's walk-off home run in the 18th inning of Game 4 of the 2005 National League Division Series capped what was at the time the longest playoff game in history at five hours, 50 minutes. Minute Maid Park was rocking when Burke lined a ball into the Crawford Boxes, and an Astros legend was born. "I never get tired of talking about it, that's for sure," Burke said. "I feel very blessed I had a moment like that, and any time you're a part of a moment like that, you realize all the pieces came together to give me the opportunity to make that swing and produce that result... It was a great game. It really was."

Burke, a former first-round pick out of the University of Tennessee, broke into the major leagues a year earlier but played in 108 games on the star-studded 2005 team, which included Craig Biggio, Jeff Bagwell, Lance Berkman, Roger Clemens, Andy Pettitte, and Roy Oswalt. Burke hit .248 with five homers and 26 RBIs that season while playing the outfield, though he came up as an infielder. For the second year in a row, the Astros won the NL wild-card on the final day of the season and were facing the Atlanta Braves in the first round. The Astros had a 2–1 lead in the best-of-five series, heading into Game 4 on October 9.

The Braves were leading 6–1 in the eighth, so a return trip to Atlanta for a decisive fifth game looked likely. Berkman gave the Astros hope with an eighth inning grand slam off Kyle Farnsworth, and Brad Ausmus tied the game with an improbable two-out solo homer in the ninth off Farnsworth, setting the stage for a long Sunday afternoon of baseball. "I felt we got off to a slow start," Burke said. "The Braves came out with more edge obviously, playing with their backs to the wall, and they jumped on us early. The big blow was Lance hitting the grand slam to get us within striking distance, and then Ausmus comes up with the biggest swing of his life, certainly the most timely. From there it was a war of attrition."

As dramatic as the home runs by Berkman and Ausmus were, they were soon overshadowed when Clemens came out of the bullpen and pitched three scoreless innings in relief (and wound up getting the win). That got the game to the bottom of the 18th inning. Burke, who entered as a pinch-runner for Berkman in the 10th inning, thought to bunt on the first pitch of his at-bat. "Chipper Jones had been playing third base for six hours," he said. But Braves rookie pitcher Joey Devine missed with a ball. The next pitch was inside, and Burke, who liked to pull the ball, was hoping to get another inside pitch so he could turn on it. He lined a 2–0 pitch just over the left-field wall for a game-winning homer, setting off a huge celebration and sending the Astros into the NLCS.

"Because I was looking at that spot, I was able to get the barrel in there, and from a hitter's standpoint, that's one of those rare moments when you're looking to drive a ball," Burke said. "I put the right swing on it and got it up and over the wall. From there it was all fun and games."

His teammates mobbed him at home plate, and Burke's place in history was secure. The ball wound up in Cooperstown, New York, in the Baseball Hall of Fame along with his jersey. He has kept the bat and the batting gloves and he has a signed picture hanging in his office of Clemens giving him a piggyback ride in the celebration. "Your team is jumping up and down, and it was a pretty big deal," Burke said. "From there it was a lot of hugs and screaming and hooting and hollering."

56 Astros Reach Fall Classic

The final out of the 2005 National League Championship Series settled in the glove of Astros right fielder Jason Lane. It turned out to be the final game at old Busch Stadium in St. Louis and a landmark moment for the Astros, who won their only National League pennant. As the Astros ran onto the field to celebrate, longtime teammates Craig Biggio and Jeff Bagwell embraced in the dugout. They were at the ends of their careers and they finally had a chance to play in the Fall Classic.

The Astros were headed to the World Series to play the Chicago White Sox, who hadn't won a World Series since 1917. The White Sox, who won 99 games and had home-field advantage by way of the American League's win over the National League in the All-Star Game, swept the Astros in a series that was decided by only six runs. The Astros were in every game but ultimately had to watch the White Sox celebrate their first championship in 88 years, winning it at Minute Maid Park. "To get the city of Houston into the World Series was fun, and if you look back, everybody is going to say, 'Well, you guys lost in four games,'" said Jeff Bagwell, who ended his career by going 1-for-8 in two starts at designated hitter for the Astros in the World Series. "We lost by six runs total. We

Chris Burke, Lance Berkman, and Adam Everett pose after winning the 2005 NLCS, which set up a World Series date with the Chicago White Sox.

didn't not show up. I enjoyed it because the city was so jacked up. It was great."

The White Sox won Game 1, getting a tiebreaking home run from Joe Crede in the fourth inning to win 5–3. Roger Clemens, a World Series veteran with the New York Yankees and Boston Red Sox, started Game 1 for the Astros and had to leave with a strained hamstring in the second inning after 54 pitches on a chilly night in the south side of Chicago. Mike Lamb homered for the Astros, becoming the first Astros player to homer in the World Series.

In Game 2 Andy Pettitte started for the Astros and gave up two runs and eight hits in six innings and didn't factor into the decision. Chad Qualls surrendered a grand slam to Paul Konerko in the seventh to put the White Sox ahead 6–4. The Astros tied the game in the ninth on a two-run single by Jose Vizcaino, but Scott Podsednik hit a walk-off homer off Brad Lidge in the bottom of the ninth to win it. Podsednik hadn't even homered in the regular season.

When the series shifted to Houston for Games 3 and 4, the Astros were still optimistic. The Astros had ace Roy Oswalt on the mound, and they were hoping to feed off a home-field advantage in the first World Series game played in Texas. The Astros wanted Minute Maid Park's retractable roof closed to help increase crowd noise, but commissioner Bud Selig ruled the roof was to be opened because the weather was consistent with conditions that led the Astros to open the roof during the regular season. "It was a little frustrating how they made us open the roof," Astros infielder/out-fielder Chris Burke said. "That was a huge part of our home-field advantage, and we were all pretty frustrated. Why they would want to take away our home-field advantage?"

Still, the Astros had a four-run lead with Oswalt on the mound in Game 3, but the White Sox scored five times in the fifth to take a 5–4 lead. The game eventually headed to extra innings with former

Astros player Geoff Blum hitting a home run in the 14th. The White Sox won 7–5 in 14 innings in the longest game in World Series history. It took 5 hours, 41 minutes.

With their backs to the wall, the Astros couldn't score in Game 4 against four White Sox pitchers, including starter Freddy Garcia. He matched Astros starter Brandon Backe by throwing seven scoreless innings, and World Series MVP Jermaine Dye's RBI single in the eighth off Lidge sent the White Sox to a 1–0 win and the sweep. "Going to the World Series and finally getting that monkey off their backs, Bagwell and Biggio, that's kind of what it was all about," Astros shortstop Adam Everett said.

57 Darryl Kile

Jeff Bagwell wasn't in much mood for a celebration. His game-winning hit scored Julio Lugo in dramatic fashion with the winning run. *So what?* Bagwell was in tears as he was congratulated by his Astros teammates after the Astros pulled out a 3–2 win in 12 innings against the Seattle Mariners on June 22, 2002. An Astros win on one of the most terrible days of his life was a footnote. It was only hours earlier that Bagwell and teammates Craig Biggio and Brad Ausmus learned of the sudden and tragic death of Darryl Kile, the former Astros pitcher who was with the St. Louis Cardinals when he died at the age of 33.

Bagwell, Biggio, and Ausmus were among Kile's best friends when he pitched for the Astros from 1991 to 1997. Kile was found dead in his hotel room in Chicago prior to the Cardinals' scheduled game against the Cubs, which was postponed. Bagwell, Biggio, and

Ausmus were so distraught they didn't take batting practice that night. Kile's No. 57 Astros jersey hung in the Houston dugout. "This was a very difficult day. I went back and forth between disbelief and sorrow," Ausmus told reporters after the game. "When you play this game for a long time, you learn to focus on the game and not on outside things, but the gravity of this was a little heavier."

Kile was a 30th round draft choice by the Astros in 1987. Blessed with a terrific curveball but at times cursed with control problems, Kile reached the majors in 1991, going 7–11 with a 3.69 ERA in 37 games (22 starts). He had a no-hitter through six innings in his first major league start on April 24, 1991, but manager Art Howe pulled him to protect his arm. Kile, though, got another shot at the no-hitter. On September 8, 1993, he threw the ninth no-hitter in Astros history when he beat the New York Mets in the Astrodome. He won 15 games and made the All-Star team that year. Kile won only 13 games combined the next two seasons before winning 12 in 1996 and going 19–7 with a 2.57 ERA in a career-high 255⅔ innings in 1997.

Kile signed with the Rockies prior to the 1998 season and went 21–30 in two years in the thin air in Colorado before being traded to St. Louis, where things came together. Kile went 20–9 with a 3.91 ERA in 34 starts in 2000. In 2002 he had gotten off to a 5–4 start before his death from coronary artery disease shocked the baseball world. Bagwell was informed of Kile's death by a phone call from former teammate Moises Alou, who was with the Cubs. "I said, 'Homeboy, what are you doing?'" Bagwell said in an MLB Network documentary about Kile's death. "'You have a game in 20 minutes.' Alou said, 'Darryl's dead. They found him in his hotel room.'" Bagwell didn't speak publicly about Kile's death until the following day, finally saying, "I am a better person because I knew Darryl Kile."

The Astros honored Kile with a memorial plaque that hangs along the left-field wall at Minute Maid Park under the 1997 National League Central championship banner, the last season Kile played for Houston before signing with Colorado. No player has worn his No. 57 since his death.

Biggio recalled a time when he hit a homer off Kile in St. Louis. As he was rounding the bases, Kile was cursing and screaming at Biggio, his friend. "I give a high five to Baggy and sit down, and Baggy comes back and says, 'How about our guy? Is that him? Is that Darryl cursing?'" Biggio said. "It was so funny. He was so pissed." Biggio said Kile called him the week before Christmas and apologized, telling him he and Bagwell have always treated him with respect.

"You're talking about one of your best friends in the game," Biggio said. "A great man, a great family man and great husband. He's gone way too soon. That was a tough day. That was a tough year. It's still hard to talk about because he's such a great person."

58 Alan Ashby

Joe Niekro, J.R. Richard, Mike Scott, and Nolan Ryan are four of the greatest starting pitchers in Astros history—with catcher Alan Ashby being the common thread among all of them. He was behind the plate for many of the greatest moments in franchise history, catching three no-hitters, and he provided a few at the plate as well, including his walk-off home run to beat the Los Angeles Dodgers in the 1981 National League Division Series.

Ashby, acquired by the Astros from the Toronto Blue Jays in a 1978 trade, is arguably the greatest catcher in Astros history. With his crooked fingers on his right hand as proof, he caught for 11 seasons in Houston and set a team record with 900 games caught before Brad Ausmus surpassed him in 2005. He was the starting catcher on the team's first two division-winning clubs in 1980 and 1986 and eventually was replaced behind the plate by Craig Biggio, who broke into the majors as a catcher before moving to second base. Ashby, a switch-hitter, remained a huge part of the Astros following his retirement, working as the team's radio analyst alongside Milo Hamilton from 1998 to 2006, as well as serving as a coach and a minor league manager in the farm system. In 2013 he returned to the club as the primary color analyst and occasional play-by-play voice on television. "I'm an Astro through and through," Ashby said.

Ashby, who grew up as a Dodgers fan in San Pedro, California, could be the answer to many trivia questions. In addition to being the man replaced by Biggio, he was the first Astros player to homer from both sides of the plate in the same game. He was in the first trade ever made by the Blue Jays, who acquired him in 1976 from Cleveland, where he caught Gaylord Perry. The Blue Jays dealt him to the Astros on November 27, 1978, for Joe Cannon, Pedro Hernandez, and Mark Lemongello in one of the worst trades in Toronto history. "That turned out to be a very good trade, and we had Craig Reynolds come over that same offseason," Ashby said. "We started playing pretty well."

In his second game with the club, Ashby caught his first career no-hitter, thrown by Ken Forsch, in a win against the Atlanta Braves. He hit just .202 that season but helped the Astros reach the playoffs for the first time in 1980 by hitting .256 with 48 RBIs in 116 games after coming over to the National League.

The 1981 season was a special one for Ashby. He caught Ryan's record-breaking fifth no-hitter on September 26, which was significant for Ashby because he grew up idolizing Sandy Koufax and had seen two of his no-hitters in person at Dodger Stadium. On October 6, 1981, he hit a two-run walk-off homer off the Dodgers' Dave Stewart in Game 1 of the NLDS, a product of the strike-shortened season. "Craig Reynolds had a pinch-hit right ahead of me," Ashby said. "I said, 'Get on base, and I'll drive you in.' He remembers me saying that, and I have no idea why I said it, but I hit the home run off Dave Stewart. It was a nice trot."

For his third no-hitter, Ashby caught Mike Scott's masterpiece to clinch the NL West on September 25, 1986, against the San Francisco Giants in the Astrodome. He was also behind the plate when Scott threw a shutout against the New York Mets in Game 1 of the 1986 NLCS a few weeks later. "Scott was a great friend of mine and still is, so it was very special in all those regards," Ashby said.

Ashby was the Astros' starting catcher on an aging club in 1989, but a back injury paved the way for Biggio to take over as the starter on May 4, 1989. He was released a week later at the age of 37. "I was a skinny kid," Ashby said. "It wasn't until my senior year in high school that I even approached any shot when I thought of becoming a catcher because I had seen Johnny Bench do it. I thought, *Hmm, I throw pretty well. I think I could maybe do something.*"

59 Brad Ausmus

For a player who was known for his defense and his ability to handle a pitching staff, catcher Brad Ausmus was an unlikely choice to come up with one of the most dramatic home runs in team history.

Yet there he was with the Astros' postseason fate in his hands with two outs in the bottom of the ninth inning in Game 4 of the 2005 National League Division Series against the Atlanta Braves. The Astros were trailing by one, and a loss meant they were headed to Atlanta for Game 5. That was a trip no one wanted to make.

Facing Kyle Farnsworth, Ausmus hit a game-tying home run to left-center field that rocked Minute Maid Park and the Braves. Lance Berkman had gotten the Astros to within a run an inning earlier with a grand slam, and Ausmus' homer forced extra innings. A lot of them. The Astros won 7–6 in 18 innings and clinched the series on Chris Burke's walk-off homer. Ausmus played the entire game, including the 13th through 15th innings at first base before being moved back to catcher. "As far as personal moments go, it's probably the highlight," Ausmus said of his home run. "I would still say that going to the World Series overall was more fun, but if I had to pick one personal moment, that would be the one that stands out."

Ausmus caught more games than any other catcher in team history and probably broke more hearts, too. He was smart—having graduated from Dartmouth—and even had the Southern California surfer thing down, making him the resident heartthrob. He was also an unlikely major leaguer. He was drafted in the 48th round by the New York Yankees in 1998 and five years later was taken by the Colorado Rockies in the expansion draft. He was traded to the Padres in 1993, playing three seasons in San Diego before being sent to the Detroit Tigers.

Ausmus played one season in Motown before a nine-player swap brought him to Houston for the 1997 season. "The team had been losing in rebuilding, and our attendance was down, and our revenue was down, and we didn't have money to get a free agent pitcher, and whatever was out there was very expensive," said Larry Dierker, who managed the club from 1997 to 2001. "We decided we had to improve our pitching with the pitchers we had, and the decision we made was to try to get the best catcher we could get and see if by having a better catcher we could improve the whole pitching staff. We went out and got Brad Ausmus. I would stay that strategy worked."

Ausmus initially played two seasons in Houston, helping the Astros win back-to-back National Central titles. The 1997 division title was especially memorable for Ausmus because it was the first for the core of that team, and he did homer in the clinching game against the Chicago Cubs (a game that was part of the live broadcast of the Chicago-set hospital drama ER). "It had been a while since the Astros made the playoffs," he said. "Confetti was falling from the Astrodome it seemed like for hours."

On January 14, 1999, he was traded with C.J. Nitkowski to the Tigers for two minor leaguers and Paul Bako, Dean Crow, and Brian Powell. After two more seasons in Detroit, the Astros brought him back in another trade with the Tigers, and he stayed eight more years (2001–08) and guided a talented pitching staff led by Roy Oswalt, Roger Clemens, and Andy Pettitte to the World Series in 2005. "I was happy about it," he said of his return to Houston. "I had enjoyed my first two years there. I knew a lot of the players, had some good friends with the Astros, and was really excited about the move back."

In 10 seasons in an Astros uniform, Ausmus hit a respectable .246 with 41 homers and 386 RBIs, winning three Gold Gloves. In his 18-year career, he was a .251 hitter and never could shake the reputation as a defensive-minded catcher. "I had decent years [at the plate] and not-so-great years," he said. "The one thing I always felt like was I didn't strike out a lot. I was a relatively tough out in terms of making the defense make the play." Ausmus paused before providing some of his self-deprecating humor. "I was a far cry from Barry Bonds."

60 Kerry Wood K's 20 Astros

The day after Cubs rookie right-hander Kerry Wood struck out 20 Astros, veterans Brad Ausmus and Craig Biggio shared a cab ride to Wrigley Field from the team hotel. The cab driver was blaring sports talk on the radio, and the topic of Wood's performance came up. The man speaking on the airwaves said Wood's stuff was no nasty that there was a player on the Astros who swung at a curveball that had bounced in the grass in front of home plate. "Brad goes, 'That's me!'" Biggio said. "That's how good his stuff was that day."

Wood tied Roger Clemens' major league record by striking out 20 hitters on May 6, 1998, during an afternoon game at Wrigley Field. Making only his fifth major league start, Wood was 20 years old and showed the kind of stuff the Cubs saw when they made him the fourth overall pick in the 1995 draft. The Astros, meanwhile, were no slouch. That club won 102 games that year and featured a future Hall of Famer in Biggio, as well as sluggers Moises Alou and Jeff Bagwell. In fact Biggio and Alou finished in the top five in National League Most Valuable Player voting that year.

Wood was so dominant that he nearly threw a no-hitter and probably should have. The only hit he gave up came on an infield single in the third inning off the bat of Ricky Gutierrez. The only other base runner he allowed came when he hit Biggio with a pitch, which isn't a shocker considering nobody in the modern era was hit by more pitches than Biggio. The Astros put only seven balls in play, including five grounders that never left the infield. "The scouting report at the time from the minor league guys said the guy's got a decent fastball and an okay curveball, and he's a two-pitch pitcher," Biggio said. "That's not the guy we saw that day."

Overshadowed that day by Wood was Astros starter Shane Reynolds. The veteran threw a complete game, working eight innings and allowing just two runs (one earned) and eight hits, while striking out 10 batters. "I remember it like it was yesterday," Reynolds recalled. "I felt like I threw a pretty good game. I think for a while he and I had the record for combined strikeouts in a game. I don't know if that's changed; I hadn't paid attention to it. It was an all-around really well-pitched, well-played baseball game where he just had stuff that was absolutely unhittable. And we had a whole lot of really good hitters."

Reynolds said Wood could have easily had the strikeout record had it not been for Gutierrez reaching base. The hit allowed Reynolds to drop down a sacrifice bunt with one out. Otherwise, he would have been another strikeout victim. "And with nobody on, I'm trying to swing away," he said. "He probably would have had 21 strikeouts instead of 20."

Astros manager Larry Dierker, who threw a no-hitter later in his career, was able to appreciate what Wood accomplished. It was still early enough in the season to where Dierker knew the game wouldn't impact the Astros' playoff chances, and he had a veteran club that would be able to shake it off. "Even though I felt bad for [my players], they were laughing themselves, coming back from the dugout because everybody knew nobody could hit that kind of stuff," Dierker said. "It was a pleasure for me to be at the front of the dugout and to be able to watch that and it was almost miraculous he was throwing his breaking ball, curveball, and slider behind in the count because he couldn't do that later in his career."

Wood finished that season 13–6 with a 3.40 ERA and was named National League Rookie of the Year despite not pitching the final month because of an injury. That would be a sign of things to come. He missed the entire 1999 season following Tommy John surgery and struggled to stay healthy, winning 86 games in 14 seasons. He couldn't quite recapture the magic of that afternoon against the Astros.

61 Astros Overcome Pujols' Home Run off Brad Lidge

The Astros were on the cusp of clinching their first trip to the World Series, and 43,470 fans at Minute Maid Park were rocking. The franchise had waited more than 40 years for this moment, and it was about to happen. It was October 17, 2005, and the Astros led the National League Championship Series over the St. Louis Cardinals three games to one and had a 4–2 lead in the ninth inning of Game 5 with closer Brad "Lights Out" Lidge on the mound. He had just struck out John Rodriguez and John Mabry to start the ninth and had two strikes on David Eckstein. The Astros were one pitch from their first pennant. The sound was deafening.

What was supposed to be one of the greatest moments in team history suddenly turned into one of the worst in a matter of minutes. Eckstein reached on a two-out single, and Jim Edmonds drew a walk. That brought feared slugger Albert Pujols—the 2005 NL MVP—to the plate, and he delivered one of the biggest home runs in postseason history by crushing a Lidge slider and sending it high over the left-field wall for a three-run homer. The ballpark was silent. Lidge crouched in disbelief. Astros pitcher Andy Pettitte could be seen on TV mouthing, "Oh my gosh!" from the dugout as the ball ricocheted off the railroad track above left field. The Cardinals won the game, forcing Game 6 in St. Louis two days later.

Lidge drew nationwide praise with the way he handled the media following the game, answering the same questions by waves of reporters. "It was a hanging slider," Lidge recalled 10 years later. "People ask me if I regret throwing that pitch, but I don't think I regret anything as long as you're trying your hardest out there. You tip your hat. He was a pretty darn good hitter."

As the Astros boarded a plane the next day and flew to St. Louis for Game 6, the charter flight was uncharacteristically quiet. "You have these kinds of things, and out of disaster, leadership emerges, and out of chaos, order is restored," former Astros manager Phil Garner said. The somber flight to St. Louis reached its cruising altitude, and the players were settling back into their seats. For the second year in a row, the Astros were going to St. Louis up 3–2 in the NLCS. They lost in seven games a year earlier, and Garner was wondering if it was time for a speech. "We get to our altitude," Garner said. "And the mic comes on and says, 'Ladies and gentleman, this is your captain speaking. We're going to be flying at about 30,000 feet today, and it's going to be a nice flight up to

Schmidt's Long Ball That Wasn't a Long Ball

Who says balls couldn't carry in the Astrodome? On June 10, 1974, Philadelphia Phillies slugger Mike Schmidt hit a Claude Osteen fastball and sent it rocketing toward center field. The ball was headed well beyond the wall before it hit a speaker hanging from the ceiling that was 329 feet from the plate and 117 above the playing surface. Astros center fielder Cesar Cedeno had retreated to the wall in center field, giving you an idea of how far the ball was hit.

Schmidt was left with a really long single. "I knew it was a good hit," said Schmidt after the game. "Running to first base, I realized it hit something up there. I didn't know what—but something. It all happened so fast. I wasn't really sure of the ground rule." Cedeno told reporters afterward he knew the ball was going out but wanted to see how far it would go. "I never saw a ball hit so far in my life," he said.

It's hard to feel too badly for Schmidt. He went on to hit 548 home runs during his Hall of Fame career, including 14 in the Astrodome.

St. Louis. Oh by the way, if you take a look to the left side of the airplane, that object you see is the ball that Pujols hit last night.'"

The plane erupted in laughter, and the ice was broken. Well, almost. "We had an off day in St. Louis, and it made it even worse because you have to wait a whole day before you get to play again," Astros first baseman Lance Berkman said. "I'm sick to my stomach and felt like we had blown maybe our best chance of going to the World Series."

Fortunately for the Astros, pitcher Roy Oswalt came through in Game 6 with one of the most clutch performances in club history. He held the Cardinals to one run in seven innings in a 5–1 win that clinched the Astros' first NL pennant. Lidge struggled in Houston, following the Pujols homer and was eventually dealt to the Philadelphia Phillies, where he had a perfect season and was the mound when they won the 2008 World Series. The Pujols homer will always be a part of his baseball resume. "It was a tough moment, but being able to get to the World Series was huge for all of us," he said.

62 Watson Breaks a Barrier

The stories of the struggles of the civil rights movement and the hell Jackie Robinson had to endure to break the color barrier in 1947 are about as real as it gets for former Astros slugger and general manager Bob Watson. "The Bull" grew up in the tumultuous 1960s, when racial tensions were high, and discrimination was still prevalent in many parts of the country. Watson experienced much of the hate and prejudice as other men of color did while beginning his professional baseball career and rose from star player to an executive in the league office.

Watson was an intimidating slugger who bashed 184 homers in his 19-year big league career, 14 years of which were spent in Houston. He was a two-time All-Star for the Astros who hit for the cycle, walloped two home runs in the World Series for the mighty New York Yankees, and scored baseball's one-millionth run. Following his career, he became the first African American general manager in Major League Baseball history when the Astros named him to the post in 1993, and three years later with the Yankees, he became the first black GM to win a World Series. Watson, who was also MLB's vice president of rules and on-field operations until the end of the 2010 season, worked in baseball as a player, coach, and executive for more than 45 years.

Following his playing career, Watson spent four years as hitting coach with the Oakland A's. While interviewing for the job with then-Oakland GM Sandy Alderson, Watson was asked what he wanted to do in baseball. "I said, 'To be honest with you, I want to sit in your chair,'" Watson said. "He said, 'You know what? I'm going to help you.'"

It was not long after when Astros owner John McMullen and GM Bill Wood called Oakland and asked permission to interview Watson to be their assistant GM. He served as assistant GM in Houston from 1988 to 1992, taking a pay cut to return to the club and pursue his goal of becoming a GM. Watson replaced Wood as GM in 1993 and spent three seasons in that role before serving as Yankees GM for two years.

The groundbreaking achievements on and off the field by Watson are even more remarkable when you consider where he came from and the prejudice he overcame. He grew up in south-central Los Angeles and really wasn't aware of what folks in the south were going through. That soon changed when Watson departed for his first spring training in Cocoa, Florida, in 1965, shortly after the Astros signed him as an amateur free agent. He was going to begin the season in Salisbury, North Carolina, and made the long bus trip with his teammates from Florida. When they arrived, Watson and two fellow African American teammates were told to stay on the bus while their white teammates disembarked. The three were taken "across the tracks" to the house of a local black man who put them up for the season.

That was only the beginning. Watson hit a home run in his first professional at-bat and received a certificate from a local restaurant for a free Salisbury steak dinner. "I went to the restaurant, and they wouldn't let me in," he said. "I'm going, 'You've got to be kidding me.' That was my first run-in."

Watson continued to have to deal with racism even as a major leaguer, especially earlier in his career. Being forced to stay at different hotels than teammates or not being allowed to eat in local restaurants was a shock to Watson, who was raised by grandparents Henry and Olsie Stewart in Los Angeles. When he encountered racism for the first time, Watson was surprised, angry, and hurt. "All of those emotions, I guess," he said. "My grandparents raised me, and I was talking to my grandmom, and she said, 'Hey, look, if Jackie Robinson went through it, you can go through it.' That was something that stuck in my mind. That was my driving force."

Watson's second year in pro ball brought more challenges and more phone calls home. He was forced to stay in a funeral home owned by an African American because he couldn't stay in apartment complexes or hotels in Cocoa when the Florida State League season started. "Again, I called my grandparents and said, 'I'm on my way home. I've got to stay in a funeral home,'" Watson said. "They said, 'What did I tell you last year? Jackie went through it, and you can go through it.'"

Watson persevered and began the 1969 season as the Astros' starting left fielder. The club was struggling at 4–19 and looking for a new catcher when it approached Watson and asked him if he would considering converting to catcher, a position he had played before. They wanted him to go to the minor leagues and gain experience, and Watson was reluctant because he had titanium pins in his shoulder and didn't want to risk further injury. "I said, 'I'll do what the club says,'" he said. "So they sent me from the big leagues in Atlanta to Savannah, Georgia. I go from the Atlanta Marriott and a big league hotel and I fly into Savannah and I was going to go check into the Hilton there, and the cab driver said, 'I'll take you there, but they're not going to let you go in the hotel and let you check in.' I said, 'Why?' And he said, 'It's a segregated hotel.'...I ended up going to the ballpark and I stayed at the ballpark for a couple of days [and] slept on the training table until a black family took me in."

Watson was in Savannah for about two weeks and grew more frustrated with life and the Astros. He told manager Hub Kittle he was going to retire and go back to Los Angeles to be with his family. He booked a flight home that included a stop in Houston. When he got off the plane in Houston, assistant general manager and farm director Tal Smith was there to inform him they had called him up to the big leagues.

Smith, who was keenly aware of the issues of racism and inequality from his days in North Carolina attending Duke University, would drive out during the spring to the homes where the black players, including Watson, Joe Morgan, and Don Wilson, were staying and drive them to the training complex. "I knew what our players were going through and tried to do what we could to make it easier for them, particularly from the standpoint of counsel and encouragement," Smith said. "No one person had the ability to change it by themselves. I was aware of all that and tried to be very understanding and sympathetic to their situation."

63 1980 NL West Tiebreaker

Needing just one win against the Los Angeles Dodgers in the final three games of the season to secure the National League West title, the Astros marched into Dodger Stadium in the final days of the 1980 season and lost three consecutive one-run games, forcing a one-game playoff for the division title the following day. "Our confidence had to be a little bit shaken, but the fact was they won it in very Hollywood style every night," outfielder Terry Puhl said. "Somebody came up and hit a dramatic home run to win it in the three ballgames. I think the most confidence that was pulled from it is we knew we had 'Knucksie' going."

Game No. 163 turned out to be one of the biggest days in Astros history thanks to a brilliant pitching performance by knuckleballer Joe Niekro and a couple of mighty swings of the bat by infielder Art Howe. Howe went 3-for-5 with four RBIs against the Dodgers on October 6, 1980, including a two-run home run in the third inning that gave the Astros a 4–0 lead. That was more than enough for Niekro, who spun a six-hit complete game to become the first Astros pitcher to win 20 games twice. The victory gave the Astros the National League West title and their first playoff berth. "I don't want to say everybody was distraught, but everybody's concerned because we just lost three games in a row and we were wondering what's going to happen," said Craig Reynolds, the Astros' shortstop. "Then 'Knucksie' gets on the bus and goes, 'Hey boys, give me a couple of runs and we got 'em. Trust me.' It wasn't hype; it wasn't a rah-rah kind of thing. It was just him telling us he's got them. Everybody believed it."

Had the Astros lost the one-game tiebreaker to the Dodgers, it would have been remembered as one of the biggest collapses in baseball. Losing a three-game lead with three games to play was difficult to do, but dropping the tiebreaker and missing the playoffs would have been nothing short of a choke. "All we had to do was win one of them to clinch the division, our first division," Howe said. "They wouldn't give in. We really felt good about Knucksie being out there for us. He was shooting for his 20th win of the season and had a tremendous year for us that year."

The Astros had champagne outside their clubhouse for the series against the Dodgers, and a large contingent of national media was in their dugout for the final three games of the season. When the tiebreaker rolled around Monday, the media had turned its attention to the Dodgers. "I said to the guys, 'That's an omen. We're going to win this thing,'" Howe said. "They were the curse being in our dugout. We had the champagne and everything the first night and they tied it up in the bottom of the ninth. It was really an emotional series. Thank goodness I had a good day on the last day of the year."

Howe had a single in the first inning after the Astros had already scored a pair of runs off Dave Goltz, but he smacked a two-run homer to left field in the third to give Houston a commanding 4–0 lead. Howe was mobbed by his teammates in the dugout. "It was funny," Howe said. "It was 1–2 on me with two outs and a man on second, and Goltz threw me a 1–2 curveball…it was strike three. I kind of tried to duck it and I froze, and Doug Harvey was the home-plate [umpire] and he called it a ball. I thought, *Wow, thank you very much.* Joe Ferguson went nuts. He was catching for the Dodgers. He was screaming at him, 'That's strike three, Doug!' I looked back at Doug, and he looked at me and said, 'Art, don't take that pitch again.' Believe it not, he threw almost the exact pitch, and I hit it out of the ballpark. When I crossed home plate, Fergie was still screaming."

Howe also had a two-run single in the Astros' three-run fourth, and they clinched the division to finish 93–70. It was a satisfying accomplishment for an Astros team that overcame the loss of All-Star pitcher J.R. Richard, who suffered a stroke in July and missed the second half. "If J.R. would have been there, I believe I'd be wearing a few rings right now," Howe said. "That's the way it goes."

64 Tal's Hill

The sight of Lance Berkman laughing after meandering up the incline in center field at what was then known as Astros Field to make an over-the-shoulder catch in the 2002 season was proof that Tal's Hill occasionally entertained fans. For 17 seasons Tal's Hill—the incline in deep center field named after longtime Astros executive Tal Smith—provided several great highlights for center fielders trying to track down a fly ball, as well as some frustration from batters who couldn't believe they hit the ball 435 feet and still didn't get the ball over the fence. "It was an interesting feature that created some conversation and uniqueness for the ballpark, and I thought it really added a dimension because now and then it was really exciting and fun to see Michael Bourn or Lance Berkman go up the hill and make a marvelous catch," said Smith, the man the hill was named after.

As part of a $15 million renovation project scheduled for after the 2016 season, the Astros were planning to get rid of Tal's Hill and the flagpole that had been in play in center field since the ballpark opened in 2000. The center-field fence, which sat 436 feet from home plate, would be moved in to 409 feet, as the Astros would use the extra space beyond the wall for more fan-friendly areas. "As you know, Tal's Hill, some people love it, some people hate it," Astros owner Jim Crane said. "We just thought it would be a better ballpark by moving that in."

Smith, who began working with the club from its inception and later served as general manager and then president of baseball operations, came up with the idea for the 10-degree uphill slope, which through time became known as Tal's Hill. When trying to come up with a unique concept for the ballpark that would bring to mind the unique characteristics of older ballparks, Smith considered iconic features like the monuments at Yankee Stadium, the Green Monster at Fenway Park, and the ivy-covered walls of Wrigley Field. Smith said when the ballpark's initial dimensions were discussed that the deep center field offset the short 315 feet down the left-field line and 326 feet down the right-field line. "We knew left field and the Crawford Boxes were going to be a hitter's haven and, as we saw in the year 2000, the pitchers learned to use center field to adjust for the short lines, particularly down left field," he said. "It proved a good balance. It's going to take a while to adjust. Shortening center field by that much in a ballpark that has a short left and where right field is not all that difficult, it creates somewhat of a dilemma for pitchers."

Tal's Hill became as much a part of Minute Maid Park as the Crawford Boxes and the retractable roof. Some fans loved it, and some hated it. Players were split as well because of the risk of injury, though no player was ever injured navigating Tal's Hill. It was rare for balls to be hit well enough to reach the Hill and even more rare for players to make it to the Hill and catch them or at least try to catch them. But from Berkman to Craig Biggio to Bourn, Tal's Hill provided a unique experience for defenders. "I saw Frank Robinson navigate [the hills at Crosley Field in Cincinnati] without any difficulty," Smith said. "It wasn't anything I particularly advocated, and the name Tal's Hill was used for an identification standpoint, and it took on a life of its own."

65 Watch a Game from the Crawford Boxes

The best seats in the house aren't always the ones closest to home plate. Just ask those fans who prefer sitting in the Crawford Boxes, the small section of seats that sit atop the manual scoreboard in left field at Minute Maid Park. "People always tell me I've got the best seats in the house," said Astros fan Clint Sparks, who has season tickets in section 101 in the Crawford Boxes. "I've been asked to upgrade several times, but this is my spot. I won't do it."

The Crawford Boxes, named for the street that runs parallel to Minute Maid Park behind the seats, provide a unique vantage. The 315-foot distance down the left field is the shortest in baseball, meaning you could spill beer on the left fielder if you—or he—isn't careful. The seats are only 19 feet above the playing surface. The manual scoreboard was inspired by the Green Monster in Boston, though fans couldn't sit atop the Green Monster in Fenway until the Crawford Boxes were already a popular seat at Minute Maid Park.

During batting practice the Crawford Boxes are extremely popular and crowded. Fans, even those who don't have tickets in that section, congregate along the railing to try and corral the dozens of home runs balls that are hit into the area. Although the Crawford Boxes are only 11 rows deep—not leaving much space for homers to fly into—any balls that strike the arched façade above them fall in the seats below, making for an easy catch and souvenir.

Sparks typically doesn't get to the ballpark early enough for batting practice, but the idea of catching a home run appeals to him. "That's the best part of being out here: the action when they're coming in hot," he said. "It's fun." Sparks had caught six home run balls in a three-year span through the end of the 2015 season. Five of the balls were hit by Astros, and the other was by Adam Dunn. Of course, if you catch an opposing player's home run in the Crawford Boxes, be prepared to be heckled into throwing it back onto the field. Sparks, though, wouldn't bite on Dunn's ball. "I just couldn't do it," he said. "It was Adam Dunn. He was a Houston boy."

During Game 4 of the 2005 National League Division Series against the Atlanta Braves, Astros fan Shaun Dean, sitting in the second row of the Crawford Boxes, caught two home runs—and not just any homers. He caught Lance Berkman's eighth-inning grand slam, as well as Chris Burke's walk-off shot in the 18th inning. Dean gave the Astros both of the balls rather than attempt to cash in. He hung out with Roger Clemens and was given a lifetime pass to Cooperstown. "On Burke's home run, it was just like I reached out and caught it," Dean told reporters. "When I went down for the press conference, I met Burke and Berkman, and Berkman asked me which one went farther. I said Burke's did, and [Berkman] said, 'No, you didn't remember right.' Everyone kind of laughed." Dean said he caught the balls with a worn-out glove that his high school coach used to call "a trash can lid."

In 2014 Astros fan Tim Pinkard of Springfield, Virginia, was in Houston for his first Astros game and also caught a pair of home run balls. But Pinkard one-upped Dean. Both of the homers he caught were off the bat of the same player: Astros slugger Chris Carter.

66 1986 NLCS

The Astros were picked to finish last in the 1986 National League West race. The club still had many of the same players who were part of the 1980 division-winning team, but the Astros muddled through four seasons (1982–85) playing roughly .500 baseball. Hal Lanier, who had been the third-base coach of the St. Louis Cardinals and came highly recommended from St. Louis manager Whitey Herzog, was hired as manager to inject some energy. A veteran club with no expectations and nothing to lose became one of the biggest stories in baseball.

The Astros jumped out to a 15–6 record and spent most of the next three months bouncing between first and second place. They were 47–41 at the All-Star break and hosted the mighty New York Mets to open the second half. The Mets, of course, were running away with the NL East behind Dwight Gooden and Darryl Strawberry and came to the Astrodome with a 59–25 record. The Mets beat the Astros 13–2 to open the second half before the Astros reeled off seven wins in a row, including five consecutive walk-off wins—two against the Mets and three against the Montreal Expos. They took control of the NL West, even though there were doubters. Dodgers manager Tommy Lasorda infamously said the Astros were "renting first place."

It was a season full of magic. Mike Scott (18–10, 2.22 ERA, 306 strikeouts) won the Cy Young Award, and Bob Knepper (17–12, 3.14) and Nolan Ryan (12–8, 3.34) came up huge in an early season three-man rotation. Rookie southpaw Jim Deshaies (12–5, 3.25) later joined the rotation and pitched well. Rookie Charlie Kerfeld went 11–2 out of the bullpen ahead of David Smith, who had 33 saves. Offensively, slugger Glenn Davis made a run at the NL Most Valuable Player by hitting 31 homers and driving in 101, while Alan Ashby, Bill Doran, Denny Walling, Jose Cruz, Billy Hatcher, and Kevin Bass all played huge roles. With Scott being a dominant force in a strong pitching rotation, the Astros were the one team who could scare the 108-win Mets. "There was a lot of mutual respect between the two teams," Doran said.

The two teams faced off in the National League Championship Series. The Astros won Game 1 of the NLCS 1–0 in the Astrodome behind Scott's five-hit shutout and a solo homer by Davis off Gooden. The Mets evened the series by winning the second game, setting the stage for three memorable games at Shea Stadium in New York. Lenny Dykstra hit a two-run, walk-off homer off Smith to win Game 3 (6–5) before Scott pitched a three-hit complete games to lead the Astros to a 3–1 win in Game 4 to even the series. The Mets took a 3–2 lead by winning Game 5 in 12 innings on a walk-off hit by Gary Carter off Kerfeld. "Game 3 really hurt us," Lanier said. "Dykstra hits a two-run homer that won the game for them, and I think that turned the momentum."

The series shifted back to the Astrodome with the Astros needing to win twice. But Game 6 was pretty much a must-win for the Mets, too. Scott was waiting in the wings for a possible Game 7, and they had no answer for his split-fingered fastball. "Whoever won Game 6 was going to win the World Series," Davis said. Ashby said the Mets didn't want Game 7 to happen: "What would have come out of it, who's to say? I know the Mets didn't want to play that game. All you've heard was that, 'Well Mike Scott's throwing the next one.'"

Game 6 proved to be one of the greatest playoff games ever played. The Astros had a 3–0 lead entering the ninth before Knepper was tagged for three runs to force extra innings. The Mets took a 4–3 lead in the 14th inning before Hatcher tied it with a dramatic homer off the left-field pole. But the Mets scored three times in the 16th—only to watch an Astros' two-run rally come up short when Jesse Orosco struck out Bass to win the series and break the Astros' hearts. "You don't get a chance to be involved in something like that very often," Doran said. "There are guys who go through their whole career and never get that opportunity. People will ask now, and I'll say, I would have rather been involved in it and come up short than not being involved in it at all. It was quite a ride. It really was."

67 Rusty Staub

Baseball players didn't make big money in the 1960s, and most worked extra jobs to make ends meet. Rusty Staub, who was signed by the Colt .45s at age 17, made his debut in the big leagues at 19 years old in 1963 after signing a $100,000 major league contract under the bonus rule, which meant players must stay on the big league roster for two years. During the offseason Staub worked with the team to help ticket holders make the transition from Colt Stadium—the place the club called home for its first three years of existence—to the Astrodome prior to the 1965 season. "You had all the people that wanted to buy tickets to the Astros," Staub said. "I was in there six days a week in that building, even before it was finished, before the architects took the braces off in the middle of the field. I had seen a lot of that." And when the Astrodome opened in 1965 with an exhibition game between the newly renamed Astros and the New York Yankees, it was the toughest ticket the city of Houston had ever seen. "I was in right field," Staub said. "I had an easy ticket."

Staub played the first six of his 23-year career in Houston, where he was a two-time All-Star and a two-time club MVP. He hit .333 with a league-leading 44 doubles in 1967. He had great appeal to the new franchise because he was a young, good-looking guy who could really swing the bat. The problem was he was on a veteran expansion club, and upper management tried to make him the face of the franchise, which may have caused resentment among the older players who were more accomplished in the major leagues. "That made it difficult for Rusty," said longtime Astros executive Tal Smith. "I don't think it set the right tone. I think this has happened in other cases in those years where a club tried to market their young players before they were ready, and sometimes the young player is not ready to handle that and doesn't react the same way." Astros general manager Spec Richardson didn't think Staub would have a long career and traded him to Montreal on January 22, 1969. It turns out his career was just starting. Staub finished with 2,716 hits and 292 home runs and was one of the best pinch-hitters in history.

The trade to the Expos, however, wasn't without controversy. Montreal was to send outfielder Jesus Alou and first baseman Donn Clendenon to Houston, but Clendenon had played for Astros manager Harry Walker with the Pittsburgh Pirates and wasn't up for a reunion. He refused to report to the Astros and attempted to retire. Major League Baseball commissioner Bowie Kuhn stepped in and said Clendenon could stay with the Expos, and Montreal instead sent Jack Billingham, Skip Guinn, and $100,000 cash to Houston. Clendenon was traded to the New York Mets midway through the 1969 season and was the World Series MVP that year.

Staub was embraced in Montreal as the expansion Expos' first star player, and the New Orleans native became known as "Le Grande Orange" for his red hair. His No. 10 was the first retired by the Expos. Staub was traded to the Mets in 1972 and became the first Mets player to drive in 100 runs when he knocked home 105 in 1975. He later had a stint with the Detroit Tigers. (In 1978 he was the first player to play all 162 games at designated hitter.) He also returned to the Expos in 1979, played with the Texas Rangers, and finished up his final five seasons with the Mets (1981–85). Staub retired only 284 hits shy of 3,000 and was the only major league player to have 500 hits with four different teams. "Rusty was probably the best fastball hitter I'd seen for a long, long time," said former teammate Bob Watson. "Even when he went to Montreal and went off to Detroit and the Mets, you couldn't throw a fastball by him."

68 Glenn Davis

Not since the days when Jimmy "Toy Cannon" Wynn was rocketing home runs into the far reaches of the Astrodome had the Astros seen the kind of power of Glenn Davis. A country strong first baseman with a fitting nickname of his own—"The Big Bopper"—Davis walloped 166 home runs and drove in 518 runs in seven years with the Astros, making All-Star teams in 1986 and 1989 and finishing second to Mike Schmidt in the 1986 National League Most Valuable Player race. He hit 31 homers and drove in 101 runs that year to help lead the Astros to the NL West division title.

Davis' rise to become one of the game's most feared sluggers was a tribute to his resiliency. He overcame a troubled childhood in which he often had thoughts of suicide, according to a 1986 interview he did with *People* magazine. His parents divorced when he was six years old, and Davis was caught in the middle. Davis was

Glenn Davis homers during the NLCS against the Mets in 1986, a year in which he hit 31 homers and had 101 RBIs.

angry and got into fights in school. When he was in high school, he befriended a teammate named Storm Davis, who also went onto the big leagues, and wound up living with the family following graduation. Glenn Davis played college baseball at the University of Georgia before transferring to Manatee Junior College to make himself eligible for the draft. The Astros drafted him with the fifth pick of the secondary phase of the draft in 1981.

He showed tremendous power throughout the minors and made his debut in September of 1984, hitting .213 with only two homers in 18 games. Still classified as a rookie in 1985, he played 100 games and hit .271 with 20 homers and 64 RBIs, establishing himself as the Astros' first baseman of the future. "Glenn was a good hitter with power and was a reliable force in the middle," said former Astros second baseman Bill Doran. "Teams normally don't win unless they have a guy like that, so having Glenn in the middle of that lineup and not only hitting with power but driving in other key runs—he was a huge force."

The year 1986 proved to be the best of Davis' career, and over the next four years, he averaged 30 homers and 96 RBIs and made the All-Star team twice. He made the final out at first base on Mike Scott's division-clinching no-hitter on September 26, 1986, and he walloped a solo homer off Dwight Gooden of the New York Mets for the only run in a 1–0 win in Game 1 of the National League Championship Series. "That was a diamond of a year," Davis said. "That was a true team. We had a lot of chemistry, but the way we functioned was just masterful."

Davis hit a career-high 34 homers in 1989 and would have put up some huge power numbers had he not played most of his career in the cavernous Astrodome. The Astros were falling out of contention by that time, and management was ready to turn the page. Davis was traded to the Baltimore Orioles in what turned out to be a terrific trade by general manager Bill Wood. He acquired outfielder Steve

Finley and pitchers Curt Schilling and Pete Harnisch for Davis, who battled injuries in Baltimore and never came close to the production he had in Houston. He retired after the 1993 season.

It's his time in Houston, for which he is most fondly remembered. "It was some of the greatest years I experienced in my baseball career, and my heart is with Houston and it's always going to be there," Davis said. "I was born and bred in that organization and I'll go to my grave being an Astro. I'm very grateful for the investment they made in me. I'm very thankful for the people who spent time to help me develop."

69 The Talent and Tragedy of Dickie Thon

Long before Carlos Correa was turning heads as a hotshot rookie in 2015 for the Astros, another young Puerto Rican shortstop was on the path to stardom in Houston. Dickie Thon, who was signed by the California Angels as an amateur free agent and made his big league debut at age 20, was traded to the Astros from the Angels on April Fool's Day of 1981 in exchange for pitcher Ken Forsch, who made the All-Star team for the Angels that season. Despite Forsch's success in Anaheim, the trade turned out pretty well for the Astros, too.

Thon was born in Indiana while his father was a senior at Notre Dame but was raised in Puerto Rico in a baseball family. His father played semi-pro ball, and his grandfather played professional baseball in Puerto Rico with Negro League legends Monte Irvin, Josh Gibson, and Satchel Paige. Thon earned his first significant playing time in 1982 when he appeared in 136 games for the Astros, hitting

.276 with 10 triples and 37 stolen bases. In 1983 he hit .286 with 20 homers, 79 RBIs, and 34 steals, getting named to the All-Star team, winning a Silver Slugger Award, and finishing seventh in the Most Valuable Player voting. The Astros found their shortstop of the future. And then tragedy struck.

On April 8, 1984, in a game against the New York Mets in the Astrodome, Thon was struck in the face by a pitch thrown by Mike Torrez. Anyone who was at the game or listening on the radio can remember the sickening sound of the ball hitting Thon's eye, knocking him to the ground. The pitch broke the orbital bone around his eye and ended his season, altering his career forever. Thon returned to the field a year later, but he had ongoing problems with depth perception and never was the same, though he played 10 more years. "Dickie was probably going to be a Hall of Fame player," teammate Enos Cabell said. "He knew how to play. Dickie became a really good ballplayer even after the head injury."

Back in 1982, Thon had to work hard to get into the lineup and wound up starting 114 games with Craig Reynolds backing up. He started all but eight games at shortstop in 1983 and opened the 1984 season poised for greatness. "Most of my career I was a leadoff hitter, but I remember in spring training [in 1983] they asked me if I wanted to hit third, and I said, 'Yeah, I would love to hit third,'" Thon said. "That helped me a lot because the pitchers were a lot more aggressive with me because I had [Jose] "Cheo" Cruz behind me and other very good hitters, and they attacked me more. I saw a lot of fastballs and I think it was good for me."

But on the day Torrez hit him with a fastball, Thon admitted he wasn't seeing the ball well that day. Thon doesn't blame Torrez or anyone for the incident, chalking it up as an accident. "It happened, and I had to deal with it," he said. "I was not the same player after that because my vision was never the same, but I battled and worked hard and I tried to do the best I could with what I had. I was lucky enough to play 10 more years after that, but it hurt my career."

Thon said playing winter ball in his native Puerto Rico, where he played against up-and-coming stars like Don Mattingly, Wade Boggs, Cal Ripken Jr., and Rickey Henderson, helped him remain as sharp as he could. He retired following the 1993 season with 1,176 hits in his 15-year career, and many more what could-have-beens. "I don't really think he threw at me to hurt me," said Thon, who reunited with Torrez for the first time about 25 years later. "I don't blame him. He was trying to throw inside, and the ball slipped, and I should have gotten out of the way. I have no hard feelings. It was part of the game."

70 Hello, Analytics

On-base percentage, WAR, and defensive shifts have become as much a part of the baseball lexicon in the mid-2010s as more traditional terms like double play, hit-and-run, and grand slam. Baseball, a game rooted in more than 100 years of tradition, has adapted to the technological world surprisingly quickly. Since the release of the groundbreaking book *Moneyball* in 2003, baseball front offices have been looking beyond the conventional numbers and scouting reports and using high-tech computer systems and statistical trends to try to find an advantage. Like it or not, analytics are here to stay, and the Astros are one of the teams on the forefront of the movement.

Jeff Luhnow, who took over the club as general manager prior to the 2012 season, got into baseball in 2003 following a diverse career that included management consulting and technology entrepreneurship. He spent eight years with the St. Louis Cardinals (2003–11) as vice president of baseball development, player procurement, and scouting and player development before being hired by Jim Crane shortly after he bought the club. Luhnow sold Crane, in part, with his commitment to analytics, convincing him the Astros could tap into statistics, data, and sabermetrics unlike any other club to get a leg up on the competition. "This organization had not invested heavily in one information stream, which is analytics," Luhnow said. "They had done a really nice job of having scouts and player development and getting medical information and other pieces of information that are part of the puzzle, but there was one obviously missing piece compared to the environment I had been in and the environments I knew existed in baseball."

One of Luhnow's first hires was Sig Mejdal as the team's director of decision sciences. Mejdal grew up in the Bay Area of California as a fan of the Oakland A's and was always interested in baseball stats. As a kid, he even had a membership in the Society for American Baseball Research. He earned two engineering degrees at the University of California-Davis and later completed advanced degrees in operations research and cognitive psychology/human factors. He has also worked at Lockheed Martin in California and for NASA, so naturally baseball was next. "The information available now is different than what it was a generation ago and even a few years ago," Mejdal said. "The more progressive teams aren't arguing or putting their energies in whether this data matters or belongs in the hands of decision makers but instead figuring out exactly how to combine it."

The goal was to present the manager, farm director, and scouting director with data like never before, giving them more information to make better decisions. Technology such as Pitch f/x gave teams the ability to track every pitch thrown in every game,

Trailblazers

The Astros were the first team to open a baseball academy in Venezuela in 1989 in an effort to take advantage of an untapped pipeline. Scout Andres Reiner blazed the trail that led the Astros to sign future stars Johan Santana, Bobby Abreu, Carlos Guillen, Richard Hidalgo, and Freddy Garcia.

The growing political unrest in Venezuela played a part in shuttering the academy in 2009, but the Astros also wanted to develop players quicker and with fewer costs. They added a minor league team to play in the Gulf Coast League and built a new facility in the Dominican Republic, which served as their headquarters in Latin America.

According to the 2008 book, *Venezuelan Bust, Baseball Boom: Andres Reiner and Scouting on the New Frontier*, Reiner and his staff signed 77 Venezuelans between January 1990 and the end of 2000. By September of 2007, 19 of those players had reached the major leagues, including five who represented Venezuela in the World Baseball Classic.

including location, acceleration, movement, and velocity. Nerds rejoiced, and fans began noticing the effects on the field as teams started shifting, putting three infielders on the right side of the infield for lefties who pull the ball, and vice versa. That was just the start. "With all the information that's out there via TV and online, it's accessible now, easily accessible," Luhnow said. "There's all these websites that show information, and the broadcasters are starting to talk about it more. Clearly, the shift is a great example. We started doing it aggressively and we're one of the few teams that stood out. Now it doesn't stand out anymore because everybody else is doing it, which unfortunately means we've lost some of the advantage."

Other advances, such as Statcast, developed by MLB Advanced Media, took analytics to a new level. It uses radars and cameras to track players' movements in real time as they field a ball. Ultimately, the game still comes down to players making the plays, but analytics have changed the way the game is played. "As long as we're making good decisions based off of the best available data, we can't control the outcome because there's a lot of other things that are out of our control," Luhnow said. "But if we do that more often than the next team, we're going to eventually have a sustainable advantage."

71 Rainout in Astrodome

If you've lived in Houston for any length of time, you know just how quickly an afternoon rainstorm can fill the streets with water and make them impassible. So you can imagine the scene when the city received between 10 and 15 inches of rain in a few hours during an afternoon deluge on June 15, 1976. The Astros were scheduled to play the Pittsburgh Pirates that day at the Astrodome, and the players were already arriving when the streets around the Dome began to fill with water.

As more and more rain fell, it made it more difficult for fans and stadium employees to reach the Astrodome, which sits 45 feet below ground level and was taking on some water itself. About three hours before first pitch, the umpires, who were staying at the nearby Shamrock Hilton hotel, called Astros team officials and told them they couldn't make it to the ballpark. Without umpires or hardly any fans, the Astros-Pirates game was rained out, or, more fittingly, "rained in." The postponement was the first of its kind for the Eighth Wonder of the World.

"It was one of those things," Astros slugger Bob Watson said. "It was a typical summer afternoon with a 10 percent chance of rain or something like that. No big deal. It was 90 degrees, and the humidity was at 100 [percent]. We went in and started taking batting practice, and it got cloudy, and they turned the lights on in the Dome, and then some leaks started popping up. One was around first base, one was around second base and center field and whatever.

"Then they came and said, 'Look guys, it's raining real hard on the loading dock,' where we parked the cars in those days. It was filling up with water, and they told us we need to move our cars. We ran out there in uniform and moved our cars over into the regular parking lot and went back in and continued to take batting practice. It was raining hard. The next thing we know, we get word that it's flooding out there. Everybody is in a panic that it might come in the Dome through the big door in center field. We were saying, 'Oh my goodness. You have to be kidding me!'"

Water never made it to the field, but neither did the umpires. Of course, everyone who managed to make it to the Astrodome was stranded, so they improvised. Concession workers set up tables behind second base, and dinner was served. The meals that had been prepared to be served in the suites on the ninth level were brought to the floor so players from both teams, coaches, and stadium employees could eat while the rain fell. "They put all this good food out there, and both teams and the fans and we sat and had a good dinner while it was flooding outside," Watson said. Astros pitcher Larry Dierker killed time by climbing on the catwalk atop the Astrodome.

The water on the streets began to subside in the middle of the night, and the players decided to try to venture home. For infielder Enos Cabell, that meant getting in his pink Cadillac with some of his teammates and heading down the Gulf Freeway. "The water was up to the hood of the car, and we were trying to get through," he said. "We didn't have big trucks at the time. It was pretty different. The whole parking lot in the Astrodome flooded. It was unbelievable. It must have been 15 feet of water. It was a tropical storm or something and just rained all night. It was flooded all the way to my house."

Watson, who drove a Chevy Blazer at the time, also carried home a few of his teammates who lived close to him. Some of them stayed overnight at his house in southwest Houston, and they all went back to the ballpark the next day and played the Pirates. "It was a strange event, to say the least," Watson said.

72 Other Astros Hall of Famers

Craig Biggio's induction into the National Baseball Hall of Fame in 2015 was a crowning achievement for a franchise that's had a surprisingly rich history. Biggio played his entire 20-year career with the Astros and became the first player to have an Astros logo on his cap in Cooperstown, though he's not the first Hall of Famer to have played for the Astros.

Biggio was the eighth former Astros player to be enshrined into the Hall of Fame. Most of those players had a cup of coffee in Houston, while others—such as pitcher Nolan Ryan and second baseman Joe Morgan—spent substantial time with the Astros, only to have another team's logo on their plaque. In Ryan's case he was inducted as a member of the Texas Rangers, the team with whom he spent the final five years of his career despite the fact he played nine of his 27 major league seasons in Houston.

Here's a look at the seven Hall of Fame players who spent time in Houston (not including Biggio):

Randy Johnson (with Astros in 1998)—The Big Unit came to the Astros in a blockbuster trade in the minutes leading up to the non-waiver trade deadline in 1998. He was 34 years old at the time and had one Cy Young under his belt during his 10 years with the Seattle Mariners. Johnson was 9–10 with a 4.33 ERA in 23 starts for Seattle when the Astros sent three prospects—pitcher Freddy Garcia, infielder Carlos Guillen, and pitcher John Halama—to the Mariners to get him for their playoff run.

Johnson was nothing short of spectacular for the Astros, going 10–1 with a 1.28 ERA in 11 starts and helping the Astros capture the National League Central with a club-record 102 wins.

A 2015 Hall of Fame inductee, Randy Johnson went 10–1 with a 1.28 ERA with the Astros and helped them capture the National League Central with a club-record 102 wins.

The Astros lost to the San Diego Padres in the National League Divisional Series, but Johnson did his part despite losing both of his starts. In 14 innings in the playoffs, he allowed three earned runs, 12 hits, and struck out 17 batters as the Astros offense was shut down by San Diego.

Astros owner Drayton McLane made an effort to re-sign Johnson, who wound up going to the Arizona Diamondbacks and winning four consecutive Cy Young awards (1999–2002) and the 2001 World Series championship. That cemented him as a Hall of Famer, and he was inducted in 2015 with a D-backs logo on his cap. In the weeks leading up to his induction, however, Johnson said the two months he spent in Houston were the best he's pitched in his career.

Don Sutton (with the Astros from 1981 to 1982)—The right-hander began his career with the Los Angeles Dodgers in a rotation that included fellow Hall of Famers Don Drysdale and Sandy Koufax. He helped the Dodgers reach the World Series five times and capped his career with a World Series ring in 1988. He went 324–256 and struck out 3,574 batters in his 23-year career, including 16 in Dodger blue.

Coming off an ERA title with the Dodgers in 1980—where he spent the first 15 seasons of his career—Sutton signed a four-year, $2.85 million deal with the Astros on December 3, 1980, and joined a rotation that included Nolan Ryan and Joe Niekro. He went 11–9 with a 2.61 ERA in 23 starts with the Astros in 1981, a season that ended prematurely when he broke his kneecap while batting against former teammate Jerry Reuss. Still, Sutton delivered more quality work in '82, going 13–8 in 27 starts before the Astros traded him to the Milwaukee Brewers.

The Astros dealt Sutton to the Brewers for outfielder Kevin Bass and left-handed relievers Frank DiPino and Mike Madden in a trade that was criticized by Astros third baseman Ray Knight.

DiPino was an effective reliever in Houston, finishing sixth in the National League Rookie of the Year race in 1983, while Bass blossomed into an All-Star and a key figure on Houston's NL West division-winning club in 1986. Sutton won his 300th game with the California Angels in 1986 before finishing his career where it started—with the Dodgers. He was inducted into the Hall of Fame in 1998 with a Dodgers cap on his plaque.

Nolan Ryan (1980–88)—One of the biggest sports stories in the history of Houston took place on November 19, 1979, when the Astros signed Ryan—a star pitcher with the California Angels who had thrown four no-hitters—to a contract to return to his home in Houston. The Astros were set to pay him $4.5 million over four years. Ryan grew up in nearby Alvin, Texas, and became the first player in major league history to make $1 million in a season.

Ryan spent the first eight years of his career in Southern California and went 138–121 with a 3.07 ERA with the Angels and led the AL in strikeouts seven times with his 100-mph fastball. He was 32 years old when he signed with the Astros and wound up playing nine seasons in Houston. He won 106 games, threw his record-breaking fifth no-hitter (in 1981), broke Walter Johnson's all-time strikeout record (1983), and led the league in ERA (1981 and 1987) and strikeouts (1987–88) while with the Astros.

Ryan left the Astros following a contract dispute at the end of the 1988 season and signed with the Texas Rangers at 42 years old, planning to play one more season and call it quits. Much to the dismay and frustration of Astros fans, Ryan played five seasons in Arlington and cemented his legacy as a Texas legend by throwing two more no-hitters—as well as getting into his infamous fight with Robin Ventura of the Chicago White Sox in 1993. Ryan was inducted into the Hall of Fame in 1999.

Robin Roberts (1965–66)—Elected to the Hall of Fame in 1976, the right-hander was nearing the end of his 19-year career when he spent parts of two seasons with the Astros, going 8–7 with a 2.77 ERA in 23 games (22 starts) in 1965 and 1966. Roberts, of course, won 234 games for the Philadelphia Phillies, leading the league in wins, complete games, and innings pitched in four straight years (1952–55).

Joe Morgan (1963–71, '80)—Morgan played 10 of his 22 major league seasons with the Astros, but those two stints came on the bookends of his most productive seasons as part of Cincinnati's Big Red Machine of the 1970s. Morgan was signed as an amateur free agent by the Colt .45s after the 1962 season and played nine years in Houston before an infamous trade to the Reds. Morgan, Ed Armbrister, Jack Billingham, Cesar Geronimo, and Dennis Menke were sent to Cincinnati for Tommy Helms, Lee May, and Jimmy Stewart in 1971.

Morgan was a two-time All-Star in his first stint in Houston but became a superstar in his eight years in Cincinnati, hitting .288 with 152 homers, 612 RBIs, and 406 steals for the Reds. He was an All-Star all eight seasons in Cincinnati, was named league MVP in 1975 and 1976 (the two seasons the Reds won the World Series), and won five Gold Gloves.

Morgan re-signed with the Astros prior to the 1980 season and hit .243 in 141 games while helping Houston reach the playoffs for the first time by winning the NL West. Trading Morgan to the Reds is generally considered the worst trade in Astros history and one of a handful under general manager Spec Richardson.

Eddie Mathews (1967)—One of the greatest third basemen in history, Mathews was a nine-time All-Star who won NL home run titles in 1953 and '59 for the Milwaukee Braves, for whom he played much of his career. He was traded to the Astros prior to the 1967 season and slugged his 500th career homer, which came off Juan Marichal of the San Francisco Giants, that season. He was traded to the Detroit Tigers late in the 1967 season after playing 101 games with the Astros.

Nellie Fox (1964–65)—A 12-time All-Star and league MVP (1959) for the Chicago White Sox, the diminutive second baseman spent his final two seasons (1964–65) in Houston for the Colt .45s and the Astros. Hall of Famer Joe Morgan, another small second baseman, grew up using a Nellie Fox model bat featuring a thick handle, and Fox convinced the rookie Morgan to switch to a bat with a thin handle to maximize his power. The two remained friends until Fox died at the age of 47 in 1975.

Aspromonte Homers for a Blind Child

Bob Aspromonte's most notable home run in his 13-year career may have been in 1965, when he clubbed the first regular-season dinger for the Astros in the Astrodome. It came off Vern Law of the Pittsburgh Pirates in the sixth inning of the Astros' 5–0 win on April 24 of the year the Eighth Wonder of the World opened. Aspromonte hit only 60 homers in his career, so it wasn't like he was known as a slugger. That didn't stop a nine-year-old fan, who was temporarily blinded by a lightning strike and who later befriended Aspromonte, from asking him on three separate occasions to hit a home run for him, and that didn't stop Aspromonte from coming through for young Bill Bradley.

The story began on April 20, 1962, when Bradley, playing for a church league in El Dorado, Arkansas, and his team were chased off their practice field by an oncoming thunderstorm. Bradley beat his teammates to a water fountain that was under a large oak tree and he was bent over quenching his thirst when a bolt of lightning struck the tree and—attracted by the water fountain—struck Bradley on the top of his head. "It basically did kill me," Bradley said. "It knocked me to the ground, and luckily one of the coaches, Creed Nance, worked at a refinery there in town and just a month earlier had a first-aid course, and if not for that, I probably would have died." Nance gave Bradley CPR and got him to the hospital.

Bradley remembers waking up the next day and doctors telling him they didn't think he would see again because they thought he had retina and optic nerve damage. "They could see the lens in front of my eyes had been fried like an egg," Bradley said. Bradley's family went to Houston to visit ophthalmologist Dr. Louis Girard, who was the founder of the Texas Eye Bank. While in Houston awaiting a series of operations, Bradley listened to Colt .45s games on the radio and became a fan of Aspromonte. Bradley's case drew some local and national coverage, and Aspromonte and teammate Joe Amalfitano came to visit him in the hospital. "When he was visiting Houston, he called the ballclub and said, 'Can I meet Bob Aspromonte?'" Aspromonte said. "I visited him in the hospital and took him a glove and ball. The kid was blindfolded and couldn't see anything. That's how it all started."

Bradley said they brought him a transistor radio and a pair of Colt .45s pajamas. "I thought the pajamas were the coolest thing," he said. "I never had a pair that looked like that before. I wore them out. As a nine-year-old, that's really cool stuff."

When Aspromonte was leaving the hospital, Bradley asked Aspromonte if he could hit a home run for him in the game later that night. Bradley was allowed to go to the game, but the doctor told him he had to be back in bed by 10 PM because he was having surgery the next day. And wouldn't you know it, in his final at-bat, Aspromonte homered with Bradley listening on the radio back in the hospital. The next year, with Bradley back in Houston, he again asked Aspromonte to hit a homer, and again Aspromonte came through—this time with a walk-off grand slam.

After undergoing several procedures and regaining some of his eyesight, Bradley came to Colt Stadium in 1963 and was finally able to see Aspromonte play in person for the first time. And, of course, when meeting Aspromonte prior to the game, he asked him to hit a home run. "I said, 'Billy, you're really pushing your luck,'" Aspromonte said. "'Will you settle for a couple of base hits?'" Considering Aspromonte was in a slump, a couple of hits would have been asking a lot.

But in a game against the New York Mets on July 26, 1963, and with Bradley watching every pitch, Aspromonte swung at a first-inning pitch from Tracy Stallard with the bases loaded and sent it over the left-field wall for a grand slam. The story of the relationship between Aspromonte and Bradley had been well documented by this time, so the game was stopped while the two embraced. "As I'm crying and everyone is going crazy, I gave him the ball," said Aspromonte, who still keeps in touch with Bradley to this day. "You should have seen his reaction. What a spark of life that came over that kid."

Bradley wound up getting back on the field himself and pitched in his Little League in Arkansas, throwing a no-hitter several years after his accident. He mailed the newspaper clipping of a story that was written about his feat to Aspromonte. "I said, 'This one's for you, Bob,'" he said. "I didn't hit you a home run, but I pitched you a no-hitter."

A few years later, Aspromonte ironically was partially blinded in one eye when a car battery exploded in his face. Bradley called him to offer support, and the two remained friends and talked on and off for years. "It's amazing and it really makes you wonder about stuff like that, divine intervention or whatever," said Bradley, who lives in Memphis. "A little kid just suffered an injury, a nearly fatal injury like that, and it definitely lifted my spirits and just really helped me to kind of get back to normal."

74 Terry Puhl

When Terry Puhl broke into the major leagues with the Astros in 1977, he was one of very few Canadian-born players in the big leagues. That meant an entire country was fully vested in his career, something the Canadian press reminded him about every time the Astros went to Montreal. "They would come and say, 'You're carrying the flag,'" Puhl said. No pressure, right? Puhl wound up making Canada and Astros fans proud during a 15-year career (14 in Houston) in which he hit .280 with 62 homers and 435 RBIs and had one of the greatest postseason performances at the plate in the 1980 National League Championship Series. He was an All-Star in 1978.

Puhl was signed by the Astros in September 1973 by a scout named Wayne Morgan, who saw him win the Most Valuable Player at a national tournament and became enamored with his left-handed swing. Puhl began his career at Covington of the Appalachian League and put up some impressive numbers in his three-plus years in the minor leagues. "The Astros had some pretty good minor league managers at that time," he said. "You might remember in A ball I had Bob Cluck [at Dubuque in 1975]. It was his first year of managing. He didn't play me the first month in A ball, and I was on the bench and he pinch ran me at third base on a sacrifice fly, and I knocked over the catcher and scored the winning run, and he said, 'That's a tough Canadian. We're going to have to play him more.'"

He was called up to the big leagues on his 21st birthday in 1977 and became a fixture in the outfield for the Astros for the next 14 seasons. Puhl wasn't flashy, but he was as dependable as they come in the field and at the plate. "A true professional who hardly ever made mistakes," said former Astros general manager Tal Smith. "He was an excellent right fielder and became an excellent center fielder…just a true professional, conducted himself in every respect in a first-class way."

Puhl's tenure in Houston spanned a couple of different Astros eras. He arrived when the young Astros were on the move and eventually made their first playoff appearance in 1980, beating the Los Angeles Dodgers in a one-game playoff for the division crown, and he was there in 1986 when they won the National League West and lost a heartbreaker to the New York Mets in the NLCS. His final year in Houston was 1990, when he was teammates with future stars Craig Biggio and Ken Caminiti. "Winning in 1980 at Dodger Stadium and finally the Astros had a [division] pennant was the No. 1 thing I carry," Puhl said. "That still goes down as the No. 1 deal for me and always will. Individually, I would say the '80 playoffs were big for me, and the '78 National League All-Star team selection."

In the memorable 1980 NLCS against the Philadelphia Phillies, who won the best-of-five series in five thrilling games (four in extra innings), Puhl went 10-for-19 (.526) to break Pete Rose's record for most hits in an NLCS. When Puhl got his 10th hit of the series with a single in the eighth inning of Game 5, a message was posted on the scoreboard informing the fans Puhl had broken Rose's record. And first baseman Rose was there to greet him at first. "He looks over at me, and they're flashing on the big scoreboard that Terry Puhl just set a new record for hits, and it eclipses Pete Rose," Puhl said. "Pete winked at me and he said, 'Records are made to be broken.'"

75 Shane Reynolds

Shane Reynolds credits pitching coach Brent Strom with turning him into the pitcher he became for the Astros. Reynolds was a fledging right-hander in the minor leagues when he went to Venezuela to pitch winter ball in 1991. Strom, the minor league pitching coordinator at the time, asked Reynolds if he wanted a long career in the major leagues or one in the minor leagues. Reynolds, of course, wanted to be a major league pitcher and worked with Strom to change his mechanics. Strom also taught Reynolds how to throw a split-fingered fastball, and he was in the majors in 1992. "I pretty much owe him everything," Reynolds said.

Reynolds played 13 seasons in the big leagues (1992–2004), leaving his mark with the Astros. The workhorse won 103 games in 11 years in Houston, including a 19–8 season during the Astros' record 102-win campaign of 1998. He was an All-Star in 2000, started five consecutive Opening Days for the Astros, and won 14 games in 2001 before injuries derailed him. A mucky departure from the Astros sent Reynolds to Atlanta, where he won 11 games in 2003 before retiring after throwing only one game for the Arizona Diamondbacks in 2004. "He always had that little chip on his shoulder and worked extremely hard," Strom said.

A native of Louisiana, Reynolds was taught hard work by his father and played college baseball at Faulkner University in Montgomery, Alabama, before transferring to Texas. It was in Austin that Reynolds clashed with Longhorns legendary coach Cliff Gustafson, who left Reynolds off his roster for the College World Series as a junior. Reynolds took the snub to heart and continued to work hard and was drafted in the third round by the Astros in 1989.

Reynolds joined the major league club around the time Astros legends Craig Biggio and Jeff Bagwell were coming into their own and he was a key starter, along with Mike Hampton, Darryl Kile, Jose Lima, and others on a team that won four division championships in a five-year span (1997–99, 2001). "The nucleus of those guys was just kind of getting there," Reynolds said. "What I remember most about 1994 is when Terry Collins was the manager, and he gave me the ability to start the season and make the team out of the 'pen, which was great. It wasn't until '97 when we won our division, but it took three or four years with the young nucleus we had. Mike Hampton was coming onto the mix, and a lot of young kids were getting their feet wet with Biggio and Bagwell. I think it really led to a good stretch of winning baseball."

During the 2002 season, Reynolds was only able to make 13 starts before having surgery to repair a pinched nerve in his back. He signed a one-year deal to return to the Astros in 2003 and was released after a rough spring in which he went 0–1 with a 5.87 ERA in five starts. His velocity was down considerably. Reynolds said management told him to take his time to recover from the injury in the spring, so the release caught him by surprise. "I was taking my time and making sure I was healthy and going to be 100 percent, and the next thing you know they released me," he said. "That was tough. I definitely wanted to stay and had been there my whole career…I had been there for so long and didn't want to go anywhere, but they made their decision."

76 Joe Morgan

Second baseman Joe Morgan forged his Hall of Fame career in eight years as the catalyst of the Big Red Machine in Cincinnati, where he was named the National League's Most Valuable Player in both years the Reds won the World Series (1975–76). What many people don't remember is that Morgan played most of his career in Houston, beginning his time as a big leaguer with the Colt .45s in 1963 and coming back to the Bayou City after his terrific run with the Reds to help the Astros win the National League West division title in 1980.

Morgan, signed as an amateur free agent in 1962, established himself as an All-Star with the young Houston franchise. He made his major league debut on September 21, 1963, for the Colt .45s against the Philadelphia Phillies at Colt Stadium, where only 2,231 fans were on hand. The 20-year-old Morgan had just been called up from the Durham Bulls of the Carolina League when he pinch hit for pitcher Don Nottebart in the third inning and popped out to second base.

"When you're a kid growing up, you say you want to make it to the major leagues, and when you reach that dream, that's what it's all about," Morgan said. "I can still remember buttoning my last button in that Colt clubhouse. I can still remember where I was standing and the whole thing. That's your first major league game, your first time putting on a major league uniform, and that's something special."

That also was the start of a brilliant major league career for Morgan, a 10-time All-Star who was inducted into the Hall of Fame in 1990. Throughout his career, which spanned 22 seasons,

Morgan kept close ties to Houston, where his career began. "I was fortunate enough to play on two World Series championship teams, but the first day I put on that uniform is still the highlight of my career."

Morgan had been a part of a young, up-and-coming nucleus with the Astros that included Cesar Cedeno, Jimmy Wynn, Bob Watson, and Rusty Staub before being traded following the 1971 season in one of the handful of poor trades made by former general manager Spec Richardson. Morgan was traded with Ed Armbrister, Jack Billingham, Cesar Geronimo, and Denis Menke to the Reds for Tommy Helms, Lee May, and Jimmy Stewart.

He never wanted to leave the Astros, but Richardson was trying to add more power to the lineup. "I loved Houston and wanted to continue to play here, and a lot of my friends were here," Morgan said. "Jimmy Wynn was my roommate, and me and Rusty Staub were great friends. I would have loved to stay here."

Morgan returned for one season in 1980 and started at second base for an Astros team that won the NL West in a one-game playoff against the Los Angeles Dodgers. Morgan, like just about everybody else who played on the Astros that season, believes Houston may have won the World Series that year had star pitcher J.R. Richard not suffered a stroke midway through the season. "Joe had been a free agent, and this was getting toward the end of his career, and there wasn't the same market for him," said former Astros general manager Tal Smith. "Tom Reich was his agent, and Tom and I had a very good relationship. We had done a number of deals and so on. I was a little bit concerned about how Joe would adapt to coming back depending on what his role might be."

Smith had manager Bill Virdon come to Houston and meet with Morgan and Reich at the Shamrock Hotel. Morgan and Virdon sat alone because Smith wanted Virdon to go over all the playing time possibilities. "He's very good about that, very straightforward, wanting to know how Joe was going to react if he was not the regular second baseman," Smith said. "Obviously, we got the right answers. Joe joined the club and was really a catalyst from the standpoint of his leadership and he came up with some very big contributions for us."

Morgan can't help but wonder what would have happened had the Astros been more patient in the 1960s and waited for their young players to mature. "Maybe we would have won a championship here instead of me winning two in Cincinnati," he said.

77 Watson Scores Millionth Run

Sometimes being at the right place at the right time can lead to something special. Of course, when you add a little hustle to make sure you're at the right place at the right time, that's when lucks meets opportunity. Former Astros slugger Bob Watson was never known for his speed during his 19-year career—he stole only 27 bases and was caught stealing 28 times—but it was the churning of his legs that propelled him into major league history on May 4, 1975.

The Astros and Giants were forced to play a Sunday doubleheader at Candlestick Park in San Francisco; the doubleheader was necessary because of a rare rainout the day before. The first game of the twin bill started at 12:05 PM and was among a full schedule of games that afternoon. All eyes were on the out-of-town scoreboard because history was going to be made. Baseball was going to celebrate its millionth run scored and entered the day about 10 runs shy of the mark. The chance to make history was something the Astros didn't ignore. "We knew there was going to have to be 10 runs scored [league-wide] or something," Watson said. "And by the time I came up in the second inning, it was down to three runs that needed to be scored."

Watson was batting cleanup and playing first base that day and began the second inning by walking. He stole second base—a rarity for him during his career—and was followed by Jose Cruz, who drew a walk. Next up was Milt May, who launched a three-run homer to right field. Watson began to casually jog toward third base when he started to hear some yelling from the bullpen, which was down the left-field line. Watson's teammates in the bullpen were telling him to "Run! Run! Run!" "So I take off on a sprint and I scored the run," he said. "Lo and behold, at the same time Dave Concepcion of the Reds hits a home run, and he's racing around the bases."

Watson's teammates knew that if Watson touched home plate before Concepcion he would score the millionth run in the history of the major leagues. "I beat him by a second and a half," Watson said. A representative from the Baseball of Hall Fame took Watson's shoes and uniform, which meant Watson was going to have to break in a new pair of cleats. Fortunately for him, he didn't play in the second game of the day. May's bat was also headed to the Hall of Fame.

The Astros lost the game 8–6, and Watson went 0-for-3 with two runs scored. Still, the attention was just beginning for Watson. The millionth run was sponsored by the candy Tootsie Roll, which awarded Watson with one million of its chewy treats. Watson donated half of the candy to the Boy Scouts of America and the other half to the Girl Scouts of America. The company also awarded him one million pennies ($10,000), which he donated to charity. Watson was also presented with a platinum watch from Seiko, which he keeps inside a safety deposit box. He has never worn it.

Watson also earned a dose of national fame. "My fan mail was something like four or five letters a week, or something like that," he said. "Scoring the millionth run, it increased to 50 to 100 per week. It got me on the map a little bit, and I ended up being the answer to a trivia question."

78 Billy Wagner

John Hudek was hurt, and Todd Jones soon joined him in the trainer's room. The 1996 Astros were suddenly in need of a closer, and manager Terry Collins decided he'd give fireballing left-hander Billy Wagner, a former first-round draft pick, a shot at the job. Wagner took to closing like a pig to slop, becoming the most successful closer in Astros history as a key part of an up-and-coming team that won four division titles in five years. "You get to pitch every day and be a part of the team and be a factor," Wagner said. "For me that was fun."

The Astros drafted Wagner in the first round in 1993 out of Ferrum College in Virginia. He didn't get many college offers because he was throwing in the mid-80s in high school, but by his sophomore year at Ferrum, he was in the mid-90s. Since he was a left-hander, he became a hot commodity. "I give 100 percent credit to scouting director Dan O'Brien and to our scouting personnel," former Astros general manager Bill Wood said. Wagner came up through the Astros system as a starting pitcher before making the transition after getting called up to Houston in 1995.

His fastball was hard to ignore, but it wasn't until Wagner learned to throw his breaking pitches for strikes that he became a force. He saved a club-record 225 games in his nine years with the Astros, making three All-Star teams and finishing fourth in the 1999 National League Cy Young Award. He stood only 5'10", threw 100 mph, and had a Virginia county accent, all of which made "Billy The Kid" one of the most popular Astros of his time. "I put in some time and I was part of that era that got everything

Houston Astros closer Billy Wagner, who saved 225 games during his nine years with the Astros, reaches back to fire a pitch on July 12, 2002.

started," Wagner said. "Honestly, me and my family thought I'd retire in Houston."

Wagner's departure from the Astros became ugly, and years later he admits he probably "helped myself out the door." At the end of the 2003 season, he criticized management for not being fully invested in winning. "You're part of that community, and then all of a sudden it changes, it throws you for a loop," Wagner said. "Maybe I brought all this on myself. I still think at the end of the day the whole point was I wanted to win."

The Astros traded Wagner to the Philadelphia Phillies for promising pitching prospects Ezequiel Astacio, Taylor Buchholz, and Brandon Duckworth. Neither amounted to much in Houston, while Wagner went on to save another 197 games for the Phillies, New York Mets, Boston Red Sox, and Atlanta Braves and became an All-Star four more times. He retired having built a Hall of Fame resume that included a staggering 11.92 strikeouts-per-nine innings and a .187 opponents' batting average, both of which are by far the best career totals of any pitcher in major league history.

In 1998 Wagner endured the scariest moment of his career when he was struck on the head by a line drive on July 15 in Arizona. He was carried off the field and spent the night in the hospital and had to overcome vertigo to get back on the mound later that summer. "I've always felt like my life had been an obstacle, trying to get over one thing, and something always tried to keep you down," he said. "I was blessed it wasn't more serious."

Wagner admits he didn't know much about his place in the game when he came up with the Astros. He said veterans like Doug Henry and Mike Magnante took him under his wing and showed him what it meant to be a major leaguer. He said they made it easy for him to be successful. "When you're young, you don't really know the ramifications of being good," he said. "You have no damn idea of what's going on, and I had no idea. And so I just rolled out there and let it eat. I didn't even know that, 'Hey, you do this long enough, somebody is going to say you're good, and there will be expectations.' I just competed."

79 Crazy Injuries

Forget strained hamstrings, torn ligaments, and pulled muscles. Some of the strangest injuries in sports have been courtesy of baseball players, who for whatever reason have fallen victim to some bizarre moments. There was Milwaukee Brewers knuckleballer Steve Sparks dislocating his shoulder while ripping a telephone book in half, Baltimore Orioles outfielder Marty Cordova scorching his face in a tanning bed, and St. Louis Cardinals outfielder Vince Coleman getting rolled up by a tarp in the 1985 playoffs.

The Astros haven't been immune to their share of strange injuries, and here are some of the most notable bizarre injuries they've had:

- In 1985 Hall of Fame pitcher Nolan Ryan was bitten by one of three coyote pups, which he had brought back to his house after he had roped them. The coyote that bit him had to be put down so it could undergo a test to its brain for rabies. That prevented Ryan from going through a series of painful rabies shots himself. In his next start, Ryan threw a complete game against the San Diego Padres in the Astrodome, leaving the Padres in pain.
- Outfielder Moises Alou, who hit .312 with 38 homers and 124 RBIs in his first season in Houston in 1998, missed the entire 1999 season after tearing a knee ligament when he fell

off a treadmill while training at his home in the Dominican Republic shortly before spring training. Alou was hurt when he tried to adjust the controls on a treadmill that was going too fast. Alou slipped and caught himself in the crevice between the treadmill belt and frame.

- Third baseman Ken Caminiti was known for his hard-nosed style of play and staying on the field despite injury, but he sustained three fractures in his lower back after falling from a deer stand during a hunting trip in Laredo, Texas, in the fall of 1999. That was during Caminiti's second stint in Houston, which drafted him and developed him. He returned to the Astros after helping the Padres to the World Series in 1998.

- Outfielder Lance Berkman, known affectionately during his career as the "Big Puma" after joking about his cat-like reflexes—or lack thereof—certainly wasn't too graceful when he tore the anterior cruciate ligament in his right knee while playing flag football at his church following the 2004 season. The next spring Berkman signed a six-year, $85-million deal that forbade any more flag football games. "It's good to be the highest-paid [defensive back] in the country," Berkman quipped.

- Outfielder Richard Hidalgo was shot in the left forearm during an apparent carjacking in his native Venezuela following the 2002 season. Hidalgo was in his hometown of Valencia, about 90 miles from Caracas, when two men approached his car. As he drove away, one of the men fired a shot into the car, striking Hidalgo. The slugger, who signed a four-year, $32 million contract with the Astros prior to the 2001 season, came back in 2003 and hit .309 with 28 homers and 88 RBIs for the Astros.

- Outfielder Hunter Pence suffered several cuts and lacerations on his hands and knees after falling through a glass door at his spring training home in Kissimmee, Florida, in 2008. Pence, who called it a "silly accident," went through a sliding glass door he didn't realize was closed. "I didn't think I would go through a glass door," he said. "Normally, it wouldn't shatter like that. Somehow, it shattered, and I was stuck in the middle of a bunch of broken glass."

80 Hunter Pence

His swing was a little unconventional. He threw from the outfield with an awkward sidearm motion. Quirky Hunter Pence blossomed quickly into one of the Astros' top prospects while coming through the system after being drafted in the second round out of the University of Texas-Arlington in 2004. The fact that Pence's mechanics, as well as his personality, were a little offbeat didn't stop him from becoming a fan favorite in Houston long before he became a cult icon, winning World Series titles with the San Francisco Giants.

The trade that sent Pence to the Philadelphia Phillies at the trade deadline in 2011 was a hard one to swallow for Astros fans, who had a tough time coming to grips with a popular young player getting traded away in the prime of his career. The Astros, who a year earlier had dealt away Lance Berkman and Roy Oswalt, were rebuilding and sent Pence to Philadelphia for four prospects. Pence helped the Phillies reach the playoffs in 2011 and was traded to the Giants a year later and became one of the cornerstones on the 2012 and 2014 championship teams. His time in Houston, though, remained dear to his heart. In fact, Pence kept Houston as his offseason home after leaving the Astros. "I have extremely fond memories," he said. "I played with a lot of incredible players and played for a lot of really great minds. [Owner] Drayton McLane was wonderful to play for, and playing in my home state and for the Astros fans—it was a lot of fun."

The Astros were a force in the National League when they drafted Pence in '04, a season in which they went to the National League Championship Series and lost to the St. Louis Cardinals. They advanced to their first World Series a year later and were still considered a longshot contender when they came to spring camp in 2007. Pence hit .571 with two homers and nine RBIs in spring training in 2007, but the Astros didn't put him on their Opening Day roster. The team gave the center-field job to begin the season to Chris Burke, the 2005 playoff hero and former first-round draft pick who was blocked at second base by Craig Biggio. Burke hit .219 through the first 21 games, and, with Pence hitting .326 with 21 RBIs in 25 games at Triple A Round Rock, the Astros called up Pence to the big leagues on April 28.

Pence's impact in Houston was immediate. He led the National League in batting average at the All-Star break and wound up finishing third in the Rookie of the Year voting, hitting .322 with 17 homers, 69 RBIs, 11 stolen bases and a high-flying style of play that endeared himself to Astros fans. With Biggio in his final season in '07 and an aging team looking to get younger, Pence was becoming the face of the franchise. He showed remarkable consistency the next three seasons, hitting .278 while averaging 25 homers and 82 RBIs. That's what made the events of July 29, 2011, so gut-wrenching for Astros fans. It was no secret the Astros were rebuilding, and Pence had been rumored to be on the block for weeks. During the fifth inning of a game against the Brewers in Milwaukee, Pence was pulled from the game and hugged team-mates in the dugout before disappearing into the clubhouse.

His time with the Astros was over. "It's always bittersweet to get traded," Pence said. "Everywhere you play, you're grateful, but at the same time, another door is opening as one door shuts. I had an opportunity to play baseball and meet some new baseball minds, new teammates. I've been very blessed and grateful for everything I've gotten."

81 Go to Spring Training

It's one of the ultimate rituals in baseball. It's where fans can get closer to the players than at any other point in the year and where the optimism is as bright as the sunny Florida skies. Any baseball fan should take a trip to see the Astros play in spring training.

The Astros called Osceola County Stadium in Kissimmee, Florida, their home since 1985, when they moved from their previous home in Cocoa, Florida.

When owner Jim Crane purchased the Astros more than three years ago, he immediately began exploring a new spring training home. The lack of proximity to major hotels meant long commutes from players, staff, and fans to Osceola County Stadium. "We're just trying to get something that's a good location, easy for the fans to get in and out," Crane said. "And the two-team facilities do make it more economical."

Crane joined Major League Baseball commissioner Rob Manfred and general manager Jeff Luhnow, dignitaries from the Washington Nationals, and other political leaders at a November 9, 2015, ceremonial groundbreaking in West Palm Beach, Florida, at the 160-acre site where the new facility will sit. The $144 million project, which took years of negotiations and planning, will open in 2017 as The Ballpark at the Palm Beaches, giving the area five teams. The Miami Marlins and St. Louis Cardinals share a facility in Jupiter, which is about 19 miles north of West Palm Beach, and the New York Mets are in Port St. Lucie, which is about 32 miles north of Jupiter. "One of our goals is to make sure that as many people as possible have an opportunity to enjoy spring training," said Manfred, who has a house near the site. "It's such a great part of our year, and I think two additional teams here ensure we have a sufficient body of teams in southeast Florida to keep it going."

The facility, located between Haverhill Road and Military Trail near the intersection of I-95 and 45th Street, is scheduled for completion in January 2017. The site was previously a dumping ground for debris. Both the Nationals and Astros will have their own practice fields and training facilities and will share a 6,500-seat stadium that also has seating available on outfield berms. "Getting a new spring training facility was high on our list of priorities," Crane said. "A lot of hard work went into getting this done. We appreciate the great support we've received from the county and the governor. We will have a first-class facility that will be great for our players and will have a great impact on this neighborhood."

The new spring training facility enabled to Crane to check off another major initiative he had since purchasing the team. The team had finally negotiated a new television deal the year before and made the playoffs in 2015 after undergoing a rebuild when Crane took over. "When we started we had a lot of things we wanted to fix, starting with the baseball team," he said. "This was high on the list to get a better location for spring training. Our facilities weren't as good as the other teams. This will give us a state-of-the-art facility, and the players won't have to travel as much and will be closer than other teams."

The Astros held their first spring training in Apache Junction, Arizona (1962–63), before moving to Cocoa Beach, Florida, in 1964. They stayed there until moving to Kissimmee in 1985. Osceola County Stadium was built in 1984 to welcome the Astros to Osceola County. After the success of the Astros, who made the playoffs in 1997–99 and 2001, Osceola County Stadium was remodeled and expanded in 2003.

82 Bill Doran

Former Astros shortstop Dickie Thon believes Billy Doran was one of the more underrated players of his era. Hall of Fame second baseman Craig Biggio has praised Doran relentlessly for showing him how to play the game, both on the field and off. After all, it was Doran who helped Biggio make the transition to second base from catcher, paving the way for a Hall of Fame career. And if you ask anyone who followed the Astros in the 1980s, Doran was as much of a key contributor to the 1986 National League West division championship club as anyone.

Doran was a steady, dependable, and wildly popular player for the Astros for nine seasons and was named the team's Most Valuable Player in 1985 and 1987. Drafted by the Astros in the sixth round in 1979 out of the University of Miami (Ohio), he wound up playing 12 seasons in the major leagues and was a lifetime .266 hitter with 84 homers, 497 RBIs, and 209 stolen bases. The numbers don't blow you away, but Doran is the best second baseman in Astros history not named Craig Biggio or Jose Altuve. "He was very underrated," Thon said. "To me, he was maybe the best second baseman in the league—even when [Ryne] Sandberg was there. The one year [1987] Billy had only six errors the whole year, and they gave the Gold Glove to Sandberg, who had more errors. Billy had better range and a lot of double plays. He could hit and run the bases very well. He could bunt. He could do everything. He was a very good player. They don't say enough about Billy in Houston."

Phil Garner started the first 136 games at second base for the Astros in 1982 before having to move to third in September to replace the injured Art Howe. Doran was called up on September 6, 1982, to take over at second base and started 991 games at the position over the next seven seasons, including all 162 games in 1987. Doran finished 11th in the National League Most Valuable Player voting in 1986 when the Astros won the NL West. That season Doran hit .276 with a .368 on-base percentage with only 37 RBIs and 42 stolen bases as the team's leadoff hitter. He slugged a two-run home run against the New York Mets in Game 3 of the 1986 National League Championship Series.

As much as Doran was liked by the Houston fans, the feeling was mutual. "We just always had a great group of guys," Doran said. "The fans were always wonderful. You get around the other places and you see how certain guys are treated, and that was just never an issue in Houston. Through the good times, through the bad times, the people were always great and supportive. I look back, and, of course, it's been a long time, but I have nothing but fond memories of the entire time that I was there. It was just a full package."

The Astros couldn't quite recapture the magic of the 1986 season in the following years and started to dismantle a veteran team, sending Doran to his hometown Cincinnati Reds for three players to be named later on August 30, 1990. The Reds won the World Series that year, but Doran wound up having back surgery and didn't play in the postseason.

He spent three seasons in Cincinnati before finishing his career with the Milwaukee Brewers in 1993, but he remained a popular figure in Houston. "I'm thankful for the upbringing that I had with Phil Garner and Jose Cruz and the guys that were out there playing every day," Doran said. "Every now and then, the people that surround you kind of make you better because you're a small piece that fits into a larger piece, and I think that's kind of where I fell into. I had to fit with that group and today I'm thankful for that. Sometimes you can be the same guy in a different organization on a different team, and the fit isn't quite right. In Houston with the guys that I was around, it was a good fit for me."

83 Yogi Berra

Shortly after Hal Lanier was tabbed to manage the Astros in the winter of 1985, owner John McMullen called him and discussed with him—perhaps told him—that Hall of Fame catcher Yogi Berra would become bench coach. McMullen, who was from New Jersey and a former minority partner in the New York Yankees, and Berra were friends. There was no way Lanier was going to go against the owner's wishes, and why would he have wanted to anyway?

Berra played 19 seasons in the big leagues with the Yankees, winning three American League Most Valuable Player awards and getting elected to 15 consecutive All-Star Games. He played in 14 World Series, winning 10 of them. He managed the Yankees twice and the New York Mets once. He had the kind of experience a first-time manager like Lanier wanted, and it didn't hurt that Lanier had known him a long time.

Lanier's father, Max, played in the big leagues, and Berra would come to their house in St. Petersburg, Florida, during spring training when Hal was a kid. Lanier and his sisters would serve Berra food and drinks. "I knew Yogi at a very young age," Lanier said. "I was told that I had to accept Yogi as bench coach, and I said, 'Wow, what a great time this is going to be.' Of course, that was my first year. He really helped me out a lot with the players during the game, after games. There would be somebody that would get sent down, and he talked to them and he helped me out, especially when we went to New York. There's so much media attention there, and half of them went to Yogi, and half of them went to me after a game. Yogi apologized for that, and I said, 'Yogi, I wish they would all go to you.' What a great baseball man, player, coach, manager, but what a great man he was off the field. I was very fortunate to be able to spend time with him and get to know him for three years."

Berra spent three seasons as the Astros bench coach. Lanier said he was instrumental in the team winning the National League West title in 1986 and provided invaluable help to the players. Veteran relief pitcher Larry Andersen said Berra told him not to throw so much in the offseason. "He said I could get ready in two weeks, and it really made a difference in my career," Andersen said. "I was fresher during the whole season by not throwing so much during the offseason. That was right from Yogi."

Hall of Fame second baseman Craig Biggio credits Berra with helping him get drafted by the Astros. While with the Astros, Berra went with coach Matt Galante to Seton Hall to scout a top prospect for the 1987 draft. Biggio, like Berra, was a catcher. The Astros wound up taking Biggio with their top pick in the draft, and he was in the big leagues a year later. Biggio, of course, played 20 seasons, amassed more than 3,000 hits, and joined Berra in the National

Baseball Hall of Fame. "I'm an Astro because he had something to do with it," Biggio said.

Biggio, a native of Long Island, used to live on the East Coast and would play golf and attend hockey games with Berra and McMullen, who also owned the NHL's New Jersey Devils. Their friendship evolved to the point Berra would call Biggio on his birthday each year. Biggio and the rest of the baseball world mourned when Berra died on September 22, 2015, at 90 years old. "He's just a great man," Biggio said. "The man lived his life right. He's one of the most recognizable people in the world, but you wouldn't ever know it."

84 Norm Miller and the 24-Inning Game

When Norm Miller touched home plate in the Astrodome at 1:37 AM on April 16, 1968, he could have never dreamed the moment would follow him for the rest of his life. Miller had witnessed much bigger moments during his career. He saw Mickey Mantle hit the first home run in the Astrodome in 1965 and he was a teammate of Hank Aaron when he broke Babe Ruth's all-time home run record in 1974. Yet the one thing Miller continued to get asked about decades after he played his final game was about the run he scored that day. "Everybody's got to be known for something, right?" he said.

Miller scored the only run in what at the time was the longest night game in Major League Baseball history, crossing home plate in the bottom of the 24th inning in a 1–0 win for the Astros against the New York Mets. Miller was on third base when Bob Aspromonte hit a grounder to shortstop Al Weis, who allowed it to skip through his legs and end the game after six hours, six minutes. "It didn't take a bad hop," Weis told reporters after the game. "I just blew it. It went right through my legs."

Miller started in right field and went 0-for-7 before leading off the 24th inning with his first hit. He went to second on a balk, and the Mets intentionally walked slugger Jimmy Wynn. The bases were loaded with one out when Aspromonte hit what should have been an inning-ending double-play ball. "It was so strange because I actually remember the moment Aspromonte hit that ball, and I'm sure I said, 'Oh shit,'" Miller said. "It was a perfect double-play ball, and I remember stepping on home plate. We didn't have big greetings at home plate for things like that. I think if anybody came out, they came out and told me, 'It's about time you got a hit.'"

Hall of Famer Tom Seaver started the game for the Mets and held the Astros to two hits in 10 innings. Astros starter Don Wilson held the Mets to five hits in nine innings, and Houston reliever Jim Ray struck out 11 batters and allowed two hits in seven innings. Neither team came close to scoring a run for much of the game, and Astros owner Judge Roy Hofheinz reportedly grew weary as the night wore on. As the Astros came to bat in the 22nd inning, the scoreboard flashed the message: "The Judge says he's ready to go to bed. Let's score a run."

A picture of Miller scoring the run was displayed in the National Baseball Hall of Fame in Cooperstown, New York, and Miller often pulls out a similar picture to relive the memory. Miller, who played 10 seasons in the big leagues, penned a self-deprecating book about his career called, *To All My Fans From Norm Who?* "All I did was run down and step on home plate," Miller joked. "Whenever I was introduced for years, people would try to find something to say about me and they'd say, 'He scored the winning run!' And it sounded so magnificent. It's so strange because what the hell was I was supposed to do? I'm lucky Al Weis missed it, or nobody would have ever heard about me. I remember not getting any balls in right field for 15, 20 innings. Between innings, [I was] lying on the ground. Back then the Astroturf was so hard, and Jimmy Wynn and I were lying on our backs and resting our knees."

85 Bill Virdon

Manager Bill Virdon demanded the best from his players. Tough but honest and fair, Virdon guided the Astros for eight seasons and took them to their first playoff berth in 1980. He went 544–522 as skipper in Houston from 1975 to 1982 and still ranks first in club history for the most wins.

Astros slugger Bob Watson said Virdon was a disciplinarian. He had a lot of rules, but the players enjoyed playing for him because he got the most out of them. Watson said Virdon told him he retired as a player because he caught himself watching an airplane in center field one day, and a ball was hit that he didn't catch. It cost his Pittsburgh Pirates the game, and Virdon couldn't deal with a lack of focus. "He went in there and told [manager Danny] Murtaugh he was retiring," Watson said.

Watson said Virdon had a managerial rule—which once led to Cesar Cedeno sitting on the bench—that you had to take infield practice in order to be in the lineup. "That's the type of guy he was," Watson said. "[Virdon] was very intense. He was on top of his game, though. He understands what your strengths and weaknesses were and he definitely wanted you to give him your best at all times."

Virdon was the 1955 Rookie of the Year after hitting .281 with 17 homers and 68 RBIs for the St. Louis Cardinals. That was the start of a 12-year major league career, including 11 years in Pittsburgh. He was a center fielder who batted left-handed and threw right-handed. He hit .267 with 91 home runs in his career and was the starting center fielder on the Pirates' 1960 World Series championship team. Virdon managed the Pirates a decade later. He won 96 games as Pirates manager in 1972 and took the National League East crown. He spent 1974–75 as the manager of the New York Yankees before coming to Houston late in the 1975 season.

Shortly after Virdon was fired by the Yankees, he and his wife and daughter were renting a home in Oyster Bay, Long Island. It wasn't far from the home of Tal Smith, who had returned to Houston to be general manager after a brief stint as the executive vice president with the Yankees. "Bill was dismissed by the Yankees, and I told him if I ever had a chance I would hire him," Smith said. The Astros fired Preston Gomez, who had gone 128–161 in parts of two seasons. "We had not done well and were not drawing well, and it was obvious changes needed to be made," Smith said. "Losing can really wear on you, and I think perhaps that had become an issue with Preston, who was very dedicated and wanted to do everything he could."

With Virdon at the helm late in the 1975 season, the team went 17–17, and then the rebuilding Astros won 80 games in 1976 and 81 in 1977 before Virdon led the club to its first pennant race. The 1979 Astros, using speed and pitching, opened up a 10½-game lead over the Cincinnati Reds in the National League West on July 4 that year and couldn't hold it. They finished in second place, one-and-a-half games behind the Reds. In 1980 the Astros won the National League West, beating the Los Angeles Dodgers in a one-game playoff for their first taste of the postseason. They lost in five heartbreaking games to the Philadelphia Phillies in the

National League Championship Series. Nolan Ryan, who joined the Astros in 1980, knew of Virdon's no-nonsense style from when Virdon managed him in the minor leagues. "You played the game right and you respect the game and you worked hard," Ryan said. "If you did those things, you got along well with Bill."

Virdon was let go late in the 1982 season and later managed the Montreal Expos, but he is remembered fondly in the Astros organization. "Bill is a great manager, very fair, very direct," Smith said. "Players knew exactly what he expects, and I think they responded well. I've heard many players say Bill was the finest manager they played for. They had great respect for him."

86 Bob Watson and The Bad News Bears

The royalty checks still occasionally come in the mail for Bob Watson, though they're never more than $5 or $10. Nearly 40 years after his brief speaking role in the movie *The Bad News Bears in Breaking Training*, Watson still gets some modest residuals from his cameo on the big screen, as well as some modest laughs when he sees the movie on television while he's flipping channels.

The comedy was the sequel to the hit film *The Bad News Bears* and didn't do quite as well critically. The plot has the ragtag Bears facing a team called the Houston Toros in the Astrodome between games of an Astros doubleheader for a chance to play a team from Japan. In the second inning of what was supposed to be a four-inning game, officials call it off because it ran over its allotted time. The Bears coach, played by actor William Devane, protests—as a few Astros players in rainbow uniforms appear in the dugout. Finally, Watson speaks up with his famous line: "Hey, c'mon, let the kids play!" Soon, both teams and the fans are chanting "Let them play!"

"The plot was they're playing this game between games of a doubleheader," Watson said. "The game was going to run a little long, and they wanted to stop the game and they wanted the Astros players to come out and say, 'Hey, let the kids finishing playing their games.' I guess the Bad News Bears were traveling across the country. I don't even know why they were in Houston. They were playing this game, and so I don't even know how I got the lead to come out and say, 'C'mon, let the kids play!'"

A few of Watson's teammates could be seen in the scene as well, including Cesar Cedeno, Enos Cabell, J.R. Richard, Ken Forsch, and manager Bill Virdon. The scene was shot during an Astros day off, Cabell said, and they had to be at the ballpark at 6:00 AM. The Astros had played a night game the day before, so it was an early wake-up call. Cabell joked that he was hitting .330 before the scene was shot and watched his average drop to .300 in a week or 10 days. "So I wasn't happy," he joked. Nevertheless, Cabell came away with a new appreciation for acting. "It was pretty interesting to do it and see what the actors and stuff go through," he said. "You have a newfound realization of what they do. They shot different shots from four, five, six directions and they add it all up and they make a movie out of that. It was pretty trying."

Watson said it took about 25 takes to complete the scene, which lasted about five minutes. Astros players were on screen for only a few seconds. "And I'm going, 'Gee whiz, there's no way I want to be in movies and be a movie star if you have to keep doing this over and over and over,'" Watson said. "We had to get the lights just right. All the people that were sitting in the stands, they had to be just right. It was terrible, but we enjoyed doing the actual scene."

Watson hit 184 homers in his 19-year big league career, 14 years of which were spent in Houston. He scored baseball's one millionth run and also became the first African American general manager in Major League Baseball history. And thanks to the Bad News Bears, he has acting on his resume as well. "A lot of people have seen that picture over the years, and every once in a while," Watson said, "a trivia question asks about the *Bad News Bears*."

87 Carlos Correa

He was one of the Astros' most anticipated prospects in history, and shortstop Carlos Correa didn't disappoint in his first season in the big leagues. Correa made his major league debut on June 8, 2015, and instantly became a force in the Astros' lineup. He set the franchise record for home runs as a shortstop and by a rookie en route to joining Jeff Bagwell (1991) as the only Astros to be named Rookie of the Year. And to think he played most of the season at 20 years old.

In 2015 Correa hit .279 with 22 doubles, 22 home runs, 68 RBIs, 14 stolen bases, and a .859 OPS in only 99 games. Among American League rookies, he ranked first in home runs, slugging percentage (.512), and OPS, while ranking second in RBIs, on-base percentage (.345), and third in batting average. He became the youngest shortstop to homer in the playoffs and the third player in history (following Joe DiMaggio and Mickey Mantle) to hit in the third spot in the batting order in a playoff game at age 21 or younger.

Correa was drafted by the Astros with the No. 1 overall pick in 2012 out of Puerto Rico and zoomed through the minor leagues. At 6'4" and with the poise of a polished veteran on and off the field, Correa put himself on a crash course with superstardom. "What happens with players with his ability is we focus on the talent, but the preparation and the work he puts in is remarkable for a 20-year-old that's new to this league," Astros manager A.J. Hinch said. "He doesn't rely on talent. He has a ton of preparation. He

Carlos Correa connects for an RBI double in July of 2015, a year in which the 20-year-old rookie hit .279 and 22 home runs.

has a routine, he has a great passion for being great, and that's why he continues to contribute. He's not getting by on talent alone."

Correa is mature beyond his years in many ways, but it's not by accident. He was just eight years old when he began assisting his father, Carlos Sr., on construction sites in their native Puerto Rico and admits he had to grow up faster than other kids who were playing video games while Carlos was handing his dad supplies on the job site. "Then when I was 12, I was working a lot harder with him, especially in the summers when I was out of school," Correa said. "I was working with my dad in construction and helping him build houses and all this stuff. I had to learn to do all this stuff at that young age and I could see how hard he had to work to get to where he was."

His parents married as teenagers and had Carlos at a young age. His father was a baseball fan and always had the game on television. He was especially a fan of Pedro Martinez, the Dominican Hall of Fame pitcher. One day when Carlos Sr. was watching a game, little Carlos said he wanted to play. Carlos Sr. came across a team that needed a first baseman and was willing to make room for little Carlos. Soon, he was hitting two or three homers per game at five and six years old in a league where kids are flipped balls by adults. The team wanted to utilize Correa's talent to the fullest and moved him to shortstop, a position where balls were being hit the most. Correa started to be recognized all around Puerto Rico and began having dreams of the major leagues. "The work ethic was always there," said Correa, who grew up idolizing former Yankees great Derek Jeter. "I learned that from my dad. I started working with them at the academy. I would go back home and work with my dad. It was a routine I did for three years, and I think it paid off. I was able to get drafted first overall by the Astros."

Correa was a hot commodity in the 2012 draft, and the Astros studied him closely because they had the first pick. Astros scouting director Mike Elias had seen Correa as a 15-year-old and was impressed. The Astros became even more impressed when they got to know Correa and his family better through a series of interviews. They eventually took him with the No. 1 pick and signed him for $4.8 million. "I'm really thankful for the support the fans in Puerto Rico have given me so far, and that's something I will always appreciate," he said.

88 Buy Astrodome Memorabilia

The Astrodome can live forever in your den—if your significant other doesn't mind a piece of Houston history serving as a reminder of the city's sports glory years. Those of us who grew up going to Astros and Oilers games in the Astrodome can preserve those memories by buying some Astrodome memorabilia, which is readily available on the web at sites like eBay as well as from individual sellers.

The future of the "Eighth Wonder of the World," which closed in earnest following the 1999 baseball season when the Astros moved downtown to what is now Minute Maid Park, is still up in the air. County officials have determined that no matter what happens to the Astrodome that it's no longer viable as a sports venue. In recent years the stadium's seats—orange, red, yellow, blue, and gray—were removed and sold off in pairs at $200 a pop to fans eager to preserve history. The seats were sold in "as is" condition, meaning decades of Astrodome grime and dirt that had to be removed.

The Astros held a yard sale late in 2013, in which tons of items removed from the stadium were put up for grabs, including lockers, turnstiles, employee uniforms, and pieces of the Astroturf. A 12-inch by 12-inch piece of Astroturf went for $20. The red jackets worn by ushers and the space-age astronaut helmets worn by the grounds crew in the Dome's early years also were sold.

Even if you can't have a piece of the actual Astrodome, you can have the next best thing—a miniature Astrodome replica. Several versions of Astrodome replicas have been produced over the years, including a few that have been handed out at Astros games through the years. Those are available on the Internet for between $75 and $100. One of the most impressive and meticulous replicas of the Astrodome was sold by the Danbury Mint in the 1990s, but it is no longer available for purchase.

Tickets and programs to some of the Astrodome's earliest games are worth thousands of dollars, and only time will tell if some of the same keepsakes from the Dome's latter days will have monetary value as well. But any Astros fan, no matter if you saw games in the Astrodome or not, should try to get their hands on a piece of Houston sports history.

Opened in 1965 the Astrodome was the first of its kind. It was the first domed stadium and the first to use Astroturf, the revolutionary synthetic playing surface that would spring up in stadiums throughout professional sports. The Astros played their home games in the Astrodome from 1965 to 1999, the NFL's Houston Oilers played there from 1968 to 1996, and the University of Houston football team called the Astrodome home from 1965 to 1997. In addition the Astrodome hosted an NBA All-Star Game, an NCAA men's basketball Final Four, the legendary "Battle of the Sexes II" tennis match between Billie Jean King and Bobby Riggs in 1973, and many other big-time sporting events.

89 Cardinals Hack the Astros

There may have been no better rivalry in baseball in the late 1990s and early 2000s than the Astros and Cardinals, two National League Central division foes who were stacked with big talent and bigger expectations. The two teams dominated the division for a decade, combining to win 10 of 11 division championships from 1996 to 2006. In fact, the Astros and Cardinals finished in the top two spots in the division six times during that decade and met in the National League Championship Series twice—with the Cardinals winning in seven games in 2004 and the Astros in six games a year later.

The Astros' move to the American League following the 2012 season put the Astros and Cardinals in different leagues, essentially putting the kibosh on the rivalry. Even in their final years together in the same division, the rivalry was fading. The Cardinals were still contending in the division each year, but the Astros were also-rans.

Then Jim Crane, who used to park cars at old Busch Stadium in St. Louis when he was younger, purchased the Astros following the 2011 season and plucked away Jeff Luhnow from the Cardinals to be his general manager. Luhnow was the director of player procurement with the Cardinals and helped them build one of the best farm systems in baseball. Upon his arrival in Houston, Luhnow brought with him a few more former Cardinals employees, including Sig Mejdal (director of decision sciences) and Mike Elias (scouting director). One of the model franchises in baseball, the Cardinals' influence was strong in Houston.

The rivalry between the clubs was renewed in 2014, but it had nothing to do with what was happening on the field. Around May 2014, Luhnow learned of a security breach in the team's internal database, which included correspondence between team officials regarding trade talks with other clubs, some of which were about deals that came to fruition. Several text messages containing the confidential material were made public about a month later on the website Deadspin.com, and the Astros quickly issued a statement revealing they were working with Major League Baseball security and the FBI to determine the party or parties responsible for the leak. In the statement the Astros said the information was obtained illegally from an outside source and that they intend to prosecute those involved.

The New York Times reported a year later the FBI and Justice Department had launched an investigation into allegations that the Cardinals may have obtained unauthorized access to Houston's computer system, which includes proprietary information regarding player personnel and evaluation. In an interview with *Sports Illustrated*, Luhnow said: "At the time when it happened a year ago, it was like coming home and seeing your house has been broken into. You feel violated when someone does that without permission. As far as whether it affected our ability to execute our plan, it's difficult to assess the effect, but we have continued to execute our plan and we are making progress. I had to call the other 29 GMs and apologize that private notes our organization had made had been made public. Those were not fun calls to make. But I've made several trades since then, and I've had no problems getting anybody on the phone."

In July of 2015, the FBI concluded its investigation and recommended that at least one Cardinals employee be charged. The Cardinals soon dismissed scouting director Chris Correa, who was hired by Luhnow in St. Louis, but the team didn't give specifics why Correa was let go. Five month later Correa pled guilty to five criminal charges in connection with unauthorized access of the Astros' database. Correa faced a maximum penalty for each of the five counts of five years in prison and a fine of up to $250,000 and restitution. Even in cyberspace the Astros-Cardinals rivalry rages on.

90 Back-to-Back No-Nos

Even though they played for different teams, Jim Maloney and Don Wilson combined to pull off one of baseball's rarest—and yet to be duplicated feats—when they pitched no-hitters in consecutive games—Maloney for the Cincinnati Reds against the Astros and Wilson for the Astros against the Reds.

Both pitchers were hard throwers and had great careers that were cut short. In Maloney's case it was an Achilles injury that kept him from pitching for Cincinnati's Big Red Machine in the 1970s (his final season was 1971), and Wilson died tragically in his garage in 1975. From 1963 to '69, Maloney was one of the best pitchers in the game, going 117–60 with a 2.90 ERA and 68 complete games during that seven-year span.

Maloney, who was called up at 20 years old in 1960, showed no-hit stuff early in his career. He threw 10 scoreless, hitless innings and struck out 18 batters against the New York Mets on June 14, 1965, before Johnny Lewis led off the 11th with a homer to beat Maloney. About two months later (August 19, 1965), he no-hit the Chicago Cubs in a 1–0 win in 10 innings in the first no-hitter in which the pitcher went more than nine innings. He threw 187 pitches in that game, which seems unfathomable now.

No one knew it at the time, but Maloney's no-hitter he threw on April 30, 1969, in a 10–0 win over the Astros at Crosley Field was on the front end of history. That's because Wilson came back the next day and also pitched a no-hitter (the second of his career) in a 4–0 win. It was the second time two pitchers had thrown back-to-back no-hitters, joining Gaylord Perry and Ray Washburn a year earlier.

Wilson won double-digit games for the Astros for eight consecutive years (1967–74), including 16 games twice. Signed by the Colt .45s as an amateur free agent out of Compton, California, in 1964, he made his debut at 21 years old in 1966 and went 104–92 in 266 career games, including 245 starts for Houston. He threw his first no-hitter on June 18, 1967—the first no-no pitched in a domed stadium and on artificial turf. He struck out 15 batters in a 2–0 win over the Atlanta Braves and fanned Hank Aaron to end the game.

Nine days before no-hitting the Reds, Wilson was rocked for seven runs in five innings in a 14–0 loss to Cincinnati in the Astrodome. The Astros took exception to Reds pitcher Clay Carroll throwing a 3–2 curveball for a strikeout in the ninth inning, and Wilson called the Reds clubhouse and told catcher Johnny Bench he was going to hit him in the head the next time he faced him.

During his no-hitter nine days later, Wilson indeed hit Bench with a pitch in the fifth inning that glanced off his shoulder and struck him in the head. Bob Watson, who grew up with Wilson in California and was on the bench that night, said that when Bench got to first base, he was asked by Astros first baseman Curt Blefary why he didn't charge the mound. "And he said, 'I'll take him deep sometime during this game,'" Watson recalled the conversation between Bench and Blefary. "That was the last base runner."

91 Tour Minute Maid Park

There aren't many places in baseball better to watch a game than Minute Maid Park in downtown Houston. The best way to see all of what Minute Maid Park has to offer is to take a daily tour. Those tours last an hour to 90 minutes and include checking out the historic Union Station, the broadcasting booths, the press box, the luxury suites, the field, the bullpen, and the manual scoreboard in left field.

Game day tours give fans an opportunity to get into the game and view the sights and sounds prior to the gates opening. The game day tour takes fans through the upper deck, the suites, the club level, and to the field level to watch batting practice for 30 minutes from the diamond club.

Those who really want to see behind the scenes can take the clubhouse tour. They are conducted about once a quarter based on scheduling opportunities. It cost $30 (but can vary on different promotions) but includes a trip to the Astros clubhouse, the Astros wall of honor, the press conference room, weight room, batting cages, and dugouts. There's also a field lap that includes trips to the dugout, bullpens, and manual scoreboard as well.

The daily tour ($14.25 for adults, $9.12 for kids under 14, and $11.17 for those 65 and older) starts on the ground floor of Union Station, the former train station that sits beyond the left-field wall and now houses the Astros offices and reception areas. Opened in 1911, Union Station served as the main passenger rail terminal for Houston for more than 60 years, closing to rail traffic in 1974. When the Astros were looking for a site to build their downtown ballpark, the area around Union Station became a focal point.

Marble columns and 45-foot ceilings with trim molding were discovered and restored during renovations.

From Union Station the daily tour proceeds to the main concourse. What makes it unique is fans can walk around the entire circumference of the ballpark and be able to see the field of play on 45-foot wide concourses. The next stop is the terrace deck, the top level of the ballpark. From there fans can get sweeping views of the ballpark and downtown buildings. If the retractable roof is closed, you can get an up-close view of the hurricane-proof glass panels. It's also the best place to see the 19th century locomotive reproduction that serves as an homage to Union Station's past that sits on tracks high above left field.

The tour then takes you to the suite level. Minute Maid Park has 63 suites that can be purchased for $100,000 per season. The next stop is the club level, which brings air-conditioned comfort to the concourses as well as unique food and beverage choices. That level also includes a stop in the press box and a peek inside the television announcing booth.

The tour then takes you below the ground to the field level and a look at the diamond club. Gourmet food in the lounge and plush seats behind home plate can be had for $400 per game, assuming you're ready to purchase them for the entire season. And that's after a one-time $20,000 personal license fee per seat. Sitting in the front row of the diamond club means you're closer to the batter's box than the pitcher. Finally, the tour takes you to the field and a stop in the Astros dugout. Fans can take a lap around the field's warning track, peeking inside the bullpens and going behind the manual scoreboard in left field. You'll leave with a greater appreciation for the ballpark, as well as some dirt on your shoes.

92 Hal Lanier

Hal Lanier's first managerial job in the major leagues turned out to be his only shot. Groomed under Hall of Fame manager Whitey Herzog of the St. Louis Cardinals, Lanier led the Astros to the National League West championship in his first year as manager in 1986. During a three-year stay in Houston, he went 254–232 before being fired after the 1988 season with one year on his contract. He never managed in the big leagues again.

Needless to say, Houston remained a special place for Lanier—even years after he last managed there. "It was great," he said. "I loved the city. I had a lot of friends there." Lanier took an Astros team picked to finish last in 1986 and engineered one of the most memorable seasons in club history. The Astros won 96 games and took the division by 10 games before losing to the New York Mets in six games in the National League Championship Series in one of the greatest playoff series ever played. "It was tough to swallow, but sometimes you're going to win them, and sometimes you're not," he said.

Lanier was destined for a life in the game. His father, Max, won 108 games in a 14-year playing career, mostly with the Cardinals, and was a two-time All-Star in the 1940s. Hal played 10 years in the big leagues himself as an infielder with the San Francisco Giants (1964–71) and New York Yankees (1972–73). He managed in the Cardinals' minor league system before joining Herzog's staff in 1981, winning a World Series in 1982. Herzog recommended him to take over the Astros. He was chosen over Joe Torre and Jim Leyland, who combined to win more than 4,000 games and five World Series titles. Lanier's fiery personality worked at first in

Houston, and he brought an aggressive style on the field. He was named the NL Manager of the Year in 1986. "Hal was tough," catcher Alan Ashby said.

Bill Wood was assistant general manager to Dick Wagner of the Astros in 1986 and 1987 and said Lanier's personality could be abrasive. That may have led to his departure from the Astros dugout. "To have the kind of year we had [in 1986] with the performances from the players, I thought Lanier and his staff did a great job," Wood said. "Things just didn't go well after that."

Lanier isn't sure why former Astros owner John McMullen decided to fire him, even though he was successful. He tried to get other jobs, but he heard he was blackballed. He's not sure why. "I really didn't have too much to say about it," he said. "It hurt a great deal because I did have 22 games over .500, but I accepted what Dr. McMullen was going to do. An older manager once told me, 'You never win your first year. You win your second and third year and then you get a three-year contract extension.' And he was right. I never did get another opportunity."

Lanier was the bench coach of the Philadelphia Phillies in 1990 and 1991 and interviewed for other managerial positions without any luck. He was out of baseball until 1996 when he was hired as manager of the independent minor league club Winnipeg Goldeyes and he held that job for 10 years. He later managed in the Northern League, Cam-Am League, and Frontier League and grew to love the minor league life while keeping positive memories of Houston. "I'll be able to walk away when I'm not having any fun and the bus rides are too long," he said.

93 Go to FanFest

There's no better way to prepare for the season or get up close and personal with the players than to attend the annual FanFest at Minute Maid Park. Typically held in late January, FanFest features more than a dozen players and members of the front office to sign autographs and answer questions from the fans.

In 2015 nearly 5,000 fans enjoyed activities for all ages, including autograph sessions with many current and former players. Fans could even take swings in the Astros batting cages, run the bases, and throw in the bullpen. In addition, there's an interactive kids zone, fan forums with front-office staff as well as current and former players, and a vendor expo. The event is free to the public with a voucher, but there's a small fee for the autographs. The majority of FanFest proceeds benefit the Astros Foundation's programs for at-risk children and teens. The autograph sessions and Q&A sessions are two of the more popular events. "FanFest has become a tradition for people. It's a great way to kick off the baseball season before we head to spring training," Astros president Reid Ryan said. "The guys are great and sign autographs and have really made this a family environment."

In recent years FanFest has capped the week-long Astros caravan, which is a fan outreach tour. The caravan makes stops all around Houston, its suburbs, and beyond as Astros players, former players, and broadcasters engage fans and get them pumped up for the season. In years past the tour has had stops in San Antonio, Austin, Corpus Christi, and Galveston, giving fans throughout Texas a chance to get up close and personal with the players. There have been stops in Louisiana as well. The caravan usually includes a stop at the Astros Urban Youth Academy, local community

Mascots

When the Astros moved to the American League in 2013, they held a fan event at Minute Maid Park to preview the team's new uniforms. They also unveiled a new mascot, who wasn't all that new. The "new" Orbit was a reincarnation of the furry alien from the 1990s who roamed the Astrodome. Orbit made his comeback with a motorcade from NASA and he lived up to the hype. He quickly became one of the more imaginative mascots in the game with his skits and penchant for playfully taunting opposing players.

In research provided by Mike Acosta, the Astros team authenticator and resident historian, the Astros' first mascot was an actual human being. It was comedian Bill Dana, who was introduced in January 1965 as the new team mascot. Dana made television appearances on *The Ed Sullivan Show*. He appeared at the Astrodome performing comedic skits before games and dressed in a full Astros uniform. Dana rubbed elbows with the likes of Neil Armstrong and Alan Shepard on Opening Day in 1965 when 22 U.S. astronauts tossed the ceremonial first pitch at the Astrodome.

Soon, more conventional mascots began invading the Astrodome. There were the "Earthmen," who dressed in astronaut suits while cleaning the Astroturf before games. The character "Chester Charge," who was the brainchild of Astrodome cartoonist Ed Henderson, appeared on the scoreboard with a bugle and later on the field in costume. Who could forget Astrojack and Astrodillo in the 1980s? Astrojack was a rabbit, and Astrodillo was—you guessed it—an armadillo. They would ride around the turf on ATVs before the game.

The team went a few years without a mascot before Orbit made his debut in 1990. He was a furry green alien with antennae who wore an Astros jersey. He was retired when the Astros left the Astrodome in 1999. Don't forget "General Admission," who debuted in 1990 and would fire his cannon from center field after each homer. The move to Minute Maid Park gave birth to "Junction Jack," a rabbit dressed in a train conductor's outfit that tied into the railroad theme that came with Union Station being attached to new Minute Maid Park. Acosta said the idea of using a rabbit stemmed from then-Astros president Bob McLaren, whose young daughter loved bunnies.

outreach centers, schools, and military facilities. "Our goal is to get out and connect with our fans on a grassroots level and let them learn who some of their players are," Ryan said.

FanFest used to encompass the Houston College Classic baseball tournament. The six-team tournament has been played since 2001 and annually features the top local baseball teams in the state, including Houston, Rice, Baylor, Texas, and Texas A&M. When the NCAA moved back the start date for the beginning of the college baseball season, FanFest and the Houston College Classic became separate events. The College Classic is now held in early March and can draw some big crowds. Alabama, Tennessee, Arizona State, Vanderbilt, LSU, North Carolina, Oklahoma State, and UCLA have also played in the tournament in years past.

94 Dave Smith

The only home run Dave Smith gave up during his rookie season in 1980 came late in the year, when Steve Henderson took him deep at Shea Stadium in New York. Smith was having a great season. He went 7–5 with a 1.93 ERA and saved 10 games, throwing a career-high 102⅔ innings. But when he gave up the homer, former general manager Tal Smith was cornered by angry team owner John McMullen after the game. "He said, 'What are we bringing that guy in for?'" Tal Smith said. "He gave up one home run all year—to a good major league hitter—and McMullen was mad."

Dave Smith didn't make too many mistakes in his career, but he might have been happier surfing than doing anything else. He was from Southern California, had blond hair (which would turn gray at early age), and certainly fit the bill as a surfer. He also had a pretty deceptive change-up and forged a path to the major leagues, saving 199 games in 11 seasons for the Astros—a club record until Billy Wagner eclipsed him, including a then-club record of 33 during his All-Star season in 1986. In a 13-year career that included two seasons with the Chicago Cubs, Smith compiled a 53–53 record in 609 appearances, recording a 2.67 ERA and 216 saves. "When you fight your tail off for eight innings and you come up one run ahead, and to have Smitty come in and have the rate of success he had, it keeps you in the game," former Astros second baseman Bill Doran said. "It keeps you going, that, 'Hey, if we just claw one out here, we have somebody dependable who's going to come in and not give it away.'"

Smith wasn't the hair-on-fire, blowtorch kind of closer you see in this day and age. His fastball was in the upper 80s, touching 90, but he certainly didn't blow anything past anybody. But Smith had the ability to remain calm in tough situations. "He smoked a lot of damn cigarettes, but other than that, his best pitch was his change-up, and he'd throw it any time," former Astros infielder Enos Cabell said. "People don't understand that. He got outs with the change-up and threw it all the time, and they still couldn't hit it. He was different. He was very different."

Smith died suddenly of a heart attack on December 17, 2008, in San Diego. He was 53 years old. Smith was the third member of the 1980 team to pass away in a two-year span, joining Joe Niekro (October 2006) and Vern Ruhle (January 2007). "That was a very close-knit team in 1980," Tal Smith said. "They played together for quite some time, and for the most part, that's been a trademark of Astro clubs—a lot of continuity, a lot of stability."

Tal Smith referred to Dave Smith as "a real stalwart," who was somewhat of a pleasant surprise when he made the team out of spring training in 1980. The pitcher made his big league debut on April 11, 1980, when he allowed one hit and walked two in a one-inning relief appearance against the Los Angeles Dodgers. Smith compiled 10 saves in his rookie season as one of three closing options. He was a right-handed complement to lefty Joe Sambito, who saved 17 games that year, along with righty Frank LaCorte, who saved 11.

But from the beginning to the end of his 11-year career with the Astros, Smith was known for his calm demeanor. "He was a surfer boy who wasn't crazy like most closers are supposed to be," former catcher Alan Ashby said. "He was quiet, and I think he was thinking about surfing most of the time. That's kind of who Smitty was, but he was very effective."

95 Big Game Brandon Backe

It was the final day of the 2004 season, and the never-say-die Astros needed to win to make the playoffs and finish off an amazing 36–10 kick to end the season. The foe was the Colorado Rockies, and the Astros liked their chances because they had eventual 2004 Cy Young Award winner Roger Clemens on the mound. If there was anyone you wanted on the mound in a big game, it was "the Rocket."

Backe was sitting at his locker about two hours prior to the game when he got a tap on the shoulder from pitching coach Jim Hickey. "He said, 'We're going to need you to pitch today,'" Backe said. "I looked up at him with a smirk and said, 'Yeah, okay, whatever dude.' He said, 'No, we have to have you pitch. Roger's sick.'" Clemens had the stomach flu and was getting fluids injected intravenously in the trainer's room. Backe, who was still coming to terms with the magnitude of what he was being asked to do, couldn't help but sneak a peek in the trainer's room to see Clemens hooked up to the IV for himself. "He gave me some words of encouragement, telling me to go out there and do what I normally do," Backe said.

As the replacement starter, Backe held the Rockies to two runs in five innings to get the win and help the Astros clinch a playoff berth, as well as adding to his reputation as one of the Astros' most clutch pitchers in history. "I'm very proud of it," Backe said. "To be recognized for what I love to do is special."

Backe was a two-sport star growing up in Galveston, Texas, where he quarterbacked the Ball High School football team before deciding to focus on baseball, which helped him get drafted in the 18th round by the Tampa Bay Devil Rays as an infielder. He switched to pitching in 2001 and was acquired by his hometown Astros prior to the 2004 season in exchange for veteran infielder Geoff Blum, who would go on to hit the game-winning home run against Houston in Game 3 of the 2005 World Series. Backe went 5–3 with a 4.30 ERA in mostly a relief role before coming through on the final day of the 2004 season.

His legacy for rising to the occasion in key situations grew when he won Game 3 of the National League Division Series against the Atlanta Braves before holding the St. Louis Cardinals to one hit in eight scoreless innings in Game 5 of the NL Championship Series, outdueling fellow Houston-area product Woody Williams. That's the game Jeff Kent ended with a walk-off homer in the ninth, putting Houston within a game of the World Series. "A lot of the fans around the area, even up to this day, bring back that memory and they tell me, specifically, that game against Woody Williams and the Cardinals in '04—Game 5—was the best game I've ever pitched. And for fans that I don't even know to bring it up, it obviously makes me feel good," he said. "I was fortunate to be around guys like Pettitte and Clemens and Oswalt, and they helped refine me as a pitcher instead of be just a thrower."

Backe's best season in the majors came in 2005, when he went 10–8 in 26 appearances (25 starts) with a 4.76 ERA. He pitched in four playoff games that year, including three starts, and threw seven scoreless innings in Game 4 of the World Series, taking a no-decision in a game the Chicago White Sox won 1–0 to clinch the title.

Backe loves to tell his underdog story of how he made it to the big leagues after having to switch positions and how he wound up getting the ball for the Astros—the team he grew up cheering for—in some of the biggest moments in franchise history. "It was an unbelievable experience," he said. "To have two unbelievable seasons where we went farther than any Astros teams had ever gone, and for me to be a part of that, it means more than words can describe."

96 Go to a Double A Game

There may be no better setting to watch a minor league game than Whataburger Field in Corpus Christi, Texas. The scenic ballpark, which opened in 2005, sits near Corpus Christi Bay with the Harbor Bridge setting the backdrop for the outfield. The Double A Hooks, a club owned by the Astros, have packed in the fans for more than a decade and have seen many of the Astros' stars of the future make their way through, including Jose Altuve, Dallas Keuchel, and Carlos Correa.

Whataburger Field occupies land once dominated by cotton warehouses at the Port of Corpus Christi. According to the team's website, the ballpark's architectural attributes—from mammoth wood beams to corrugated siding—pay tribute to the site's heritage. The scoreboard in left-center field is framed by antique cotton presses, one of which dates to the 1920s. All of the seats at Whataburger Field are close to the action, whether that includes what's going on between the lines or watching the vessels that navigate up and down the ship channel behind the stadium. The Hooks play 70 home games a year against Texas League rivals like San Antonio, Frisco, and Midland. "There's always been great synergy in the relationship," said Astros president Reid Ryan, the former CEO of Ryan-Sanders baseball. "Corpus Christi was an Astros town for 40 years before the advent of the Hooks, and the entire Coastal Bend and South Texas are critical to the success of both clubs."

Hall of Fame pitcher Nolan Ryan (Reid's father) teamed with Houston businessman Don Sanders to buy the Double A Jackson Generals in the late 1990s and founded the Round Rock Express, which plays in Dell Diamond in suburban Austin, in 2000. The Express served as the Double A affiliate of the Astros before Ryan and Sanders moved the franchise to Corpus Christi when it purchased Edmonton's Triple A team and moved it into Round Rock. The Express became the Rangers' Triple A affiliate in 2011. The Hooks have been playing in Whataburger Field since 2005 and have been an Astros affiliate since their inception. The Astros purchased the club in 2013.

Corpus Christi, situated along the Coastal Bend of Texas, is only about 210 miles from Houston, making it the Astros' only minor league affiliate within a reasonable driving distance. For that reason it's often the place the Astros send many of their rehabbing major league players, giving fans of the Hooks a few chances throughout the year to see major league talent. Tickets can be purchased by phone at 361-561-HOOK (4665), or just drop by the ballpark. Fans three years and younger are admitted for free unless the accompanying adult desires a seat for the child, in which case a reserved-seat ticket is required. Gates open 90 minutes before first pitch. Whataburger Field doesn't allow outside food or drink to be brought inside, but it does serve Whataburger, so why would you need any outside food?

Corpus Christi is also home to several beaches, the Texas State Aquarium, and the USS Lexington, which was commission in 1943 and saw extensive service through the Pacific War. Decommissioned in 1991 she was donated for use as a museum ship and in 2003 was designated a National Historic Landmark. Just east of Corpus Christi are Padre Island and Mustang Island, which are home to various municipal, state, and national parks. Most are within a short drive of Whataburger Field, meaning Astros fans can make a weekend out of a trip to see the Hooks.

97 The Don Wilson and Jim Umbricht Tragedies

Don Wilson and Jim Umbricht were two of the Astros' most promising young pitchers when their lives were cut tragically short—Umbricht died of cancer in 1964, and Wilson died in a 1975 accident. The No. 32 worn by Umbricht and the No. 40 worn by Wilson are two of 10 numbers retired by the Astros, but they are the only two that were retired in honor of players who died in the middle of their careers.

Umbricht, whose family survived the Great Depression in Chicago while he was growing up (his older brother, Bill, was killed in action in World War II), was a right-handed reliever. He was selected by the Colt .45s in the 1961 Expansion Draft from the Pittsburgh Pirates, for whom he appeared in 19 games from 1959 to 1961. In Houston, Umbricht developed into an effective reliever, posting a 4–0 record with a 2.01 ERA in 1962.

He was playing golf with Astros general manager Paul Richard during spring training in 1963 when he saw a small lump on his right leg. Umbricht eventually had it checked out and was told that he had lymphoma, which had spread to his leg, thigh, and groin. He had a tumor removed during a six-hour surgery and returned to the mound, appearing in 35 games in 1963, going 4–3 with a 2.61 ERA. His health deteriorated in the offseason, though, and he was in and out of hospitals before dying on April 8, 1964—five days before Houston's season opener. Ken Johnson pitched eight and two-third innings in a 6–3 victory on Opening Day at Cincinnati and said afterward, "I had an extra special reason for wanting to win this one—my ex-roommate."

Umbricht's family spread his ashes on the grounds of the Astrodome, which was under construction next door to Colt Stadium, by having his brother, Ed, fly a plane over the site and scatter them. That season the Colt .45s wore black armbands to honor Umbricht, and his number became the first to be retired by the team. "He was a great guy and a very fine relief pitcher," said former Astros general manager Tal Smith. "His family, his brother, and his parents remained big fans and supporters of the club for years."

Wilson was a hard-throwing right-handed pitcher who won double-digit games for the Astros for eight consecutive years (1967–1974), including 16 games twice. Signed by the Colt .45s as an amateur free agent out of Compton, California, in 1964, he made his debut at 21 years old in 1966 and went 104–92 in 266 career games, including 245 starts for Houston. "He had a tremendous fastball, a decent slider and he pitched up in the zone," said former teammate Bob Watson, who grew up with Wilson.

On June 18, 1967, Wilson threw the first no-hitter pitched in a domed stadium when he struck out 15 batters in a 2–0 win against the Atlanta Braves, whiffing Hank Aaron for the final out. He made history in 1969 when he followed up a no-hitter thrown by Cincinnati's Jim Maloney against the Astros at Crosley Field and no-hit the Reds the next day, winning 4–0, on May 1, 1969. "He was a dominant pitcher," Smith said. "In 1969 the club got off to a terrible start. They got no-hit by Jim Maloney in Cincinnati, and that made us 4–20, and Wilson came back the next night in the same ballpark and no-hit the Reds and got the club started." Sparked by Wilson, the Astros won 19 of their next 23 games to get within a game of .500.

Wilson was found dead along with his five-year-old son on January 5, 1975, in their Houston home. The pitcher was found in the passenger seat of his 1972 Thunderbird in the garage, which was attached to the house. His son was found in an upstairs bedroom as carbon monoxide gas had leaked throughout the garage and the house. The garage doors were open, and the car wasn't running because it had ran out of gas. The death was ruled an accident—not a suicide attempt. The Astros retired Wilson's number on April 13, 1975, and wore a black patch in his honor that season.

98 Famous Brawls

The Astros have been involved in their fair share of fights throughout the years—and not always against the opposition. There have been teammates who have gone at it and even a well-publicized scuffle between general manager Ed Wade and pitcher Shawn Chacon in 2008. Here are some of the most famous fights in Astros history.

Astros vs. Expos (August 12, 1996)—When Danny Darwin plunked Henry Rodriguez of the Expos with a pitch in Montreal, a 10-minute brawl ensued that covered the entire infield at Olympic Stadium. Rodriguez charged the mound, and he and Darwin hit the ground while teammates piled on. Darwin thought Rodriguez took too much time admiring a home run in his previous at-bat. The fight died down but then broke out again and got really ugly. The Astros' 5'8" John Cangelosi pulled down 6'7" Expos pitcher—and former Astros first-round pick—Jeff Juden from behind, and Juden body slammed Cangelosi, who landed several punches.

Enter Expos outfielder and future Astro Moises Alou, who threw his helmet at Astros pitcher Shane Reynolds and instead struck Astros manager Terry Collins, cutting him above his lip. Collins was ejected along with Darwin, Cangelosi, Rodriguez, Alou, Juden, and the Astros' Derrick May. "That was a real fight," Expos manager Felipe Alou said.

Brewers fan vs. Bill Spiers (September 24, 1999)—Spiers was minding his own business in right field at Milwaukee's County Stadium when a 23-year-old fan ran onto the field and attacked him. The Astros were awaiting the bottom of the sixth inning when the fan jumped onto the back of Spiers, who couldn't shake him off. "The whole thing caught me by surprise," Spiers told reporters. "I looked down and saw blue jeans wrapped around my neck. I couldn't move, so I fell down backward trying to get him off me."

Spiers and the fan fell to the ground as the entire Astros team ran onto the field to assist him. Astros pitcher Mike Hampton started to kick the attacker. "It was a scary thing," he said. "My instincts just took over. My rage took over. I was pretty furious. I wanted to get him off my teammate."

Wade vs. Chacon (June 25, 2008)—Chacon had been taken out of the Astros rotation in June of 2008 and subsequently asked for a trade. He was sitting in the lunch room in the home clubhouse at Minute Maid Park when Wade, in his first year as general manager in Houston, asked him to join him in manager Cecil Cooper's office.

Chacon told Wade that he could tell him whatever he had to tell him right there, and tensions rose. Voices were raised, and Chacon admitted to shoving Wade to the ground and grabbing his neck. Astros players rushed in to break it up. Chacon was suspended immediately and filed a grievance, but a three-person arbitration panel ruled the Astros were within their rights to terminate Chacon's contract without his entitlement to further compensation. Chacon never pitched in the majors again.

Matt Mieske vs. Mitch Meluskey (June 11, 2000)—Meluskey was a promising young catcher and a bright spot in the Astros' otherwise dismal season. According to witnesses, Meluskey was late for his turn in the batting cage and he jumped in ahead of Mieske. The two exchanged words, and Meluskey punched Mieske when the two were outside the cage. The fight happened only about an hour before the Astros' game against the Padres in San Diego and with several fans in the stands. "It has everything to do with respect," Craig Biggio told reporters. "Some people have it, and some people don't. I'm going to leave it at that. There's no way in the world something like that should happen."

Danny Darwin vs. Pedro Guerrero (August 16, 1990)—Darwin, aka "Dr. Death," and the St. Louis Cardinals slugger shouted at each other after Darwin threw inside to Guerrero in the sixth inning at old Busch Stadium. Guerrero punched Darwin in the face at first base after Darwin got an infield hit in the seventh. Both benches cleared, and Darwin and Guerrero shouted at each other outside the teams' locker rooms. According to news reports, several police officers were called to the clubhouse area as a precautionary measure. Darwin said after the game: "I still can't understand why I got kicked out." Maybe it's because he accidentally punched first-base umpire Bob Davidson.

99 Walk Around the Astrodome

She still sits there in all her glory. The Astrodome, the "Eighth Wonder of the World," remains a Houston icon. The 51-year-old stadium hasn't been used in earnest for more than a decade, but there she stands. The seats have been pulled out—along with many other things on the inside that make a stadium a stadium. But the grandeur remains. The Astrodome still stands tall, even if it's dwarfed these days by NRG Stadium, which sits next door.

It's nearly impossible to get inside the Astrodome these days, though a couple of years ago, a pair of men broke into the Astrodome and took video from all over—including from the locker rooms, the scoreboard booth, and even the roof—and posted it on the Internet. But if you want to get close to the Astrodome *legally*, you still can. A ticket to an event at NRG Park, which includes the football stadium, grants access to the Astrodome—or at least the outside. Get there early and take a walk around the Astrodome. Soak it in. Walk up and peek inside the gates. Take a picture of the skylights still glistening in the sun like they have been for half a century. Take a minute and imagine the history. Luv Ya Blue, The Killer B's, Elvis Presley, Muhammad Ali, Evel Knievel all took center stage here.

Go Go Astros

It's a corny tune with cheesy lyrics and a playful piano chorus, but, man, was it catchy. And if you went to the Astrodome in the late 1970s or the 1980s, it was hard to get it out of your head. "Go Go Astros" was written by Mack Hayes, a garage band rocker from Texas City. He was the same guy who wrote the Oilers' "Luv Ya Blue" fight song.

In 1978 when the Oilers were the biggest thing in Houston, Hayes and his wife performed a parody of "The Twelve Days of Christmas" on local TV called "The Twelve Days of Oiler Christmas." The response was overwhelming, and it was played on the radio. Oilers owner Bud Adams summoned him to his office and asked him to write a song to spearhead a promotion called "Luv Ya Blue." The song was introduced during the Oilers' pep rally following their loss to the Pittsburgh Steelers in the AFC Championship Game and was a hit. Hayes played the song at Oilers home games through much of the 1980s with his Luv Ya Blue Band.

Hayes then had an idea: maybe the Astros would like a fight song, so he recorded "Go Go Astros." He recorded a Spanish version on the flip side called "Vamos Vamos Astros." Hayes doesn't speak Spanish, but he got someone to help him with the proper Spanish pronunciations. "It has all been great fun for me," Hayes said. "And I still hear from folks around the country about the songs and still get requests to play them at some of my gigs."

The Astrodome was the first of its kind when it opened in 1965 to much fanfare. It was the first domed, air-conditioned stadium in the United States. Looking at the Dome today, you can still appreciate the architecture and marvel at what it must have been in 1965. You can't help but applaud the vision of Judge Hofheinz. You can't help but feel the history of Houston pouring out of its beams.

Talking a walk around the Astrodome is nothing short of a history lesson. Billie Jean King beat Bobby Riggs in the infamous tennis match billed as "Battle of the Sexes II" in 1973. Behind Elvin Hayes, the University of Houston men's basketball team

Say what you will about "Go Go Astros," but it remains timeless. And unlike "Luv Ya Blue" and the Oilers, the Astros are still around. Here are the "Go Go Astros" lyrics:

Go Go Astros!
Here come the Astros
Burnin' with desire!
Here come the Astros
Breathin' orange fire!
Here come the Astros
With winning on their mind!
Here come the Astros
No. 1 every time!
Go Go Astros!
Go Go Astros!
Way down south in Houston
Baseball's come alive!
From pitching to the outfield
It's flashing orange and white!
Stealing 'round the bases
Driving in the runs
No place else but Houston
Astros No. 1!

upset mighty UCLA and Lew Alcindor before more than 52,693 fans—the largest crowd to attend a college basketball game for the next 35 years—in the "Game of the Century." It even became a place of hope when it served as a refuge for Hurricane Katrina evacuees in 2005. More than 20,000 fans came to the Astrodome on April 10, 2015, to celebrate its 50th birthday.

The Astrodome might not be here forever. Harris County voters in 2013 voted down a $213 million referendum to renovate and covert the Astrodome into a state-of-the-art convention center and exhibition space, so its future remains unclear. "The Dome should remain erect as a symbol of the first architectural feat of its kind," said Larry Dierker, former Astros pitcher, broadcaster, and manager. "There were people who said it couldn't be done. I think it's worthy of staying here even if nothing's done with it. The ideal solution is what the county judge suggested—that we find some way to use all that air-conditioned indoor space for entertainment for citizens of Houston because they own it. What form does that take? I don't know. Judge Hofheinz was pretty special to be able

The San Diego Padres and the Houston Astros stand for the national anthem during a 1998 playoff series at the Astrodome, a structure that is still worth visiting.

to imagine that this could happen. But there has to be another person with the imagination like Judge Hofheinz that will step forward and come up with something that we can all work on and get done."

100 Eat Chicken and Waffles in a Cone

The chicken waffle cone is exactly what you thought it would be. Take a waffle cone, add a big scoop of mashed potatoes, and top it with chicken bites. Then pick your choice of toppings—gravy, honey mustard, or barbecue. Any trip to Minute Maid Park would be incomplete without tackling the chicken waffle cone, which is available at The Street Eats stand on the main concourse at section 126 (the first-base side).

This thing is too big to eat without a fork, at least initially. It's served lying on a small basket, so your plan of attack should be to reach down into the cone for some mashed potatoes and scoop up a few chicken bites at the same time. If you finish it all—and it's a lot of food—and you still want to eat the cone, go for it. Chances are you'll probably be too full to continue, but you'll be letting your friends down if you don't finish. The mashed potatoes are real and made from potatoes peeled each morning at Minute Maid Park. Not bad for $9.

If chicken and mashed potatoes in a waffle cone isn't your thing, don't worry. There are plenty of other options around the ballpark. In addition to the chicken waffle cone, Street Eats features chicken fried bacon on Texas toast with lettuce, tomato, and three pepper mayo; smoked pork sandwich dip slow roasted with roasted peppers, cheddar cheese, and crispy jalapenos; Texas Hold'em, barbecue chicken with golden cheddar cheese, tomato, fries, and slaw on Texas toast; chicken bahn mi, Asian chicken with cucumber, pickles, carrots, cilantro, and chili mayo; and pulled pork taco, two pulled pork tacos in corn tortillas with cabbage slaw and hot sauce.

The Texas Legends Grill (section 134) features burgers with beef from Nolan Ryan's farm. There's the eight-ounce single burger, a bacon burger, a mushroom Swiss burger, and a New York strip steak sandwich topped with white cheese horseradish sauce and fried onions. The H Town Grille (sections 109, 125) has burgers, grilled chicken sandwiches, brisket sausage, veggie dogs, and more. The Home and Away Ballpark Classics (sections 113, 129, 156) has traditional ballpark fare including hot dogs, chili cheese dogs, Bavarian pretzels, and more.

The Texas Smoke stand (section 124) is as good as it sounds. It features brisket sandwiches, loaded baked potatoes, barbecue baked potatoes, and side items, including baked beans, potato salad, and coleslaw. The Casa Nacho stand (section 111) also has some quality food.

Foamer Nights

The details of exactly how Foamer Nights operated are somewhat ambiguous 40 years later. The simple concept was this: when an Astros player hit a home run when the digital clocks in the Astrodome were lit red, indicating an even number of minutes, fans got free beer for a limited amount of time. The promotion, instituted by Astrodomain CEO Sidney Shlenker in 1974, lasted about two years or so.

The Astros didn't hit many home runs back in those days, so there weren't many chances for free beer. Astros fans, though, were able to do some damage on "Foamer Nights." When the promotion started, Lee May hit the first two winning homers in the early innings of different games. Astros fans responded by tipping 123 kegs of free beer.

There are also some great drink options, too. Stockyard Bar at section 156 serves a variety of domestic and imported beers, including Saint Arnold Amber Ale and Goose Island 312 Urban Wheat Ale, as well as a variety of wines. And Corona Cantina (section 119) features Corona on draft, Negra Modelo, Pacifico, and other bottled beers.

And don't forget the popular Saint Arnold's Bar located in the atrium of Minute Maid Park. It plays host to happy hours prior to each Friday game with plenty of beers from Saint Arnold on tap—including Summer Pils, Elissa IPA, Santo, Fancy Lawnmower, and Amber Ale—as well as ZiegenBock and Bud Light.

Acknowledgements

When I was deliberating taking on this project, I exchanged emails with Susan Slusser of the *San Francisco Chronicle* and Dan Connolly of *The Baltimore Sun*, both of whom had done similar books on the A's and the Orioles, respectively. As two of the best in the business, I trusted their input. They both told me the same thing: it would be a heck of a lot of work, but it would be worth it. They were right on both fronts. So first, I want to thank them for their brutal honesty and pointing me in the right direction to get started.

I want to thank Tom Bast at Triumph Books for jumping on board with the project and editor Jeff Fedotin, who provided encouragement and solid input while never letting me forget my deadline. It was a pleasure working with you. I couldn't have taken on his project without the blessing of Dinn Mann, the executive vice president of Major League Baseball Advanced Media and the man who plucked me away from newspapers and brought me to MLB.com in 2009. I'm thankful every day. Writing a book about the Astros wasn't something I took lightly considering Dinn's grandfather, Judge Roy Hofheinz, was the Astros' first owner and was the vision behind the Astrodome. I thank you for your trust in me, as well as your help on this project, and throughout the years. I would also like to thank my other wonderful bosses at MLB.com: Bill Hill and Jim Banks and my longtime friend, Carlton Thompson.

I received some early input on the book from Mike Acosta, Kevin Eschenfelder, Bill Brown, and Alyson Footer and appreciate their willingness to help. Acosta, whose knowledge of the Astros has few equals, was a frequent source of information. A special thanks to the Astros media relations team of Gene Dias, Steve Grande,

Chris Peixoto, Dena Propis, and Jake Holtrop. Thanks also to Astros owner Jim Crane and president of business operations Reid Ryan. Brad Horn of the Hall of Fame, another Houston product who grew up cheering for the Astros, assisted as well.

This project would have absolutely not been possible without the input of Tal Smith and Larry Dierker. Smith, who was around in the infancy of the franchise, met with me over coffee for more than an hour so I could pick his brain. And he was repeatedly a source of information, including another hour-long interview over the phone. Dierker also gave me more than an hour of his time and helped me track down some Astros alumni. Larry has seen it all when it comes to the Astros. Thanks for sharing your memories and time.

When it was time to find someone to write the foreword, only one name came to mind: Craig Biggio. The greatest Astro of them all and a Hall of Famer, Biggio graciously agreed to write the foreword and gave me some terrific insight. I can't thank Craig enough for being such a huge part of this project. It was a privilege to be there when he was inducted into the Hall of Fame, and I'm honored to consider him a friend.

I wound up interviewing close to 50 people for the book, ranging from former players, owners, managers, and others. I would like to thank: Larry Andersen, Alan Ashby, Brad Ausmus, Brandon Backe, Jeff Bagwell, Lance Berkman, Geoff Blum, Bill Bradley, Chris Burke, Enos Cabell, Jose Cruz, Glenn Davis, Bill Doran, Morgan Ensberg, Adam Everett, Matt Galante, Phil Garner, Mack Hayes, A.J. Hinch, Art Howe, Gerry Hunsicker, Mike Lamb, Hal Lanier, Jason Lane, Brad Lidge, Jeff Luhnow, Drayton McLane, Norm Miller, Roy Oswalt, Hunter Pence, Terry Puhl, Tim Purpura, Chad Qualls, Shane Reynolds, J.R. Richard, Nolan Ryan, Chris Sampson, Brent Strom, Dickie Thon, Billy Wagner, Bob Watson, Bill Wood, and Jimmy Wynn. Thank you for being gracious with your time. There were several other interviews I did in the past couple of years I used for this book, including Bob Aspromonte, Al Spangler, Mike Scott, Billy Hatcher, Cesar Cedeno, Rusty Staub, John Mallee, Jeff Kent, Jim Deshaies, and Joe Morgan. Thanks to all.

The most important people in this whole project are my family. My father, Patrick, and mother, Margaret, sacrificed everything they had to come to this country from Scotland in 1975 and to give us a better life, and I'm forever grateful. I hope I made you proud. My late father took me to my first Astros game in the mid-1970s, and we attended many more together. We shared all kinds of sports together, including his beloved Glasgow Celtic, and he was my soccer coach. He pushed me and wanted the best for me. I miss him dearly. My late sister, Bridget, was six years older than me and always there for me during times of need. I miss her every day. My mother and stepfather Ralph Anderson have always been strong and supportive. My brother, John, helped me during some tough times, and I'm grateful. See you in Seattle.

Most importantly, I need to thank my teammates. And what a team I have. My wife, Lisa, has allowed me to live this crazy life covering baseball because she knows how much I love it. I couldn't do any of this without her support and love. She holds down the fort when I'm out of town, which isn't easy. She's the team MVP, and I'm sure she was tired of me telling her I had to go "write a few chapters." Thanks for being so supportive and a wonderful mother. I can't imagine coming home from a road trip and not seeing the faces of her and my precious daughters, Erin, Emily, and Amy. I thank them for letting Daddy live a dream and I'm proud of the young ladies they've become. I'm honored to have a front-row seat in their lives and I can't wait to see what's next. You're all a force to be reckoned with.

Finally, thank you to Astros fans everywhere for reading and reaching out over the years. I hope you enjoyed this book.

Sources

Newspapers and Wire Services
Houston Chronicle
USA TODAY
Ottawa Sun
Associated Press
The Houston Post

Magazines
Sports Illustrated
Baseball America
People

Websites
BaseballReference.com
Baseballhall.org
AstrosDaily.com
MLB.com
Astros.com

Books
Dene Hofheinz Mann, *You Be The Judge*, 1965, Premier Printing Company
Larry Dierker, *This Ain't Brain Surgery*, 2003, Simon and Schuster
Jimmy Wynn, with Bill McCurdy, *Toy Cannon: The Autobiography of Baseball's Jimmy Wynn*, 2010, McFarland & Company, Inc., Publishers
Norm Miller, *To all my fans...From Norm Who?*, 2009, Doubleday Productions

J.R. Richard, with Lew Freedman, *Still Throwing Heat*, 2015, Triumph Books

James Gast, *The Astrodome: Building An American Spectacle*, 2014, Aspinwall Press

Clifton Blue Parker and Bill Nowlin, *Sweet '60: The 1960 Pittsburgh Pirates*, 2013, Society for American Baseball Research (SABR)

Fran Zimniuch, *Shortened Seasons: The Untimely Deaths of Major League Baseball's Stars and Journeymen*, 2007, Taylor Trade Publishing

Rob Rains, *Nolan Ryan: From Alvin To Cooperstown*, 1999, *The Sporting News*

Robert Reed, *Colt .45s: A Six-Gun Salute*, 1999, Gulf Publishing Company

Edgar W. Ray, *The Grand Huckster*, 1980, Memphis State University Press

Campbell B. Titchener, *The George Kirksey Story*, 1989, Eakin Press